Advance Prais... ...avid R... ...riffin's
The New Pearl Harbor... ...g Questions about the

"David
reviewing
persuasiv
administ

"This is
that shou
thoughtf

"An extra
to becom

"David F
dispassion
account
administr
mind-sto
history-st
con and

...orr., *who was killed in the North Tower of*
...d co-founder of September 11th Families
for Peaceful Tomorrows

"This is a very important book. David Ray Griffin's carefully researched and documented study demonstrates a high level of probability that the Bush administration was complicit in allowing 9/11 to happen in order to further war plans that had already been made. A must read for anyone concerned about American foreign policy under the present administration."
—*Rosemary Radford Ruether, Carpenter Professor of Feminist Theology, Graduate Theological Union, Berkeley, California*

"This is a must-read for all who want to get past the conspiracy of silence and mystification that surrounds these events."
—*John B. Cobb, Jr., Professor of Theology, Emeritus, Claremont School of Theology and Claremont Graduate University*

"That 9/11 has become a defining moment in our history cannot be gainsaid. But its exact significance is an exceedingly contentious question notwithstanding the seeming clarity of prevailing accounts. David Ray Griffin deconstructs those accounts with a host of unresolved puzzles strongly suggestive of some sort of culpable complicity by US officials in the event. His book presents an incontrovertible argument of the need for a genuinely full and independent investigation of that infamous day."
—*Douglas Sturm, Presidential Professor of Religion and Political Science, Emeritus, Bucknell University*

"This book is as full of research and authoritative notes as a field full of springtime daisies. The author raises frightening questions, and the questions beg for answers. One thing we can conclude for certain. The events surrounding 9/11, both before and after, cannot be simply swept under the rug of conventional wisdom…. This book gives us a foundation to discover the truth, one that we may not wish to hear."
—*Gerry Spence, trial lawyer and author of* How to Argue and Win Every Time

"David Griffin's *The New Pearl Harbor* belongs on the book shelves of all those who, in any way, doubt the veracity of the accounts presented to the public by the Bush administration concerning the worst terrorist attack in America's history. The facts presented in this book are disturbing—and they should be. Griffin's book goes a long way in answering the age-old question inherent in American political scandals: What did the President know, and when did he know it?"
—*Wayne Madsen, author, journalist, syndicated columnist*

THE NEW PEARL HARBOR

Disturbing Questions about the Bush Administration and 9/11

by David Ray Griffin

foreword by Michael Meacher, MP

ARRIS BOOKS
An imprint of Arris Publishing Ltd
Gloucestershire

First published in Great Britain in 2004 by

Arris Books
An imprint of Arris Publishing Ltd
12 Main Street
Adlestrop
Moreton-in-Marsh
Gloucestershire GL56 0YN
www.arrisbooks.com

ISBN 1 84437 036 4

Printed and bound in Great Britain by
Biddles Ltd, Kings Lynn, Norfolk

To request our complete catalogue, please call us at **01608 659328**, visit our web site at:
www.arrisbooks.com, or e-mail us at: **info@arrisbooks.com**

CONTENTS

ACKNOWLEDGMENTS

In writing this book, I received an enormous amount of help and support. The greatest help came, of course, from the authors upon whose work I drew. Without the work of Nafeez Ahmed and Paul Thompson, this book would not have even been begun, and without the books by Thierry Meyssan and Michel Chossudovsky, it would have been far less complete. And then there are all those reporters and researchers who have published relevant material in newspapers and magazines, on television shows, or on the Web, some of whom were laboring away long before Ahmed and Thompson began their work. To some of these reporters and researchers I am indebted only indirectly, through their influence on my primary sources; to others, I am directly indebted. I have acknowledged the work of at least many of them in the notes. The attempt to discover the truth about 9/11 and bring it to light has been a very cooperative enterprise, one involving hundreds of intensely dedicated, mostly unpaid, investigators.

I have received help from many other people, including Tal Avitzur, John Cobb, Michael Dietrick, Hilal Elver, Richard Falk, Allison Jaqua, Gianluigi Gugliermetto, Colleen Kelly, John McMurtry, Pat Patterson, Rosemary Ruether, Pamela Thompson, and Sarah Wright. I wish also to thank all those who took time to express in writing their support for this book.

I am indebted to Richard Falk for reasons that go far beyond his gracious willingness to write the Foreword. It was through his influence that I first began working on global political matters. He has been my main discussion partner about these matters. And it was through him that I became connected with Olive Branch Press of Interlink Publishing.

I am especially grateful for this connection. The two people with whom I have worked at Olive Branch—Pamela Thompson and Michel Moushabeck—have not only been delightful collaborators. They have also manifested the kind of commitment to this book that authors usually only dream about.

I am appreciative of my institution, the Claremont School of Theology, and especially its president, Philip Amerson, and its dean, Jack Fitzmier, for their unstinting support of academic freedom and their recognition of the need for the school's faculty to write about vital public issues of the day.

Finally, I am, as usual, most indebted to the ongoing support from my wife, Ann Jaqua.

FOREWORD

Never in modern history has an event of such cataclysmic significance been shrouded in such mystery. So many of the key facts remain unexplained on any plausible basis, and so many of the key actors have put forward contradictory accounts, only to be forced to retract or cover up later.

David Griffin is a good person to guide sceptical readers through the miasma of spin and pretence that has clouded the truth. He is dismissive of conspiracy theories that abound, round shock killings of the famous like the Kennedy assassination and the Princess Diana fatal crash. He rightly believes that investigators should stick firmly to established facts, or carefully measured likelihoods, rather than try to prove predetermined theories. His technique, rightly, is to raise questions fearlessly and then test possible answers rigorously against all the available evidence.

And the unanswered questions are quite stunning. When eleven countries supplied detailed and specific intelligence to the American government in the months before 9/11, why did the US fail to follow it up in any systematic way? The former US federal crimes prosecutor, John Loftus, has said: "The information provided by European intelligence services prior to 9/11 was so extensive that it is no longer possible for either the CIA or FBI to assert a defence of incompetence."

Mossad gave the US government in August 2001 a list of 200 terrorists said to be preparing a big operation. It included the names of at least four of the hijackers. None were arrested. Why? Zacarias Moussaoui, a French Moroccan flight student now thought to be the twentieth hijacker, was arrested in August 2001 after an instructor reported his suspicious interest in learning how to steer large airliners. When French intelligence then told the Americans he was a radical Islamist, his captors sought a warrant to search his computer, which contained clues to the 9/11 mission. The FBI turned them down. Why?

And so on.

Most difficult to explain of all, how could the US, the biggest military power with the most advanced technologies in the world, fail to scramble any of the fighter aircraft in the F16 squadron at the US

Andrews Airforce base, just ten miles from Washington DC, for one and a half hours after the hijack was discovered until the Pentagon was hit at 9.38 AM? How did the standard mandatory FAA intercept procedure to tackle hijacked aircraft, which the US military had operated 67 times in the previous nine months, so signally fail to be operated in the far more catastrophic circumstances of 9/11?

The book is entitled *The New Pearl Harbor*, which might itself suggest a conspiracy slant since President Roosevelt is widely believed to have received advance warning about the Japanese attack on 7 December 1941, but the information never reached the US fleet, and the ensuing national outrage induced a reluctant US public to join the Second World War. However, the link was not first made by David Griffin. It was originally made by the Bush neo-conservative think-tank Project for the New American Century and published at the time of the Presidential election campaign in September 2000. In this document, future members of the Bush administration said that the process of transforming the US into "tomorrow's dominant force" was likely to be a long one, in the absence of "some catastrophic and catalysing event–like a new Pearl Harbor." There is no need for conspiracy theories when they themselves state their aspirations.

David Griffin's book is an excellent exposé of so many of the deeply troubling questions that must still be answered fully and transparently if democratic control over political and military leaders is to mean anything at all.

—Michael Meacher, MP

INTRODUCTION

The attacks of 9/11 have often been compared with the attacks on Pearl Harbor. Investigative reporter James Bamford, for example, has written about President Bush's behavior "in the middle of a modern-day Pearl Harbor."[1] CBS News reported that the president himself, before going to bed on 9/11, wrote in his diary: "The Pearl Harbor of the 21st century took place today."[2]

This comparison has often been made for the sake of arguing that the American response to 9/11 should be similar to the American response to Pearl Harbor. Just after the president's address to the nation on September 11, 2001, Henry Kissinger posted an online article in which he said: "The government should be charged with a systematic response that, one hopes, will end the way that the attack on Pearl Harbor ended—with the destruction of the system that is responsible for it."[3] An editorial in *Time* magazine that appeared right after the attacks urged: "For once, let's have no fatuous rhetoric about 'healing.'...A day cannot live in infamy without the nourishment of rage. Let's have rage. What's needed is a unified, unifying Pearl Harbor sort of purple American fury."[4]

Some of the comparisons have pointed out that the attacks of 9/11 did indeed evoke a response, calling for the use of US military power, similar to that produced by Pearl Harbor. Quoting a prediction made in 2000 by soon-to-be top officials in the Bush administration that the changes they desired would be difficult unless "a new Pearl Harbor" occurred,[5] Australian journalist John Pilger wrote: "The attacks of 11 September 2001 provided the 'new Pearl Harbor.'"[6] A member of the US Army's Institute for Strategic Studies reported that after 9/11, "Public support for military action is at levels that parallel the public reaction after the attack at Pearl Harbor."[7]

These comparisons of 9/11 with Pearl Harbor do not seem unjustified. The events of 9/11, virtually everyone agrees, were the most important events of recent times—for both America and the rest of the world. The attacks of that day have provided the basis for a significant restriction on civil liberties in the United States (just as Pearl Harbor led to restrictions on the civil liberties of Japanese Americans).[8] Those attacks have also been the basis of a worldwide "war on terror" led by the United States, with the wars in Afghanistan and Iraq being the two major episodes thus far.

The Bush administration's "war on terror" is, moreover, widely perceived as a pretext for a more aggressive imperialism. Phyllis Bennis, for example, says that 9/11 has resulted in "foreign policy imposed on the rest of the world through an unchallenged law of empire."[9] Of course, a few historians have been pointing out for some time that American leaders have long desired an empire covering the whole world.[10] But most critics of US foreign policy believe that the imperialism of the Bush II administration, especially since 9/11, has been much more explicit, far-reaching, and arrogant.[11] Richard Falk has, in fact, referred to it as "the global domination project."[12] Although there was an outpouring of good will toward America after 9/11 and a widespread willingness to accede to its claim that the attacks gave it a mandate to wage a worldwide war on terrorism, this good will was quickly exhausted. American foreign policy is now criticized around the world more widely and severely than ever before, even more so than during the war in Vietnam. The American answer to all criticism, however, is 9/11. When Europeans criticized the Bush administration's intention to go to war against Iraq, for example, several US opinion-makers supportive of the war explained the difference in perception by saying that the Europeans had not suffered the attacks of 9/11.

The Failure of the Press

Given the role of 9/11 in leading to this much more explicit and aggressive imperialism, some observers have suggested that historians will come to look back on it as the real beginning of the 21st century.[13] Nevertheless, in spite of the virtually universal agreement that 9/11 has been of such transcendent importance, there has been little public scrutiny of this event itself. On the first anniversary of the 9/11 attacks, the *New York Times* wrote: "One year later, the public knows less about the circumstances of 2,801 deaths at the foot of Manhattan in broad daylight than people in 1912 knew within weeks about the Titanic."[14] That was the case in part because the Bush administration, arguing that an investigation would be a distraction from the needed "war on terrorism," resisted the call for a special commission. But the public's lack of information about 9/11 was also due in large part to the fact that the *Times* and the rest of the mainline press had not authorized investigative reports, through which the public's lack of knowledge might have been overcome. Another year later, furthermore, the situation remained virtually the same. On September 11, 2003, a writer for the *Philadelphia Daily News* asked: "why after 730 days do we know so little about what really happened that day?"[15]

The American press has, in particular, provided no in-depth investigation of whether the official account of what happened fits with the available evidence and is otherwise plausible.[16] Many newspaper and television stories have, to be sure, raised several disturbing questions about the official account, showing that there are elements of it that do not seem to make sense or that seem to contradict certain facts. But the press has not confronted government officials with these apparent implausibilities and contradictions. The mass media have not, moreover, provided the public with any comprehensive overviews that lay out all the disturbing questions of which they are aware. There have been many very important stories by a number of journalists, including the internationally known, award-winning journalist Gregory Palast and Canada's award-winning Barrie Zwicker (see notes 16 and 18). But such stories, if even seen, have been largely forgotten by the collective consciousness, as they have remained individual products of brilliant and courageous reporting, having thus far not been allowed to add up to anything significant. Finally, although strong criticisms of the official account have been presented by many otherwise credible individuals, the mass media have not exposed the public to their views.

Criticisms of the official account are, to be sure, inflammatory, for to reject the official account is to imply that US leaders, including the president, have constructed a massive lie. And if they did construct a false account, they would have done so, most people would assume, in order to cover up their own complicity. And that is indeed the conclusion of most critics of the official account. That would certainly be an inflammatory charge. But how can we claim to have a free press— a Fourth Estate—if it fails to investigate serious charges made against a sitting president on the grounds that they are too inflammatory? The charges against President Nixon in the Watergate scandal were inflammatory. The charges against President Reagan in the Iran-Contra affair were inflammatory. The various charges brought against President Clinton were inflammatory. In all these cases, however, the press reported the issues (albeit in the first two cases rather belatedly). It is precisely in such situations that we most need an independent press.

But the press has failed to do its job with regard to 9/11 even though, if the official account of 9/11 were found to be false, the consequences would be enormous—much more so than with any of those prior scandals. The official account of 9/11 has been used as the justification for the wars in Afghanistan and Iraq, which have resulted in the deaths not only of thousands of combatants but also of far more innocent civilians than were killed on 9/11. This account has been used as the justification for dozens of other operations around the world, most of which are largely unknown to the American people. It has been used to justify the USA PATRIOT Act, through which the civil liberties of Americans have been curtailed. And it has been used to justify the indefinite incarceration of countless people in Guantánamo and elsewhere. And yet the press has been less aggressive in questioning President Bush about 9/11 than it was in questioning President Clinton about his relationship with Monica Lewinsky, a very trivial matter by comparison.

The failure of the American media in this regard has been admitted by some insiders. For example, Rena Golden, executive vice-president and general manager of CNN International, was quoted as saying in August of 2002 that the American press had censored itself on both 9/11 and the war in Afghanistan. "Anyone who claims the US media didn't censor itself," Golden added, "is kidding you. And this isn't just a CNN issue—every journalist who was in any way involved in 9/11 is partly responsible."[17] As to why this has been the case, CBS anchorman Dan Rather has said:

> There was a time in South Africa that people would put flaming tires around people's necks if they dissented. And in some ways the fear is that you will be necklaced here, you will have a flaming tire of lack of patriotism put around your neck. Now it is that fear that keeps journalists from asking the toughest of the tough questions.[18]

Rather's confession surely explains at least part of the press's reticence to question the official account, especially since journalists perceived as unpatriotic are in danger of being fired.

One of the chief critics of the official account, Thierry Meyssan, suggests that Americans have viewed any criticism of the official account to be not only unpatriotic but even sacrilegious. On September 12, Meyssan reminds us, President Bush announced his intention to lead "a monumental struggle of Good versus Evil."[19] On September 13, he declared that the next day would be a National Day of Prayer and Remembrance for the Victims of the Terrorist Attacks. And on September 14, the president himself, surrounded by Billy Graham, a cardinal, a rabbi, and an imam as well as four previous presidents and many members of Congress, delivered the sermon. In this sermon, he said:

> Our responsibility to history is already clear: to answer these attacks and rid the world of evil. War has been waged against us by stealth and deceit and murder. This nation is peaceful, but fierce when stirred to anger....In every generation, the world has produced enemies of human freedom. They have attacked America, because we are freedom's home and defender. And the commitment of our fathers is now the calling of our time....[W]e ask almighty God to watch over our nation, and grant us patience and resolve in all that is to come.... And may He always guide our country. God bless America.[20]

Through this unprecedented event, in which the president of the United States issued a declaration of war from a cathedral, Meyssan observes, "the American government consecrated...its version of events. From then on, any questioning of the official truth would be seen as sacrilege."[21]

9/11 and the Left

If raising disturbing questions about the official account would be seen as both unpatriotic and sacrilegious, it is not surprising that, as both Rena Golden and Dan Rather admit, the mainline press in America has not raised these questions. It is also not surprising that right-wing and even middle-of-the-road commentators on political affairs have not raised serious questions about the official account. It is not even surprising that some of them—including Jean Bethke Elshtain, a professor of social and political ethics—have declared that the accusation of official complicity is beyond the pale of reasonable debate, so that any arguments on its behalf can simply be ignored. Elshtain, calling the suggestion that American officials, including the president, were complicit in the attacks "preposterous," adds: "This sort of inflammatory madness exists outside the boundary of political debate" and therefore does not even "deserve a hearing."[22] From this perspective, it is not necessary to examine the evidence put forward by critics of the official account, even though some of these critics are fellow intellectuals teaching in neighboring universities—such as two well-respected Canadian academics, economist

Michel Chossudovsky and social philosopher John McMurtry.[23] Although Elshtain points out that "[i]f we get our descriptions of events wrong, our analyses and our ethics will be wrong too,"[24] she evidently thinks it unnecessary to consider the possibility that the official description about the events of 9/11 might be wrong. Although this attitude is unfortunate, especially when it is expressed within the intellectual community, it is not surprising.

What *is* surprising, however, is that America's leftist critics of US policy, who are seldom worried about being called either unpatriotic or sacrilegious, have for the most part not explored, at least in public discourse, the possibility of official complicity.[25]

These critics have, to be sure, been extremely critical of the way in which the Bush administration has responded to 9/11. They have, in particular, pointed out that this administration has used 9/11 as an excuse to enact policies and carry out operations that have little if any relation to either punishing the perpetrators of the attacks or preventing further such attacks in the future. They have even pointed out that most of these policies and operations were already on the agenda of the Bush administration before the attacks, so that 9/11 was not the cause but merely the pretext for enacting them. These critics also know that the United States has many times in the past fabricated an "incident" as a pretext for going to war—most notoriously for the wars against Mexico, Cuba, and Vietnam.[26] But few of these critics have seriously discussed, at least in public, whether this might also be the case with 9/11, even though a demonstration of this fact, if it were true, would surely be the most effective way to undermine policies of the Bush administration to which they are so strongly opposed. Abjuring a "conspiracy theory," they accept, at least implicitly, a "coincidence theory," according to which the attacks of 9/11 were, from the administration's point of view, simply a godsend, which just happened to allow it to carry out its agenda.

An example is provided by Rahul Mahajan, a brilliant and outspoken critic of US imperialism. He analyzes the themes of US imperialism since 9/11 in the light of the document alluded to earlier that mentioned the need for a "new Pearl Harbor," this being *Rebuilding America's Defenses*, which was prepared by the Project for the New American Century. Three of the major themes of this document, Mahajan emphasizes, are the need to place more military bases around the world from which power can be projected, the need to bring about "regime change" in countries unfriendly to American interests, and the need for greatly increased military spending, especially for "missile defense"—explicitly understood not as deterrence but as "a prerequisite for maintaining American preeminence" by preventing other countries from deterring *us*. Mahajan then points out that "[t]he 9/11 attacks were a natural opportunity to jack up the military budget" and that the other ideas in this document, in conjunction with the well-known preoccupation of Bush and Cheney with oil, provided the major themes of their post-9/11 imperial strategy. Mahajan also notes that this document said that the desired transformation of the military would probably be politically impossible "absent some catastrophic and catalyzing event—like a new Pearl Harbor." And Mahajan even adds that "within a year they [the authors of this document] had their Pearl Harbor and the chance to turn their imperial fantasies into reality." After pointing out all of this, however, Mahajan opts for coincidence over conspiracy, saying: "Conspiracy theorists will no doubt rejoice, but this, like so many events in the history of US foreign policy, is simply another example of Pasteur's famous axiom that 'Fortune favors the prepared mind.'"[27]

Mahajan may, of course, be right. But he gives us no reason to think so. He, in particular, reveals no sign of having studied the evidence provided by those who have argued that the attacks could have been successful only through the complicity of the US government.

How This Book Came About

Whether or not it is true that Mahajan dismissed the evidence without examination, it was certainly true of me. Until the spring of 2003, I had not looked at any of the evidence. I was vaguely aware that there were people, at least on the Internet, who were offering evidence against the official account of 9/11 and were suggesting a revisionist account, according to which US officials were complicit. But I did not take the time to try to find their websites. I had been studying the history of American expansionism and imperialism quite intensely since 9/11, so I knew that the US government had fabricated "incidents" as an excuse to go to war several times before. Nevertheless, although the thought did cross my mind that 9/11 might likewise have been arranged, I did not take this possibility seriously. It seemed to me simply beyond belief that the Bush administration—*even* the Bush administration—would do such a heinous thing. I assumed that those who were claiming otherwise must be "conspiracy theorists" in the derogatory sense in which this term is usually employed—which means, roughly, "crackpots." I knew that if they were right, this would be very important. But I was so confident that they must be wrong—that their writings would consist merely of loony theories based on wild inferences from dubious evidence—that I had no motivation to invest time and energy in tracking these writings down. I fully sympathize, therefore, with the fact that most people have not examined the evidence. Life is short and the list of conspiracy theories is long, and we all must exercise judgment about which things are worth our investment of time. I had assumed that conspiracy theories about 9/11 were below the threshold of possible credibility.

But then a fellow professor sent me an e-mail message that provided some of the relevant websites. Knowing her to be a sensible person, I looked up some of the material on the Internet, especially a massive timeline entitled "Was 9/11 Allowed to Happen?" by an independent researcher named Paul Thompson.[28] I was surprised, even amazed, to see—even though Thompson limits himself strictly to mainline sources[29]—how much evidence he had found that points to the conclusion that the Bush administration did indeed intentionally allow the attacks of 9/11 to happen. At about the same time, I happened to read Gore Vidal's *Dreaming War: Blood for Oil and the Cheney-Bush Junta*, which pointed me to the most extensive book on 9/11, *The War on Freedom: How and Why America Was Attacked September 11, 2001*, by Nafeez Ahmed, an independent researcher in England.[30] Ahmed's book provides an organized, extensively documented argument that directly challenges the accepted wisdom about 9/11, which is that it resulted from a "breakdown" within and among our intelligence agencies.[31] Ahmed, like Thompson, suggests that the attacks must have resulted from complicity in high places, not merely from incompetence in lower places. Ahmed's and Thompson's material taken together, I saw, provided a strong *prima facie* case for this contention, certainly strong enough to merit an extensive investigation by the American press, the US Congress,[32] and the 9/11 Independent Commission,[33] all of which had thus far operated on the assumption that 9/11 resulted from intelligence and communication failures.

I also saw, however, that the work of Thompson and Ahmed was not likely to reach very many of the American people. Thompson's timelines, while extremely helpful for researchers with the time and patience to work through them, were not easily readable by ordinary citizens, partly because they were available only online and partly because, as the name "timeline" indicates, the evidence was arranged chronologically rather than topically.[34] And, although Ahmed's evidence was in a book and was arranged topically, the book was quite long and contained far more material than needed to support the basic argument. Much of this additional material was, furthermore, in the book's early chapters, so that one had to work through several chapters before getting to the evidence that directly contradicted the official account. If the important information provided by Ahmed and Thompson were to reach many people, including busy members of Congress and the press, something else would be needed.

I decided, accordingly, to write a magazine article that would summarize the main evidence and also point interested readers to the studies of Thompson, Ahmed, and others presenting a revisionist account of 9/11. But that article grew into a book-length manuscript, because I soon found that, even though I tried to limit myself to the most important evidence, it was impossible within the confines of an article to present an intelligible account that would do justice to the evidence that has been provided by these researchers.

After I began writing, furthermore, I learned of the work of the previously mentioned French researcher, Thierry Meyssan, in particular his hypothesis that the aircraft that hit the Pentagon could not have been a Boeing 757, which is what Flight 77 was, but must have been a guided missile. When I first learned of this revisionist hypothesis, I—probably like most people now reading my report of it—assumed it was completely absurd. Surely the difference between a gigantic 757 and a relatively small missile is so great that if the Pentagon had been hit merely by a missile, Pentagon officials could not have convinced anyone that it was a 757! Did we not learn from press reports that the hole created in the side of the Pentagon was 200 feet wide and five stories high? Had we not learned from one of the passengers on Flight 77—TV commentator Barbara Olson—that it was headed toward Washington? And had not eyewitnesses identified it? Virtually everyone, including most critics of the official account of 9/11, accepted the idea that the Pentagon was hit by

Flight 77. How could they all be wrong? Nevertheless, after I got Meyssan's books and read them for myself, I saw that his case, as absurd as it had seemed at first glance, is quite strong. I eventually became convinced, in fact, that it is with regard to the strike on the Pentagon that—assuming Meyssan's descriptions of the evidence to be accurate—the official account seems most obviously false. Or at least that it is tied for first place for this honor. The fact that the official account of the strike on the Pentagon is still widely accepted provides an especially good example, therefore, of the fact that most of the public has simply not been exposed to the relevant evidence. The present book seeks to bring together all the major strands of this evidence.

No previous book has done this. Ahmed's book, while easily the most comprehensive, does not have much of the evidence contained in Thompson's timelines and in Meyssan's books. And Meyssan's books, while containing important evidence not available elsewhere, do not have most of the information provided by Ahmed and Thompson. The same is true of the other most important book in English on the subject, Michel Chossudovsky's *War and Globalisation: The Truth Behind September 11.* As its subtitle indicates, it focuses on the background to 9/11, dealing with 9/11 itself only briefly. In the present book, I have brought together what seems to me the most important evidence found in these[35] and some other sources.[36]

The Book's Contents

As I see it, five major types of evidence have been raised against the official account. The first type, which involves inconsistencies and implausibilities in the official account of what happened on 9/11 itself, is discussed in the four chapters of Part I. The four other types of evidence are discussed in Part II. All this evidence is organized in terms of a number of "disturbing questions,"[37] which are disturbing precisely because they suggest that the official account is, as the title of the English translation of Meyssan's first book on the subject calls it, a "big lie."[38] They are also disturbing because they suggest the revisionist thesis that the attacks of 9/11, which President Bush has rightly called *evil,* were carried out with the complicity of some officials of the Bush administration itself.

In the Conclusion, I ask whether the best explanation of the evidence presented in the prior chapters is indeed, as the revisionists suggest, official complicity in the attacks of 9/11. I then discuss the implications for the kind of investigation now needed.

Possible Meanings of "Official Complicity"

Although the revisionist writings on which this book draws charge official complicity in the attacks of 9/11, one thing missing in them is any careful discussion of just what they mean by "official complicity." There are at least eight possible views of what official complicity in the attacks of 9/11 might mean. In order that readers can decide, as they examine the evidence, which kind of official complicity, if any, the evidence supports, I list these eight possible views here in ascending order of seriousness—meaning the seriousness of the charge against the Bush administration that the view would imply.

1. *Construction of a False Account:* One possible view is that although US officials played no role in facilitating the attacks and did not even expect them, they constructed a false account of what really happened—whether to protect National Security, to cover up potentially embarrassing facts, to exploit the attacks to enact their agenda, or for some other reason. Although this would be the least serious charge, it would be sufficiently serious for impeachment—especially if the president had lied about 9/11 for personal gain or to advance some pre-established agenda, such as attacking Afghanistan and Iraq.

2. *Something Expected by Intelligence Agencies:* A second possible view is that although they had no specific information about the attacks in advance, some US intelligence agencies—such as the FBI, the CIA, and some intelligence agencies of the US military—expected some sort of attacks to occur. Although they played no role in planning the attacks, they perhaps played a role in facilitating them in the sense of deliberately not taking steps to prevent them. Then, having done this without White House knowledge, they persuaded the White House after 9/11 not only to cover up their guilt, by constructing a false account, but also to carry out the agenda for which the attacks were intended to gain support.

3. *Specific Events Expected by Intelligence Agencies:* A third possible view is that intelligence agencies (but not the White House) had specific information about the timing and the targets of the attacks.

4. *Intelligence Agencies Involved in Planning:* A fourth possible view is that intelligence agencies (but not the White House) actively participated in planning the attacks.

5. *Pentagon Involved in Planning:* A fifth possible view is that the Pentagon (but not the White House) actively participated in planning the attacks.

6. *Something Expected by White House:* A sixth possible view is that although the White House had no specific knowledge of the attacks in advance, it expected some sort of attacks to occur and was a party to facilitating them, at least in the sense of not ordering that they be prevented.[39] This view allows for the possibility that the White House might have been shocked by the amount of death and destruction caused by the attacks that were actually carried out.

7. *Specific Advance Knowledge by White House:* A seventh possible view is that the White House had specific foreknowledge of the targets and the timing of the attacks.

8. *White House Involved in Planning:* An eighth possible view is that the White House was a party to planning the attacks.

As these possibilities show, a charge that 9/11 involved "complicity" or "conspiracy" on the part of US officials can be understood in many ways, several of which do not involve active involvement in the planning, and *most* of which do not involve presidential involvement in this planning. One reason these distinctions are important is that they show that discussion of the idea of official complicity—whether such complicity is being charged or rejected—needs to be more nuanced than is often the case. For example, the charge that Jean Bethke Elshtain rejects as "preposterous" is the "charge that American officials, up to and including the president of the United States, engineered the attacks to bolster their popularity."[40] In so wording it, she not only equates the charge of official complicity with the eighth of the possible views listed above, which is the strongest charge, but also ties this charge to the imputation of a specific motive to the American officials allegedly involved—that of bolstering their own popularity. Having dismissed that highly specific charge as preposterous, she evidently assumes that the whole idea of official complicity has been laid to rest. But there are many other possibilities.

For example, Michael Parenti, one of the few well-known leftist thinkers to have suggested some form of official complicity, points out, like Mahajan, that the attacks were so convenient that they have provoked suspicion: "The September terrorist attacks created such a serviceable pretext for reactionism at home and imperialist expansion abroad as to leave many people suspecting that the US government itself had a hand in the event." Parenti at first seems to dismiss this suspicion as completely as Mahajan, saying: "I find it hard to believe that the White House or the CIA actively participated in a conspiracy to destroy the World Trade Center and part of the Pentagon, killing such large numbers of Americans in order to create a casus belli against Afghanistan."[41]

Parenti, however, does not stop there. Citing an article by Patrick Martin, who refers to some facts suggesting official complicity, Parenti endorses Martin's conclusion—that although the US government did not plan the details of the attacks or anticipate that thousands of people would be killed, it "expected *something* to happen and looked the other way."[42] Parenti thereby illustrates the second or, more likely, the sixth of the possible views.

In any case, I have found, as I have said, that the revisionists have made a strong *prima facie* case for at least some version of the charge of official complicity. To say that they have made a *convincing* case would require a judgment that the evidence that they cite is reliable. And, although I have repeated only evidence that seemed credible to me, I have not independently verified the accuracy of this evidence. As the reader will see, this evidence is so extensive and of such a nature that no individual—especially no individual with very limited time and resources—could check out its accuracy. It is for this reason that I claim only that these revisionists have presented a strong *prima facie* case for official complicity, strong enough to merit investigations by those who do have the necessary resources to carry them out—the press and the US Congress. If a significant portion of the evidence summarized here holds up, the conclusion that the attacks of 9/11 succeeded because of official complicity would become virtually inescapable.

I should perhaps emphasize that it is not necessary for *all* of the evidence to stand up, given the nature of the argument. Some arguments are, as we say, "only as strong as the weakest link." These are *deductive* arguments, in which each step in the argument depends on the truth of the previous step. If a single premise is found to be false, the argument fails. However, the argument for official complicity in 9/11 is a *cumulative* argument. This kind of argument is a general argument consisting of several particular arguments that are independent from each other. As such, each particular argument provides support for all the others. Rather than being like a chain, a cumulative argument is more like a cable composed of many strands. Each strand strengthens the cable. But if there are many strands, the cable can still hold a lot of weight even if some of them unravel. As the reader will see, there are many strands in the argument for official complicity in 9/11 summarized in this book. If the purported evidence on which some of these are based turns out to be unreliable, that would not necessarily undermine the overall argument. This cumulative argument would then simply be supported by fewer strands. And some of the strands are such that, if the evidence on which they are based is confirmed, the case could be supported by one or two of them.[43]

"Conspiracy Theories"

Before turning to the evidence, however, we should pause to consider the fact, to which allusion has been made, that it seems widely assumed that any such case can be rejected *a priori* by pointing out that it is a "conspiracy theory." Indeed, it almost seems to be a requirement of admission into public discourse to announce that one rejects conspiracy theories. What is the logic behind this thinking? It cannot be that we literally reject the very idea that conspiracies occur. We all accept conspiracy theories of all sorts. We accept a conspiracy theory whenever we believe that two or more people have conspired in secret to achieve some goal, such as to rob a bank, defraud customers, or fix prices. We would be more honest, therefore, if we followed the precedent of Michael Moore, who has said: "Now, I'm not into conspiracy theories, except the ones that are true."[44]

To refine this point slightly, we can say that we accept all those conspiracy theories that we believe to be true, while we reject all those that we believe to be false. We cannot, therefore, divide people into those who accept conspiracy theories and those who reject them. The division between people on this issue involves simply the question of which conspiracy theories they accept and which ones they reject.[45]

To apply this analysis to the attacks of 9/11: It is false to suggest that those who allege that the attacks occurred because of official complicity are "conspiracy theorists" while those who accept the official account are not. People differ on this issue merely in terms of which conspiracy theory they hold to be true, or at least most probable. According to the official account, the attacks of 9/11 occurred because of a conspiracy among Muslims, with Osama bin Laden being the chief conspirator. Revisionists reject that theory, at least as a sufficient account of what happened, maintaining that the attacks cannot be satisfactorily explained without postulating conspiracy by officials of the US government, at least in allowing the attacks to succeed. The choice, accordingly, is simply between (some version of) the received conspiracy theory and (some version of) the revisionist conspiracy theory.

Which of these competing theories we accept depends, or at least should depend, on which one we believe to be better supported by the relevant facts. Those who hold the revisionist theory have become convinced that there is considerable evidence that not only suggests the falsity of the received conspiracy theory, which we are calling "the official account," but also points to the truth of the revisionist theory. I turn now to that evidence.

PART ONE

THE EVENTS OF 9/11

CHAPTER ONE

FLIGHTS 11 AND 175: HOW COULD THE HIJACKERS' MISSIONS HAVE SUCCEEDED?

In many respects, the strongest evidence provided by critics of the official account involves simply the events of 9/11 itself. At 8:46 AM, one hijacked airplane crashed into the North Tower of the World Trade Center (WTC). At 9:03, another crashed into the South Tower. And at 9:38, the Pentagon was hit. In light of standard procedures for dealing with hijacked airplanes, however, not one of these planes should have reached its target, let alone all three of them. It is also far from clear how the New York attacks could have succeeded in the sense of causing the buildings of the WTC to collapse. There are, furthermore, disturbing questions about the third airliner—whether it was really the aircraft that hit the Pentagon—and about the fourth one—whether it was the one plane that *was* shot down. Finally, after examining questions that have been raised about all these matters, I will look at questions raised by President Bush's behavior that day. The present chapter, however, deals only with Flights 11 and 175 and the collapse of the WTC buildings.

American Airlines Flight 11

The first plane to be hijacked was American Airlines (AA) Flight 11, which left Boston at 7:59 AM. At 8:14, besides failing to respond to an order from FAA (Federal Aviation Administration) ground control to climb, its radio and transponder went off,[1] suggesting that it had *possibly* been hijacked. At 8:20, with FAA ground control watching its flight path on radar, the plane went radically off course, leading ground control to conclude that it had *probably* been hijacked. At 8:21, flight attendants reported by telephone that the plane had *definitely* been taken over by hijackers, who had already killed some people. At 8:28, the plane turned toward New York. At 8:44, Secretary of Defense Rumsfeld was in the Pentagon talking about terrorism with Representative Christopher Cox.

"Let me tell ya," the Associated Press quoted Rumsfeld as saying, "I've been around the block a few times. There will be another event. There will be another event."[2] And, if he in fact said this, he was right. Two minutes later, at 8:46, Flight 11 crashed into the WTC's North Tower. This was 32 minutes after evidence that the plane had possibly been hijacked and 25 minutes after knowledge that it definitely had been.

Skeptics about the official account believe that the attempt to crash an airliner into the WTC could not have been successful under normal circumstances. The basic problem, they argue, is that there are standard procedures for situations such as this and that, if they had been followed, Flight 11 would have been intercepted by fighter jets within 10 minutes of any sign that it may have been hijacked. Had the plane then failed to obey the standard signal to follow the fighter jets to an airport to land, it would have been shot down. This would have occurred by 8:24, or 8:30 at the latest, so that the question of whether to shoot down a commercial airliner over the heart of New York City would not have arisen.

As evidence, the skeptics cite FAA regulations, which instruct air traffic controllers:

> Consider that an aircraft emergency exists...when:...There is unexpected loss of radar contact and radio communications with any... aircraft.... If...you are in doubt that a situation constitutes an emergency or potential emergency, handle it as though it were an emergency.[3]

Accordingly, at 8:14, the loss of radio contact alone would have led the flight controller to begin emergency procedures. The loss of the transponder signal would have made the situation doubly suspect. The controller, after finding that it was impossible to re-establish radio contact, would have immediately contacted the National Military Command Center (NMCC) in the Pentagon and its North American Aerospace Defense Command (NORAD), which would have immediately had jets sent up—"scrambled"—from the nearest military airport. According to spokespersons for NORAD, from the time the FAA senses that something is wrong, "it takes about one minute" for it to contact NORAD, and then NORAD can scramble fighters "within a matter of minutes to anywhere in the United States."[4] "According to the US Air Force's own website," reports Nafeez Ahmed, an F-15 routinely "goes from 'scramble order' to 29,000 feet in only 2.5 minutes" and then can fly at 1,850 nmph (nautical miles per hour).[5] If normal procedures had been followed, accordingly, Flight 11 would have been intercepted by 8:24, and certainly no later than 8:30, 16 minutes before it, in the actual course of events, crashed into the WTC.

Furthermore, even if radio contact and the transponder's signal had not been lost, the fact that the plane went radically off course at 8:20 would have led the FAA to notify the military. Every plane has a flight plan, which consists of a sequence of geographic points, or "fixes," and, according to a report by MSNBC:

> Pilots are supposed to hit each fix with pinpoint accuracy. If a plane deviates by 15 degrees, or two miles from that course, the flight controllers will hit the panic button. They'll call the plane, saying "American 11, you're deviating from course." It's considered a real emergency.[6]

So, even if the FAA had waited until the plane went off course at 8:20, the plane should have been intercepted by 8:30, or 8:35 at the latest, again in plenty of time to prevent it from going into New York City.

As to what would occur upon interception, Ahmed explains by quoting the FAA manual:

> [The interceptor military craft communicates by] Rocking wings from a position slightly above and ahead of, and normally to the left of, the intercepted aircraft.... This action conveys the message: "You have been intercepted." The commercial jet is then supposed to respond by rocking its wings to indicate compliance, upon which the interceptor performs a "slow level turn, normally to the left, on to the desired heading [direction]." The commercial plane then responds by following the escort.[7]

If Flight 11 had been thus intercepted but did *not* respond, it would, according to standard procedures, have been shot down. Marine Corps Major Mike Snyder, a NORAD spokesman, after telling the *Boston Globe* that NORAD's "fighters routinely intercept aircraft," continued:

> When planes are intercepted, they typically are handled with graduated response. The approaching fighter may rock its wingtips to attract the pilot's attention, or make a pass in front of the aircraft. Eventually, it can fire tracer rounds in the airplane's path, or, under certain circumstances, down it with a missile.[8]

The question raised by critics, of course, is why this did not happen in the case of Flight 11. Why was the plane not even intercepted?

Some confusion about this matter, they point out, was created by Vice President Cheney during an interview on "Meet the Press" on September 16, in which he suggested that the "question of whether or not we would intercept commercial aircraft," as well as the question of whether it would be shot down, was "a presidential-level decision." This statement, point out the critics, confuses two matters: intercepting and shooting down, and interception is a routine matter, which occurs well over a hundred times a year.[9] The confusion of these two matters was also aided by General Richard Myers, then Acting Chairman of the Joint Chiefs of Staff,[10] in testimony to the Senate Armed Services Committee on September 13, in which he stated: "[A]fter the second tower was hit, I spoke to the commander of NORAD, General Eberhart. And at that point, I think the decision was at that point to start launching aircraft."[11] He, like Cheney, implied that fighters would be sent up to intercept flights only if ordered to by commanders at the highest level. But interception occurs routinely, as a matter of standard operating procedure, even if shooting down a plane would be, as Cheney implied, "a presidential-level decision."

Moreover, although some researchers have accepted the view that a hijacked plane could be shot down only with presidential authorization,[12] Thierry Meyssan points out that the military regulations seem to say otherwise. According to these regulations,

> In the event of a hijacking, the NMCC [National Military Command Center] will be notified by the most expeditious means by the FAA. The NMCC will, with the exception of requests needing an immediate response...forward requests for DoD [Department of Defense] assistance to the Secretary of Defense for approval.[13]

Accordingly, concludes Meyssan, the regulations give the responsibility for shooting down hijacked airplanes "to the Secretary of Defense." Furthermore, as the phrase beginning "with the exception" shows, if the Secretary of Defense cannot be contacted in time, other people in the line of command would have the authority. According to a Department of Defense document cited by Meyssan:

> It is possible to formulate to any element in the chain of command "Requests needing Immediate Response." These arise from imminently serious conditions where only an immediate action taken by an official of the Department of Defense or a military commander can prevent loss of lives, or mitigate human suffering and great property damage.[14]

According to this reading, many people in the line of command would have had the authority to prevent the "loss of lives" and "great property damage" that occurred when AA Flight 11 slammed into the North Tower of the WTC.

One might argue, to be sure, that at that time no one would have known that the plane was going to do that. But, critics of the official account would reply, that argument—besides not explaining why Flight 11 was not at least intercepted—would not apply to the *second* plane to crash into the WTC.

United Airlines Flight 175

UA Flight 175 left Boston at 8:14 AM, which was just when the FAA was learning that Flight 11 may have been hijacked. At 8:42, its radio and transponder went off and it veered off course. Knowing by then that the earlier flight had definitely been hijacked and was flying across New York City, FAA officials would surely have been ready to contact the military immediately. They, in fact, reportedly notified NORAD at 8:43.[15] NORAD should have had fighter jets intercepting this plane by 8:53. And by this time, being 7 minutes after the first hijacked plane had hit the WTC, the fighters certainly should have been ready to shoot down this second hijacked plane if it did not immediately follow orders. Instead, however, no planes intercepted Flight 175, and it crashed into the WTC's South Tower at 9:03.

Another disturbing feature about this crash, especially to the families of the victims, is that at 8:55, a public announcement was reportedly broadcast inside the South Tower, saying that the building was secure, so that people could return to their offices. Such announcements reportedly continued until a few minutes before the building was hit, and may have contributed "to the deaths of hundreds of people."[16] Paul Thompson asks: "Given that at 8:43 NORAD was notified Flight 175 was hijacked and headed toward New York City, why weren't people in the building warned?" A disturbing question, since Thompson's implication seems to be that perhaps someone other than the hijackers was seeking to ensure that a significant number of lives were lost.

In any case, given the fact that this plane hit the WTC 17 minutes after the first crash, none of the reasons that could be imagined to explain why standard procedures broke down with regard to the first plane—such as inattentive air traffic controllers, pilots at military bases not on full alert, or the assumption that the plane's aberrant behavior did not mean that it had been hijacked—could be used to explain why Flight 175 was not shot down or even intercepted. For one thing, by then all the technicians at NORAD's Northeast Air Defense Sector "had their headsets linked to the FAA in Boston to hear about Flight 11," so NORAD would have been fully aware of the seriousness of the situation.[17] Even more puzzling is why in another 35 minutes, at 9:38, the Pentagon would be hit, but we will wait until the next chapter to examine this third flight. The present task is to consider the official account of the first two flights and the response of the critics.

Why Were Flights 11 and 175 Not Intercepted?

One of the strange things about the official account, say its critics, is that there has been more than one version of it. General Myers, in his aforementioned testimony to the Senate Armed Services Committee on September 13, said: "When it became clear what the threat was, we did scramble fighter aircraft." When asked whether that order was given "before or after the Pentagon was struck," Myers—who was acting chairman of the Joint Chiefs of Staff—replied: "That order, to the best of my knowledge, was after the Pentagon was struck."[18] One problem with this statement, point out critics, is that officials at NMCC would have become clear about "what the threat was" long before the Pentagon itself was hit at 9:38. It would have been clear at least by 8:46, when the WTC was hit and another hijacked plane was heading in its direction. Another problem, of course, is that it was not necessary for officials at NMCC and NORAD to understand fully "what the threat was" in order for there to be jets in the air to intercept Flights 11, 175, and any unauthorized aircraft headed toward Washington. Standard operating procedures should have taken care of all those things.

This version of the official account was also told by at least two other officials. According to a story in the *Boston Globe* on September 15, Major Mike Snyder, speaking for NORAD, said that no fighters were scrambled until after the Pentagon was hit. And on September 16, when Tim Russert, during his aforementioned interview with Vice President Cheney on "Meet the Press," expressed surprise that although we knew about the first hijacking by 8:20, "it seems we were not able to scramble fighter jets in time to protect the Pentagon," Cheney did not dispute this statement.[19]

The major problem with this first version of the official account, of course, is that it says that military behavior completely contradicted standard procedures, which call for jets to be scrambled as soon as a suspected hijacking is reported. Despite the fact that statements by Myers and Cheney seemed to suggest otherwise, it requires no command from on high for fighter jets to be scrambled. Rather, the critics point out, an order for them *not* to be scrambled is what would require a command from on high. For example, Illarion Bykov and Jared Israel, commenting on the fact that the standard emergency systems failed on 9/11, say: "This could only happen if individuals in high positions worked in a coordinated way to make them fail."[20]

Within a few days, in any case, NORAD began saying that it *did* have planes scrambled but they arrived too late.[21] To the critics, however, this second version seems almost as strange as the first.

According to this version, NORAD was not notified by the FAA of the hijacking of Flight 11 until 8:40. This would have been 26 minutes after the plane's radio and transponder went off and 20 minutes after it went off course. Allan Wood and Paul Thompson write:

Is NORAD's claim credible? If so, the air traffic controllers...should have been fired and subject to possible criminal charges for their inaction. To date, however, there has been no word of any person being disciplined.... If NORAD's claim is false, and it was indeed informed within the time frame outlined in FAA regulations...,that would mean NORAD did absolutely nothing for almost thirty minutes while a hijacked commercial airliner flew off course through some of the most congested airspace in the world. Presumably, that would warrant some very serious charges. Again, no one associated with NORAD or the FAA has been punished.[22]

The lack of disciplinary action suggests either that this story is false or that the relevant parties at FAA and/or NORAD did what they had been instructed to do.

This account has more anomalous features. After NORAD received word of the hijacking, according to this account, it did not give the scramble order until 8:46, six minutes after it had been notified. Furthermore, NORAD inexplicably gave this order *not* to McGuire Air Force Base in New Jersey, which is only 70 miles from NYC, but to Otis Air National Guard Base in Cape Cod, which is over 180 miles away.

That would have made no difference with regard to Flight 11, of course, because 8:46 was when it was striking the WTC.

In the meantime, however, NORAD says that it had received notification at 8:43 from the FAA of Flight 175's hijacking, so the two F-15s that were given the scramble order at 8:46 were sent after this flight instead. But, inexplicably, the F-15s are said not to have taken off until 6 minutes later, at 8:52.

However, perhaps the strangest feature of this story, from the viewpoint of the critics, involves its failure to explain, even with all those delays, why the planes did not arrive in time to stop the second attack on the WTC. At 8:52, there were still 11 minutes until 9:03, when Flight 175 would hit the second tower. Lieutenant Colonel Timothy Duffy, a pilot said to have flown one of the F-15s, has been quoted as stating that he "was in full-blower all the way," which would mean he was going over 1,875 nmph.[23] At this speed, the F-15s would have been covering over 30 miles a minute. Hence, allowing the standard 2.5 minutes for them to get airborne and up to speed, they should have reached Manhattan in about 8 minutes, having a full 3 minutes left to shoot down the errant airliner. And yet, according to this second version of the official account, the F-15s were still 70 miles away when Flight 175 crashed into the South Tower.[24] Indeed, according to NORAD's timeline, it took them 19 minutes to reach the city. So, if the story about jets from Otis is even true, they must have been traveling at far less than "full blower"—in fact, if we accept NORAD's timeline, more like 700 mph.[25]

Furthermore, even if the times in this story are adjusted enough to account for the fact that the planes were late, there is still the question of why the order was not given to McGuire Air Force Base. As Ahmed says, an F-15 flying at 1,850 nmph "would cover the ground from New Jersey's Air Force Base to New York in under 3 minutes, and thus could have easily intercepted Flight 175."[26] So, the critics conclude, even if this second story is accepted, the WTC's second tower should not have been hit.

Finally, the claim that jets were scrambled to try to stop this second hijacked plane still leaves us with no explanation as to why standard procedures were not followed with regard to the *first* one. Accepting this second version of the official account would, furthermore, leave us puzzled as to how General Myers, Vice President Cheney, and the NORAD spokesman could have at first believed that no planes whatsoever had been scrambled until after the Pentagon had been hit.

Accordingly, some critics, including some with military experience, think that the second version was fabricated. For example, Stan Goff, a retired Master Sergeant who taught Military Science at West Point, concludes that no Air Force jets were scrambled until after the Pentagon was hit.[27] Andreas von Bülow, former State Secretary in the German Defense Ministry, said: "For 60 decisive minutes, the military and intelligence agencies let the fighter planes stay on the ground."[28]

Under either version of the official account, in any case, the successful attacks on the WTC should not have been possible. This view is supported by Anatoli Kornukov, the commander in chief of the Russian Air Force, who was quoted the day after 9/11 as saying: "Generally it is impossible to carry out an act of terror on the scenario which was used in the USA yesterday.... As soon as something like that happens here, I am reported about that right away and in a minute we are all up."[29] After quoting Kornukov's statement, Ahmed comments: "It is, of course, well known that the US Air Force is far superior to Russia's," adding that some reasonable inferences can be drawn from these facts—in particular, that the attacks on the WTC could have happened only if standard operating procedures were suspended.

> Standard Operating Procedures (SOP) were completely and inexplicably dropped on 11th September—something that had never occurred before. The question then remains as to who was responsible for ensuring that routine emergency response rules were not adhered to.[30]

Bykov and Israel have little doubt about who that was, saying:

> The sabotage of routine protective systems, controlled by strict hierarchies, would never have been contemplated let alone attempted absent the involvement of the supreme US military command. This includes at least US President George Bush, US Secretary of Defense Donald Rumsfeld and the then-Acting Head of the Joint Chiefs of Staff, Air Force General Richard B. Myers.[31]

This is indeed the question that must be faced: Could a plan to hijack airplanes and crash them into the WTC have been successful without "stand down" orders approved by Bush, Rumsfeld, and Myers?

As the conclusions drawn by critics of the official account of Flights 11 and 175 show, this account has evoked disturbing questions.[32] Further disturbing questions have been raised by the collapse of the buildings of the World Trade Center.[33]

The Collapse of the WTC Buildings

According to the official account, the North and South Towers (the Twin Towers) collapsed due to the impact of the airliners plus the intense heat produced by the resulting fires. Calling this the "official account," I should add, does not mean that it has been endorsed by any official body. The Federal Emergency Management Agency (FEMA) was given the task of investigating the collapse, but when it issued its report in May of 2002, it declared that "the sequence of events leading to the collapse of each tower could not be definitively determined."[34] Nevertheless, FEMA's report was filled with speculation that served to support the official theory.

This theory is widely rejected by those familiar with the facts. It was rejected already in January of 2002 in an article by Bill Manning entitled "$elling Out the Investigation," which was published in *Fire Engineering*, a trade magazine with ties to the New York Fire Department. Manning reported that a growing number of fire protection engineers had suggested that "the structural damage from the planes and the explosive ignition of jet fuel in themselves were not enough to bring down the towers."[35] In the meantime, many more objections to the official theory have been raised. Some of these objections involve special problems associated with the collapse of a third building in the complex known as Building 7 (WTC-7).

To evaluate these objections, it is necessary to review some of the facts. The North Tower (WTC-1) was struck at 8:46 AM. It collapsed one hour and 42 minutes later, at 10:28. The South Tower (WTC-2) was struck at 9:03 AM. It collapsed 56 minutes later, at 9:59. Building Number 7 (WTC-7), which was two blocks away and was not struck, collapsed at 5:20 PM. These facts immediately suggest two questions: Why did the South Tower, which was struck 17 minutes later than the North Tower, nevertheless collapse 29 minutes earlier? And why did WTC-7 collapse at all, given the fact that it was not struck? Additional details about the collapse of these three buildings raise even more questions. I will first deal with questions that have been raised about the North and South Towers, then turn to WTC-7.

The Twin Towers: According one account that became widely circulated shortly after 9/11 by being articulated on a NOVA program, the North and South Towers were caused to collapse when the heat of the fires, fed by the jet fuel, melted the buildings' steel columns.[36] It is now universally agreed, however, that the fires would not have been nearly hot enough. To melt steel, one needs a temperature in the range of 2,770°F (1,500°C), which can be produced only by some special device, such as an oxyacetyline torch. A hydrocarbon fire, such as one based on refined kerosene—which is what jet fuel is—does not get nearly that hot. As explained by Thomas Eagar, professor of materials engineering and engineering systems at MIT, the maximum possible temperature for an open fire fueled by hydrocarbons would be 1,600 to 1,700°F. Moroever, since the WTC fires were fuel-rich fires, as evidenced by the fact that they gave off much black smoke, they were not even very hot for hydrocarbon fires, "probably only 1,200 or 1,300°F."[37]

As the melting theory illustrates, some of the widely accepted explanations of the collapse of the towers are unsound scientifically. Many other theories are inadequate because they do not take account of specific facts about the buildings and the nature of the collapses. Before examining any more theories, therefore, we should look at some of these facts.

Each of the towers was about 1,300 feet tall. To support these extremely tall buildings, there were 47 steel columns in the central core of each building and 240 steel columns around the perimeter, with each column being far thicker at the bottom than at the top. The perimeter columns were connected to the core by means of steel bar-joist trusses in the concrete floors. Although there has been considerable talk of "flimsy trusses,"[38] *Scientific American* quoted engineer Robert McNamara as saying "nowadays, they just don't build them as tough as the World Trade Center." With regard to the bar-joist trusses in particular, the FEMA report said: "The floor framing system for the two towers was complex and substantially more redundant than typical bar joist floor systems."[39] Investigations of some recovered steel have found, furthermore, that far from being defective, it met or even exceeded the standard requirements.[40]

Given these facts about the towers, we can dismiss a second idea that has been widely promulgated, namely, that the impact of the airplanes would have substantially weakened the towers. Thomas Eagar says that the impact of the airplanes would have been insignificant, because "the number of columns lost on the initial impact was not large and the loads were shifted to remaining columns in this highly redundant structure."[41] "[W]ithin a few dozen seconds after the plane crash," Eric Hufschmid points out, "[t]he North tower was quiet, stable, and motionless."[42]

Those who support the official account, such as Eagar himself, generally argue that the collapses must be explained in terms of the heat from the fires. In Eagar's words: "The real damage in the World Trade Center resulted from the size of the fire." Because the steel used in buildings must be able to hold five times its normal load, Eagar points out, the steel in the towers could have collapsed only if it was heated to the point at which it "lost 80 percent of its strength," which would be about 1,300°F. Eagar believes that this is what happened.[43] The credibility of the official theory, accordingly, depends at least in part on whether there is evidence that the towers had the requisite fires.

To evaluate this issue we must acknowledge the distinction, emphasized by Eagar himself, between temperature and heat (or energy).[44] Something, such as a burning match or light bulb, can have a very high temperature but not generate much heat (energy), because it is so small. A burning match would never bring a steel beam up to its temperature. A 1,300°F fire would bring a huge steel beam up to this temperature only if it were a very big fire, so that it had lots of energy.

There is one more condition: The big fire would have to be applied to the steel beam for a considerable period of time.

For the official theory to be credible, therefore, the fires in the towers must have been moderately hot; they must have been large fires, spreading throughout the buildings; and they must have burned for a considerable length of time. All the available evidence, however, suggests that the opposite was the case. A most valuable book for examining this evidence is Eric Hufschmid's *Painful Questions*,[45] which contains the best set of photographs available.

The Twin Towers have commonly been described as "towering infernos." From the point of view of human bodies, this was a true description of the North Tower, from which many people leaped to their death to avoid the smoke and flames in the floors above the 96th floor, where the airplane hit. There is a huge difference, however, between the tolerance of human bodies and that of steel. Photographs of the North Tower provide no evidence of any fire that could have weakened its steel significantly. A photograph taken within 16 minutes of when the North Tower was hit (because the South Tower had not yet been hit) shows only a dark hole with black smoke pouring out of it. No flames are visible. As Hufschmid points out: "The lack of flames is an indication that the fires were small, and the dark smoke is an indication that the fires were suffocating."[46] Another photo, taken from another angle just after the South Tower was hit, shows some flames on floors just above the point of impact but no others. However great the flames may have been in the first several minutes, while they were being fed by the jet fuel, this skyscraper was not a towering inferno by the time 16 minutes had passed.[47]

We have all, of course, seen pictures of a huge fireball outside the South Tower.[48] There was also a fireball outside the North Tower after it was hit.[49] These fireballs were created by the burning of the jet fuel that was spilled. The South Tower had a far bigger fireball because it was hit near a corner, so more fuel was spilled outside. These fireballs generated a great amount of heat. But it was momentary, because the fuel was quickly burned up.[50] The fact that the South Tower's fireball was bigger, furthermore, does not mean that the South Tower's fires were bigger. To the contrary. Because so much jet fuel was burned up within the first few minutes, there was less to feed the fire inside the building. As Hufschmid reports, "photos show the spectacular flames vanished quickly, and then the fire remained restricted to one area of the tower...[and] slowly diminished."[51]

The facts about the fire, therefore, seem to rule out any version of the official account according to which each tower had hot, widespread, long-lasting fires. Insofar as there were hot fires, they were localized and of short duration. Such fires, even if they were 1,300°F, could not have brought much if any steel up to that temperature.[52]

Another count against the fire theory is the likelihood that, even if the Twin Towers had been engulfed in raging fires, they would not have collapsed. Prior to the alleged exceptions of 9/11, a steel-framed building had never before collapsed solely because of fire. As a report by FEMA in 1991 stated about a fire in a Philadelphia building that year, the fire was so energetic that "[b]eams and girders sagged and twisted," but "[d]espite this extraordinary exposure, the columns continued to support their loads without obvious damage."[53]

Defenders of the fire theory, however, appeal to the special characteristics of the Twin Towers. Given these special characteristics, they contend, the fire did not have to heat all the steel by spreading throughout all the floors. According to Thomas Eagar, it was sufficient to have a hot fire that covered one floor. The culprits, he says, were the "angle clips," which "held the floor joists between the columns on the perimeter wall and the core structure," and which, he says, were not designed to hold five times their normal load.[54] Articulating what critics call the "zipper" version of the truss theory, Eagar says: "Once you started to get angle clips to fail in one area, it put extra load on other angle clips, and then it unzipped around the building on that floor in a matter of seconds."[55] And then:

> As the joists on one or two of the most heavily burned floors gave way and the outer box columns began to bow outward, the floors above them also fell. The floor below (with its 1,300-ton design capacity) could not support the roughly 45,000 tons of ten floors (or more) above crashing down on these angle clips. This started the domino effect that caused the buildings to collapse within ten seconds.[56]

Something like this theory was endorsed in the FEMA report, which spoke of "a pancake-type of collapse of successive floors."[57]

There are, however, many problems with this account. First, even this more modest view of the amount of steel that had to become very hot would seem to require more heat than was present, especially in the South Tower.

Second, as Hufschmid points out: "In order for a floor to fall, hundreds of joints had to break almost simultaneously on 236 exterior columns and 47 core columns."[58]

Third, Eagar means his theory to do justice to the fact that the towers collapsed "within ten seconds." For a 1,300-foot building, however, ten seconds is almost free-fall speed. But if each floor produced just a little resistance, so that breaking through each one took a half second, the collapse of all those floors—80 or 95 of them—would have taken 40 to 47 seconds. Can we really believe that the upper part of the buildings encountered virtually no resistance from the lower parts?[59] The problem would be even worse in relation to the North Tower, at least if Hufschmid is right to say that it fell in eight seconds, which would be exactly free-fall speed. "How," he asks, "could the debris crush 100 steel and concrete floors while falling as fast as objects fall through air?"[60]

Fourth, Eagar's theory, like all other versions of the official account, cannot do justice to the fact that the collapse of the towers was *total*, resulting in a pile of rubble that, in Eagar's own words, "was only a few stories high."[61]Even if one granted that his theory might explain why the floors and outer columns collapsed, it does not explain, argues Peter Meyer, the collapse of the massive steel columns in the core of the buildings:

> Why were the lower parts of the massive supporting steel columns not left standing after the collapse? If the official story is true, that the damage was caused by the impacts and fires, which occurred only in the upper floors, and that the floors then pancaked, one would expect the massive steel columns in the central core, for, say, the lowest 20 or 30 floors, to have remained standing.[62]

Still another fact about the collapse of the towers that counts against the fire theory is the fact, mentioned at the outset, that the South Tower collapsed first. As we saw, it would take considerable time for fire to heat steel up to its own temperature. All other things being equal, then, the tower that was struck first should have collapsed first. And yet, although the South Tower was struck 17 minutes later than the North Tower, it collapsed 29 minutes earlier. This surprising fact would perhaps not create a problem if the fire in the South Tower had been much bigger. As we have seen, however, the fire in the South Tower was actually much smaller. Upon hearing that one tower took almost twice as long as the other one, therefore, one would assume that that was the South Tower. And yet the opposite was the case. This complete reversal of expectations suggests that the collapse of these buildings was caused by something other than the fires.[63]

And that is, of course, what the critics maintain. Their alternative explanation is that the collapse was an example of a controlled demolition, based on explosives that had been placed throughout the building. This theory, point out its advocates, can explain all the facts discussed thus far. With regard to why the collapse was total and so rapid, Meyer says that

> this is understandable if the bases of the steel columns were destroyed by explosions at the level of the bedrock. With those bases obliterated, and the supporting steel columns shattered by explosions at various levels in the Twin Towers, the upper floors lost all support and collapsed to ground level in about ten seconds.[64]

Also, the controlled demolition theory, in conjunction with the fact that the South Tower was struck near the corner, can account for the otherwise surprising order in which the two towers collapsed.

In both cases the fires within the buildings died down after awhile, giving off only black, sooty smoke. If the Twin Towers were deliberately demolished, and the intention was to blame the collapse on the fires... then the latest time at which the towers could be collapsed would be just as the fires were dying down. Since the fire in the South Tower resulted from the combustion of less fuel than the fire in the North Tower, the fire in the South Tower began to go out earlier than the fire in the North Tower. Those controlling the demolition thus had to collapse the South Tower before they collapsed the North Tower.[65]

There are, furthermore, some additional facts about the collapse of the Twin Towers that seem explainable only by the demolition theory. One of these is the fact that each collapse produced a lot of fine dust or powder, which upon analysis proved to consist primarily of gypsum and concrete.[66] Jeff King, examining the official account in light of what the videos show, says:

> [T]he biggest and most obvious problem that I see is the source of the enormous amount of very fine dust that we see generated during the collapse.... Where does the energy come from to turn all this reinforced concrete into dust?[67]

And as Hufshmid adds, photos of the rubble show only "a few small pieces of concrete," which means that "[v]irtually every piece of concrete shattered into dust." As a result, "Perhaps 100,000 tons of concrete in each tower was pulverized to a powder. This required a lot of energy."[68] What is especially problematic, King suggests, is

> how much very fine concrete dust is ejected from the top of the building very early in the collapse. Since it should at most be accelerating under gravity at 32 feet per second, things would actually be moving quite slowly at first.... It is very hard to imagine a physical mechanism to generate that much dust with concrete slabs bumping into each other at 20 or 30 mph.[69]

Hufschmid points out, moreover, that even concrete slabs hitting the ground at free-fall speed would not be pulverized. "In order to pulverize concrete into powder, explosives must be used."[70]

The use of explosives is perhaps even more strongly suggested by another feature of the collapses, alluded to in King's second statement, namely, that when the towers started to collapse, they did not fall straight down, as the pancake theory holds. They exploded. The powder was ejected horizontally from the buildings with such force that the buildings were surrounded by enormous dust clouds that were perhaps three times the width of the buildings themselves. The photographs in Hufschmid's book are especially valuable for helping one grasp this overwhelmingly impressive and important fact.[71] What other than explosives could turn concrete into powder and then eject it horizontally 150 feet or more? And if it be suspected that the dust simply floated out, some of the photographs show that rather large pieces of the tower were also thrown out 150 feet or more.[72]

Another startling feature of the collapse would have required still more energy. Besides powdery dust, the other major component of the rubble was, as would be expected, steel. But the steel was in short sections. "Almost every piece of steel in both towers broke at the joints."[73]

The controlled demolition theory is given additional support by the fact that some people, including some firemen, reported hearing explosions, feeling explosions, or witnessing effects that appeared to be results of explosions, both in the intermediate floors and in the subbasements of the Towers.[74]

Still more support is provided by seismic evidence that a moderately powerful earthquake was recorded as each tower was collapsing. The seismographs at Columbia University's Lamont-Doherty Earth Observatory in Palisades, New York, 21 miles north of the WTC, recorded a 2.1 magnitude earthquake beginning at 9:59:04, then a 2.3 quake beginning at 10:28:31.[75] In each case, "the shocks increased during the first 5 seconds then dropped abruptly to a lower level for about 3 seconds, and then slowly tapered off." This pattern, Hufschmid suggests, reflects the fact that the first explosives detonated were those near the tops of the towers, where the steel columns were the thinnest. The shocks get stronger as the detonation pattern, controlled by a computer program, worked its way down.

The final explosions at the base of the tower and in the basement had to break joints on columns made from 100mm thick steel, so they were powerful explosives. The seismic data peaked when the explosives in the basement were detonated. Then the explosions stopped and the rubble continued to fall for another couple of seconds, resulting in small seismic tremors.[76]

The demolition theory is further supported by reports that molten steel was found at the level of the subbasements. The president of Controlled Demolition, Inc. (in Phoenix, Maryland), Mark Loizeaux, who wrote the clean-up plan for the entire operation, has been quoted as saying that in the third, fourth, and fifth weeks, the clean-up crew found "hot spots of molten steel...at the bottoms of the elevator shafts of the main towers, down seven [basement] levels."[77]

Besides explaining the existence of the widely reported hot spots, which kept smoldering for weeks,[78] the theory that explosives had been set could explain an otherwise inexplicable fact—that after the collapse of the towers, the debris, including the steel, was quickly removed before there could be any significant investigation. The *New York Times* complained, saying: "The decision to rapidly recycle the steel columns, beams and trusses from the WTC in the days immediately after 9/11 means definitive answers may never be known." The next week, the aforementioned essay in *Fire Engineering* said: "The destruction and removal of evidence must stop immediately."[79] But it went ahead at full speed.[80] Explaining the possible significance of this fact, Meyer points out that

> [a] way to prove that the supporting steel columns of the Twin Towers had been blasted by explosives would be to examine fragments from them among the debris for evidence of what metallurgists call "twinning." But the WTC debris was removed as fast as possible and no forensic examination of the debris was permitted.... Almost all the 300,000 tons of steel from the Twin Towers was sold to New York scrap dealers and exported to places like China and Korea as quickly as it could be loaded onto the ships, thereby removing the evidence.[81]

Why this haste, critics wonder, unless the government had something to hide?[82]

WTC-7: Although the collapse of this 47-story building is generally ignored or discussed simply as an afterthought, it is in many respects the most puzzling. Because it was not struck by an airplane, the main ingredients in the typical explanations of the collapse of the Twin Towers cannot be employed. There is, in fact, no official explanation. The FEMA report provided a lot of speculation about what might have happened, but provided no consensus statement about what actually did happen.[83] The report by the House Science Committee also provided no explanation.[84] But insofar as there is an account that is widely accepted in official and media circles, it goes something like this. Although Building 7—which was 355 feet away from the North Tower and still farther from the South Tower—was not hit by any significant amount of falling debris, enough debris did cross over to start a fire. Then besides the fact that the fire chief decided, for some unknown reason, not to have his crew enter this building, the sprinkler system (inexplicably) failed to put out this little fire, and it grew until it was raging. It then came into contact with the thousands of gallons of diesel fuel stored on the ground floor. The resulting fire then became so hot that it caused the building's steel reinforcement to collapse at 5:20 PM.

This theory faces many problems. First, there is no evidence of any raging fire. "Every photo taken of building 7," Hufschmid reports, "shows only a few tiny fires in only a few windows," primarily on the 7th and 12th floors.[85]

Second, there is again the problem of how a hydrocarbon fire, even had it been raging, could have caused the collapse, especially since Buildings 4, 5, and 6 did have raging fires but did not collapse.[86] In this case, moreover, the collapse could not be partly explained by the impact and fuel of an airplane, so WTC-7 would be the first steel-framed building in history to collapse solely from fire damage.[87] If such a thing really happened on 9/11, critics point out, this would be an event of overwhelming importance. Everything that architects and building engineers have long assumed about steel-framed buildings would need to be rethought. Insurance companies around the world would need to recalculate all their rates on the basis of the realization that ordinary fires could cause steel-framed buildings to collapse. And so on. And yet the idea that WTC-7 collapsed because of fire has been accepted as if it were nothing unusual. In an essay entitled "WTC-7: The Improbable Collapse," Scott Loughrey says:

> FEMA's nonchalance about WTC-7's collapse is stunning. Structural failures of this magnitude do not normally take place.... [Do] we now live in an era when tall steel buildings can collapse in large cities without any significant discussion of why?[88]

Third, there are several features that would be difficult for the official theory because they suggest controlled demolition. Indeed, Hufschmid emphasizes, the collapse of WTC-7, unlike that of the Twin

Towers, suggests a typical demolition, because "Building 7 collapsed at its bottom."

> When Building 7 collapsed, the interior fell first, and that caused the outside of the building to move inward.... The result was a very tiny pile of rubble, with the outside of the building collapsing on top of the pile. This is how conventional demolitions operate.[89]

A significant amount of powdery dust was also produced, although in this case there was not as much dust and most of it was produced at the ground, where this collapse began, instead of in the air.[90] Seismic vibrations were registered at the time of the collapse, although they were only one-tenth the magnitude of those associated with the other towers, and there were two hot spots in the rubble from this collapse, one of which was extremely hot.[91] Molten steel was also reportedly found at this site.[92] Finally, the steel was quickly removed from this site as well, and with even less justification, for the building had long since been evacuated, so there was no need to search for survivors, as there had been at the Twin Towers. So what possible justification was there for the destruction of forensic evidence—which is generally considered a serious crime?

In conclusion, I return to the point that the FEMA report actually gave no explanation. It instead said:

> The specifics of the fires in WTC 7 and how they caused the building to collapse remain unknown at this time. Although the total diesel fuel on the premises contained massive potential energy, the best hypothesis has only a low probability of occurrence.[93]

It must be recognized, however, that FEMA had been given an impossible assignment—to explain the collapse of this building while remaining within the framework of the official theory. Not being able to suggest that the collapse resulted from a controlled demolition, the best FEMA could come up with was a theory having "only a low probability."

The same understanding must be applied to Thomas Eagar and all the other experts who have presented highly improbable explanations of the collapse of the Twin Towers. If political correctness were not a factor, so that they could simply state the most probable hypothesis, given the evidence, most of them would surely choose controlled demolition. For example, Matthys Levy, who suggested that the towers fell because their steel melted, also said: "It was very much like a controlled demolition when you look at it."[94] If it was indeed a controlled demolition, of course, that would mean that the terrorists were able to succeed in their mission to bring down the World Trade Center only because it was an inside job.

The questions raised about the official accounts of Flight 77, Flight 175, and the collapse of Buildings 1, 2, and 7 of the World Trade Center do not necessarily point to presidential complicity. But they do seem to point to official complicity at some level. Although the evidence that the collapse of the WTC was an inside job might mean that it was planned by private parties, the fact that the federal government allowed forensic evidence to be removed suggests at least the first possible view mentioned in the Introduction: official complicity in a cover-up. But then this first view—according to which no US officials played a role in facilitating the attacks—seems to be ruled out by the evidence related to Flights 11 and 175, which seems to require involvement by at least the Pentagon's NMCC and NORAD. The evidence about the flights also seems to rule out the second possible view, according to which no US agencies had any specific knowledge of the attacks in advance. The attacks on the WTC, it would seem, could not have succeeded unless some US officials had given "stand down" orders for standard operating procedures to be canceled on that particular day. And, although this might be taken to mean the fifth possible view, according to which the Pentagon gave those orders, it would be difficult to believe that such orders could have been given without White House approval. Examinations of the official account of the attacks on the WTC in relation to various relevant facts have, in any case, raised disturbing questions. Further disturbing questions have been evoked, moreover, by tensions between the facts and the official accounts of the other flights.

CHAPTER TWO

FLIGHT 77: WAS IT REALLY THE AIRCRAFT THAT STRUCK THE PENTAGON?

A Flight 77 left Dulles airport in Washington, DC, at 8:20. At 8:46, it went significantly off course for several minutes, but reportedly no fighter jets were scrambled. At 8:50, the plane got back on course, but radio contact was lost, and at 8:56 the plane's transponder went off and the plane disappeared from the air traffic controller's radar screen in Indianapolis. But no jet fighters were scrambled to find it. At 9:09, this air traffic controller warned that the plane may have crashed in Ohio.[1] *USA Today*, furthermore, later printed a story with this statement: "Another plane disappears from radar and might have crashed in Kentucky. The reports are so serious that [FAA head Jane] Garvey notifies the White House that there has been another crash."[2] In any case, Flight 77 is not heard from again—or at least, according to the official account, not until 9:25.

At 9:25, which was 29 minutes after Flight 77 disappeared, air controllers at Dulles Airport reported seeing a fast-moving plane, which, they warned, appeared to be heading toward the White House.[3] At 9:27, Vice President Cheney and National Security Advisor Condoleeza Rice were reportedly told, while in the bunker below the White House, that an airplane, being tracked by radar, was 50 miles outside Washington and headed toward it.[4] Beginning at 9:33, radar data reportedly showed the aircraft crossing the Capitol Beltway and heading toward the Pentagon, which it flew over at 9:35.[5] Then, starting from about 7,000 feet above the ground, the aircraft made a difficult "downward spiral, turning almost a complete circle and dropping the last 7,000 feet in two-and-a-half minutes."[6] At this time, Secretary of Defense Rumsfeld, according to the official account, had not been informed of the approaching aircraft and was still with Representative Cox. While they together watched the television coverage of the WTC, Rumsfeld reportedly demonstrated his predictive powers again, saying: "Believe me, this isn't over yet. There's going to be another attack, and it could be us." Moments later, at about 9:38, the Pentagon was hit.[7] As a result of the crash and the ensuing fire, 125 workers in the Pentagon, primarily civilians, were killed.

Although later that day the aircraft that struck the Pentagon was said to be Flight 77, which was a Boeing 757, this equation was evidently not immediately obvious. Danielle O'Brien, one of the air traffic controllers at Dulles who reported seeing the aircraft at 9:25, said: "The speed, the maneuverability, the way that he turned, we all thought in the radar room, all of us experienced air traffic controllers, that that was a military plane."[8] Another witness, seeing the plane from a 14th floor apartment in Pentagon City, said that it "seemed to be able to hold eight or twelve persons" and "made a shrill noise like a fighter plane."[9] Lon Rains, editor at *Space News*, said: "I was convinced it was a missile. It came in so fast it sounded nothing like an airplane."[10] Still another witness, who saw it from his automobile, was reported as saying that it "was like a cruise missile with wings."[11] The official account, however, would be that it was a much bigger aircraft, a Boeing 757—indeed, Flight 77 itself.

On that day, that connection was, however, only gradually made. At 10:32, ABC News reported that Flight 77 had been hijacked, but there was no suggestion that it had returned to Washington and hit the Pentagon. Indeed, Fox TV shortly thereafter said that the Pentagon had been hit by a US Air Force flight.[12] Only sometime in the afternoon did it become generally accepted that the aircraft that hit the Pentagon was Flight 77.

Some critics of the official account reject this identification. The chief critic of the official account of the strike on the Pentagon is the aforementioned French researcher Thierry Meyssan, president of the Voltaire Network, which the *Guardian* in April of 2002 described as "a respected independent think tank whose left-leaning research projects have until now been considered models of reasonableness and objectivity."[13]

Officials at the Pentagon have, to be sure, denounced Meyssan's theory. At a Department of Defense news briefing on June 25, 2002, spokesperson Victoria Clarke, when asked about Meyssan's theory, said: "There is no question, there is no doubt what happened that day. And I think it's appalling that anyone might try to put out that kind of myth. I think it's also appalling for anyone to continue to give those sorts of people any kind of publicity."[14] It is understandable, whatever the truth of the matter is, that the Pentagon would want to discourage reporters and other people from examining Meyssan's theory by calling it "appalling." Meyssan himself uses the same term for the official theory, calling it "the appalling fraud."[15]

But, of course, name-calling by either side of the issue should not be allowed to settle anything. The question should be which of the competing theories is best supported by evidence. And Meyssan's arguments, combined with those of other critics, do provide many reasons for concluding that it was not Flight 77 that hit the Pentagon. I will discuss five such reasons, then point out some further difficulties for the official theory about the strike on the Pentagon.

Were the Sources for the Identification Credible?

Meyssan, in addition to noting that the identification between AA Flight 77 and the aircraft that struck the Pentagon was made only gradually, argues that the original sources for this identification are dubious. In particular, he suggests, all but one of the statements on which this identification was based came from military personnel.[16] The first move toward the identification was made by a statement on the website of the Pentagon announcing that it had been hit by a "commercial airliner, possibly hijacked."[17] Then that afternoon the story that this airliner was Flight 77 spread quickly through the media. The source of this story, the *Los Angeles Times* reported, was some military officials speaking on condition of anonymity.[18] The media also started reporting that Flight 77, just before it disappeared from view, had made a U-turn and headed back toward Washington.[19] But, argues Meyssan, since the civilian air controllers were, according to the official account, no longer receiving information from either radar or the transponder, this "information" must also have come from military sources.[20]

The one other statement used to connect Flight 77 with the strike on the Pentagon was made by Theodore ("Ted") Olson, the US Justice Department's Solicitor General. He said that his wife, Barbara Olson—the well-known author and television commentator—had made two phone calls to him from Flight 77 at about 9:25 and 9:30. These conversations, as reported, said nothing about where the plane was or in what direction it was headed, but they did indicate that Flight 77 had not already crashed or exploded but had been hijacked. Flight 77, therefore, at least *might* have been the aircraft that hit the Pentagon.

Skeptics about this identification suggest that there are at least four reasons to doubt Ted Olson's testimony. First, he is very close to the Bush administration. Besides having pleaded George W. Bush's cause before the Supreme Court in the 2000 election dispute, he more recently has defended Vice President Cheney's attempt to prevent the release of papers from his energy task force to the committee investigating the Enron scandal. Second, Olson has stated that there are many situations in which "government officials might quite legitimately have reasons to give false information out."[21] Third, Olson's reports about the conversations with his wife are both vague and self-contradictory.[22] Fourth, on the other flights, telephone calls were reportedly made by several passengers and flight attendants, but Ted Olson is the only person who reported receiving a call from Flight 77. This latter fact is especially strange in light of a later report that at about 9:30 the hijackers told the passengers that they were all going to die and so should call their families. Thompson asks: "Given this announcement, why are there no phone calls from this flight except for Barbara Olson's?"[23] Thompson's question, in other words, is whether there really was a call from her. This question could presumably be answered by subpoenaing the telephone records of her cell phone company, American Airlines, and the Justice Department. Any of the alternative scenarios consistent with this question would need to explain, of course, what became of Barbara Olson, and also whether it is plausible that Ted Olson would have participated in a plan with that outcome. This issue is one of the problems mentioned in Chapter 9 that would face any complicity theory about "what really happened."

Physical Evidence That the Pentagon Was Not Hit by a Boeing 757

In addition to the argument that all the information originally connecting Flight 77 with the aircraft that struck the Pentagon evidently came from dubious sources, a second argument, provided by Meyssan, consists of physical evidence that the Pentagon was not hit by a Boeing 757, which is what AA Flight 77 was.

Most important is the evidence provided by photographs that were taken immediately after the crash. One crucial photo was taken by Tom Horan of the Associated Press just after the firetrucks had arrived but before the firemen had been deployed. (This photo is reproduced in Meyssan's *Pentagate* and on the cover of his *9/11: The Big Lie* and is also available on the Internet.[24]) When this photograph was taken, the west wing's facade had not collapsed. Another photo taken at this time shows that the hole in the facade was between 15 and 18 feet in diameter, contradicting a newspaper report that it was "five stories high and 200 feet wide."[25] This photo also shows no damage above the hole or on either side of it. And neither photo shows any sign of an airplane—no fuselage, no tail, no wings, no engines[26]—or any evidence that the lawn had been scraped.[27] Whatever struck the Pentagon made a clean hit from the air and went completely inside.

Just how far the aircraft went into the Pentagon is shown by a photograph that was taken later and published by the Pentagon (and on the cover of Meyssan's *Pentagate*). This photo shows that the inside wall of the third of the Pentagon's five rings, known as the C-ring, was penetrated, resulting in a hole about seven feet in diameter. This means that the aircraft had the power to penetrate six reinforced walls.

This photographic evidence creates enormous problems for the official account, according to which the damage was caused by an aircraft as large as a Boeing 757. The most obvious problem is that since the aircraft penetrated only the first three rings of the Pentagon, only the *nose* of a Boeing 757 would have gone inside. (This can be seen in a picture, provided by Meyssan, in which the outline of a Boeing 757 is superimposed upon an aerial photograph, provided by the Department of Defense, of the Pentagon's west wing.[28]) The rest of the airplane would have remained outside. As Meyssan comments: "We should thus be able to see the wings and the fuselage outside, and on the lawn in fact." In response, one might suggest that perhaps the plane burned up before any photographs could be taken. But, Meyssan says:

> While the plane's nose is made of carbon and the wings, containing the fuel, can burn, the Boeing's fuselage is aluminum and the jet engines are built out of steel. At the end of the fire, it would necessarily have left a burnt-out wreck.[29]

But not the slightest sign of a burnt-out wreck is shown in the photograph taken by Tom Horan or any of the other photographs.

The official story, to be sure, takes account of this problem by saying that not simply the nose but the entire airplane went inside the Pentagon. This is why it does not appear in the photographs.[30] Other features of the photographic evidence, however, create insuperable difficulties for this theory. One of these features is the fact that the orifice created by the impact, as mentioned above, was at most 18 feet in diameter. Is it not absurd to suggest that a Boeing 757 created and then disappeared into such a small hole? As Meyssan points out, the hole was big enough for the passenger cabin, which is less than twelve feet in width. But the plane's wings give it a breadth of 125 feet. Can anyone seriously believe that a 125-foot-wide airplane created and then went inside a hole less than 20-feet wide?

Evidently so. Some defenders of the official account claim that the wings, upon hitting the strongly reinforced facade of the west wing, would have folded back, allowing the entire plane to disappear within the building. According to one such defense:

> As the front of the Boeing 757 hit the Pentagon, the outer portions of the wings likely snapped during the initial impact, then were pushed inward towards the fuselage and carried into the building's interior; the inner portions of the wings probably penetrated the Pentagon walls with the rest of the plane. Any sizable portions of the wings were destroyed in the explosion or the subsequent fire.[31]

One problem with this explanation, of course, is that after the plane's forward motion was suddenly reduced when the nose hit the Pentagon, the wings would not have folded back. Unless the laws of kinetic energy were momentarily suspended, Meyssan points out, "the wings would have been propelled forwards rather than backwards."[32]

On a Boeing 757, furthermore, the jet engines, made of steel, are attached to the wings, so the wings would have hit the facade with great force. And yet prior to the facade's collapse, as we have seen, the photos reveal no visible damage to the facade on either side of the orifice, even where the engines would have hit the building.

And if that problem is not considered decisive enough, the fact that the photographs clearly show that the facade *above* the opening is completely intact and even unmarked creates a still more insuperable problem, given Boeing 757's big tail. As Meyssan says, when its tail is taken into account, the Boeing is about 40 feet high. So, unless one is going to claim that the tail obligingly ducked before entering, the fact that the facade above the opening is completely intact proves that it was not a Boeing 757 that went inside the Pentagon's west wing. For support, Meyssan quotes French accident investigator François Grangier, who said: "What is certain when one looks at the photo of this facade that remains intact is that it's obvious the plane did not go through there."[33]

The more general problem is that whatever did hit the Pentagon simply did not cause nearly enough destruction for the official story to be true. A Boeing 757, besides being so tall and having such a wide wingspan, weighs over 100 tons. Traveling at a speed of 250 to 440 miles per hour, it would have caused tremendous devastation. And yet, as a photograph supplied by the Department of Defense itself shows, "the plane only destroyed the first ring of the building."[34] The second and third rings were merely penetrated by an aircraft small enough to create a hole only seven feet in diameter.

Furthermore, if the aircraft that hit the Pentagon did too little to have been a Boeing 757, this last-mentioned fact, about the hole in the inside wall of the C-ring, shows that it also did too much. That is, Meyssan points out, the nose of a Boeing, which contains the electronic navigation system, is made of carbon fibers rather than metal. Being "extremely fragile," such a nose could not have gone through three rings of the Pentagon, creating a seven-foot exit hole in the inside wall of the third ring. The Boeing's nose would have been "crushed rather than piercing through." What *could* create such a hole is the head of a missile.

> Certain missiles are specially conceived to have a piercing effect. These missiles are weighted with depleted uranium, an extremely dense metal that heats with slightest friction and renders piercing easier. These missiles are notably used to pierce bunkers. An airplane crashes and smashes. A missile of this type *pierces*.[35]

And this is what the photographs show—that the Pentagon was pierced rather than smashed.

The notion that the Pentagon was hit by a missile rather than an airplane is supported by still another feature of the photographic evidence—the kind of fire it documented. Photos of hydrocarbon fires, such as the fires produced in the Twin Towers by the burning of the jet fuel, show yellow flames mixed with black smoke. But photographs of the Pentagon fire show a *red* flame, indicating the kind of fire produced by the type of missile described above—a much hotter and more instantaneous fire.[36] Suggesting that the Pentagon was hit by "one of the latest generation of AGM-type missiles, armed with a hollow charge and a depleted uranium BLU tip," Meyssan says that a missile of this type can cause "an instantaneous fire, giving off heat in excess of 3,600° Fahrenheit." And that corresponds with the fire started in the Pentagon:

> In traversing the Pentagon's first ring, the aircraft started a fire, as gigantic as it was sudden. Immense flames issued from the building, licking at the facades. They withdrew just as quickly, leaving behind them a cloud of black soot.[37]

The photographic evidence, in sum, provides several reasons to conclude that the Pentagon was not hit by a Boeing passenger plane but was instead hit by a military missile.

This conclusion from the photographic evidence is given additional support by the fact that the aircraft that headed toward the Pentagon was not shot down by on-site missiles. Although some news reports have said that the Pentagon, unlike the White House, has no such missiles, the Pentagon is in fact, Meyssan points out, protected by "[f]ive extremely sophisticated antimissile batteries."[38] And, although Pentagon officials claim that they had no idea that an aircraft was coming their way, an unidentified aircraft was, as we saw earlier, reported at 9:25 to be speeding in that direction. Meyssan says:

> Contrary to the Pentagon's claims, the military thus knew perfectly well that an unidentified vehicle was headed straight for the capitol. Yet the military did not react and the Pentagon's anti-missile batteries did not function. Why? The close-range anti-aircraft defenses at the Pentagon are conceived to destroy missiles that attempt to approach. A missile should normally be unable to pass. As for a big Boeing 757-200, it would have strictly no chance. Whether an airliner or a missile, an explanation needs to be found.

Meyssan then suggests a hypothesis that could account for this anomaly:

> Each military aircraft in fact possesses a transponder which...permit[s] it to declare itself in the eyes of its possessor as *friendly* or *hostile*.... An antimissile battery will not...react to the passage of a friendly missile. It is not impossible that was what happened at the Pentagon on 11 September 2001.[39]

Meyssan's hypothesis could also answer a question raised by reports that when the aircraft was making its circular approach to the Pentagon, it came very near to the White House—namely, why the White House's missile system did not shoot it down.[40]

In light of these considerations, the very fact that the aircraft that hit the Pentagon was not shot down by the Pentagon's (and the White House's) missiles can be considered physical evidence against the claim that it was a passenger plane.

Further physical evidence is provided by the simple fact that there were evidently no remains of a Boeing 757 at the crash site. As we have seen, the explanation why no such remains were visible in the photographs is that the entire plane went *inside* the Pentagon. If that is what happened (ignoring now the question of whether it is even remotely plausible), there should have been a burnt-out wreck, or at least some identifiable remnants of the plane, found inside the Pentagon after the fire was put out. But that was evidently not the case.

At a Pentagon briefing on the day after 9/11, Ed Plaugher, the county fire chief who was in charge of putting out the fire in the Pentagon, was asked whether anything was left of the airplane. He said that there were "some small pieces...but not large sections.... [T]here's no fuselage sections and that sort of thing."[41] According to Plaugher's eyewitness testimony the day after the fire, therefore, there was no fuselage or any other large pieces, such as jet engines. His testimony was, furthermore, implicitly confirmed by the Department of Defense insofar as the only parts of Flight 77 that it announced finding, other than unidentifiable fragments (which, as Meyssan points out, "could have been from something quite different"), were a beacon and the two black boxes. The black boxes were said, furthermore, to have been found at a time—4:00 AM—that makes critics of the official story suspicious.[42] Plaugher's testimony was further confirmed at a Pentagon press conference on September 15. When Terry Mitchell was asked about evidence of the plane, he said that one could see only "small pieces." Lee Evey, head of the renovation project, said that the evidence of the aircraft is "not very visible.... None of those parts are very large.... You don't see big pieces of the airplane sitting there extending up into the air."[43]

How is this testimony consistent with the idea that the Pentagon was hit by a Boeing 757? That airplane's fuselage is made of aluminum, which does not melt in an ordinary hydrocarbon fire. Its engines are made of tempered steel, which also does not normally melt. And yet the more-or-less official story was that the fire was so hot that all this metal not only melted but was vaporized.[44] Is this believable? In the first place, if the fire was that hot, how did the upper floors of the Pentagon survive? In the second place, why would the fire have been so hot if it were a hydrocarbon fire? In the third place, even if there was something about the crash that made this hydrocarbon fire extra hot—hot enough to produce the red flames and other effects shown in the photographs—would even fire this hot vaporize aluminum and steel? If the official story rests on this account of the laws of physics, it is important enough to run an experiment to test this hypothesis. And this could be done easily enough, using some worn-out Boeing 757.

Even if one believed that there was a chance that such a test might be successful, however, there would be one more condition that would have to be passed. According to at least one version of the official story, authorities were able to identify victims of the crash by their fingerprints.[45] To provide support for the official account, therefore, the fire would have to be hot enough to vaporize aluminum and steel and cool enough to leave human flesh intact. This would, of course, be impossible, so Meyssan is amazed that the Pentagon could evidently make both of these claims without fear of ridicule.[46]

In any case, such a test is no longer necessary because, as with other features of the official account of 9/11, this one evolved into a second version. As Meyssan reports, six months later, in April of 2002, the FBI claimed that enough of the Boeing 757 had been recovered to make possible its almost complete reconstitution. An FBI spokesman, Chris Murray, was quoted as saying: "The pieces of the plane are stocked in a warehouse and they are marked with the serial numbers of flight 77."[47] The following month, furthermore, this new version of the official account was supported by Ed Plaugher, who now remembered that when he arrived on the scene he had seen, he said, "pieces of the fuselage, the wings, the landing gear, pieces of the engine, seats," adding: "I can swear to you, it was a plane." He even—inadvertently contradicting the Pentagon's statement that the black boxes were not found until 4:00 AM three days later—claimed to have seen one of them.[48]

It might seem that US officials could confirm this new version of the fate of Flight 77 by simply showing the warehouse full of recovered pieces to reporters and members of the 9/11 Independent Commission. At most, however, this evidence would show only that much of the airplane had been recovered. It would not tell us that it had been recovered from the Pentagon—as opposed to Ohio, Kentucky, or somewhere else. It is not possible, therefore, to confirm this theory by pointing to this physical evidence in combination with Ed Plaugher's improved memory. Moreover, this new version, besides being in conflict with Plaugher's statements on September 12, is also in conflict with the statements of Timothy Mitchell and Lee Evey on September 15. If big pieces of the airplane, such as the engines, the fuselage, and the tail, were in the Pentagon, why did these men not see them? Why did Evey not see any "big pieces of the airplane sitting there extending up into the air"? And why have our reporters not asked such obvious questions?

Meyssan's claim that what hit the Pentagon was something other than Flight 77, we have seen, is supported by considerable physical evidence. This claim gathers a little additional support from two more facts reported by Paul Thompson. For one thing, when the flight control transcripts for the 9/11 planes were finally released on October 16, "Flight 77's ends at least 20 minutes before it crashes."[49] Although there is more than one possible explanation for this fact, one of these explanations is that government officials did not want the press and the public to hear what actually occurred during the final 20 minutes of Flight 77. The second fact is the existence of a news story according to which

> an employee at a gas station across the street from the Pentagon that services only military personnel says the gas station's security cameras should have recorded the moment of impact. However, he says, "I've never seen what the pictures looked like. The FBI was here within minutes and took the film."[50]

This report, if true—and someone could presumably interview the employee, José Velasquez—suggests that the FBI had known that an aircraft was going to crash into the Pentagon. How else can we explain that they got there "within minutes"? And, more directly germane to our present topic, it also suggests that FBI officials feared that the gas station's security cameras might have captured something about the crash scene that they did not want the press or the public to see, and this could have been the fact that the Pentagon was struck by a military missile rather than a commercial airliner. If, by contrast, the camera's pictures supported the government's claims, we would expect the government to have made these pictures public. So these two stories, while not constituting physical evidence as such, do suggest that there is (or at least *was*) physical evidence that would further undermine the official account.

What about the Reported Sightings of an American Airliner?

Whereas the physical evidence strongly counts against the official theory and instead supports the missile theory, proponents of the official theory have relied primarily upon reports that several eyewitnesses saw an American Airliner hit the Pentagon. For example, one debunker of the view that the Pentagon was not really struck by a Boeing 757 wrote in the *Sunday Times* that "the killer blow to this conspiracy is that several witnesses saw the plane hit the building."[51] How can critics of the official account reconcile their revisionist view with the fact that these reports exist? There seem to be four main approaches.

One approach builds on the standard forensic point that when there is a conflict between physical evidence and eyewitness testimony, the physical evidence is usually, once its authenticity is confirmed, given more weight. If the prosecuting attorney in a criminal trial has presented a strong case based on physical evidence, the defense attorney can seldom hope to render a "killer blow" to this case simply by presenting eyewitness testimony to the contrary. This is because the human testimony might be wrong for all sorts of reasons, such as misperception, faulty memory, or outright lying (perhaps because of bribery or intimidation). Accordingly, any allegedly eyewitness testimony that contradicts the physical evidence is explained away.

Meyssan employs this approach. The claims by witnesses to have seen an American Airlines plane could be explained, he suggests, in terms of the dynamics of the social psychology of perception and memory, which often leads people to "see" what they expect to see, or to "remember" having seen what they are expected to have seen. Given the fact that these witnesses had seen images or heard reports of airliners hitting the WTC and later heard that it was an American Airlines Boeing 757 that hit the Pentagon, it is not at all surprising that several people would report having seen such an airplane headed for the Pentagon, even if the actual aircraft was something quite different.[52]

Meyssan combines this approach with a second, which is to point out that there were also several reports of eyewitnesses who said that the aircraft looked and/or sounded like a missile or a military plane. Recall the testimony of, for example, Dulles air traffic controller Danielle O'Brien, who said that all the experienced air traffic controllers in the room thought that it was a military plane and the witness who said that it "seemed to be able to hold eight or twelve persons" and "made a shrill noise like a fighter plane" (see page 26). Meyssan, in addition to quoting the statements of these eyewitnesses and others, points out that an AGM-type missile "does look like a small civilian airplane" and "produces a whistling noise similar to that of a fighter aircraft." On this basis, he counts those who reported seeing a military plane as witnesses on behalf of the missile theory.[53]

Finally, having shown that the eyewitnesses supportive of the official theory are at least partly balanced by eyewitnesses supportive of the missile theory, Meyssan can assume that we should take these latter witnesses more seriously. That is, if what hit the Pentagon was a missile, the fact that several people said that they saw a commercial airliner hit the Pentagon is not surprising, given the dynamics of the psychology of perception and memory. But if what hit the Pentagon had been a Boeing 757, it would be *very* surprising to have reports of people—especially people with trained eyes and ears—claiming to have seen a missile or small military plane. These reports of having seen a missile or a small military plane must, accordingly, be given more weight. Properly interpreted, then, the eyewitness testimony does not contradict, but instead supports, the missile theory.

There is, however, a third way to reconcile the physical evidence and the reports of eyewitness testimony supporting the official theory. Rather than explaining away these reports by appealing to the psychology of perception and memory, one could examine the reports themselves more carefully to see if the people actually said what they were reported to have said. This approach is taken by Gerard Holmgren. Beginning with 19 accounts said by the Urban Legends website to be eyewitness testimony that an American airliner hit the Pentagon,[54] Holmgren found, for starters, that a majority of the people cited did not actually claim to have seen the Pentagon hit by a commercial airplane. Instead, "[w]hat they claimed was to have seen a plane flying way too low, and then immediately afterwards to have seen smoke or an explosion coming from the direction of the Pentagon, which was out of sight at the time of the collision." (Although this distinction might at first glance seem too picayune, these reports would be compatible with the two-aircraft thesis, to be discussed below.) With regard to the other cases, Holmgren found one or more of the following problems: the alleged witness could not be identified; the claim that the witness had seen an American Airlines plane was added by the reporter; or the witness who initially claimed to have seen the American airplane hit the Pentagon withdrew the claim under questioning—which was the case with Mike Walter of *USA Today* when he was interviewed on CBS by Bryant Gumbel.[55] "What appeared at first reading to be 19 eyewitness accounts," Holmgren concludes, "actually turned out to be none."

Then, finding ten other reports that initially appeared to provide eyewitness testimony, he found that they all suffered from similar problems. Holmgren's efforts led him to the following conclusion:

> My conclusion is that there is no eyewitness evidence to support the theory that F77 hit the Pentagon, unless my search has missed something very significant. Given the strength of the photographic evidence that whatever hit the Pentagon could not possibly have been F77, I can see no reason for not stating this conclusion with a lot of confidence, unless and until contrary evidence emerges.[56]

There is, finally, a fourth way to reconcile the physical evidence and the eyewitness testimony—a way that allows an even less skeptical approach to testimony that seems to support the official theory. This approach involves the hypothesis that there were *two* aircraft heading toward the Pentagon. According to this two-aircraft thesis, both sets of eyewitnesses—those who reported seeing a missile (which they may have called a small military plane) and those who reported seeing a passenger jet (which they may have specifically identified as an American airliner)— were correct. Dick Eastman, who develops this both/and position, says that eyewitnesses divide up into three sets: (1) those who reported seeing "an airliner, shiny, red and blue markings, with two engines, in a dive, and flying 'low' in terms of one or two hundred feet, and silent"; (2) those who reported seeing an aircraft coming in "at tree-top level, at '20 feet' all the way, hitting lamp posts in perfect low level flight...engines roaring; pouring on speed; smaller than a mid-sized airliner"; and (3) those such as Kelly Knowles, in an apartment two miles away, who "saw two planes moving toward the Pentagon, one veering away as the other crashed." Eastman's analysis can also explain the testimony of those witnesses who combine features of the first two categories by supposing that they *saw* the American airliner while *hearing* the missile. Eastman's main point, in any case, is that at least most of the testimony of most of the witnesses can be accepted as accurate, but that the only witnesses who stated the full truth were those in the third category—those who reported seeing *two* aircraft.

Eastman's theory, in other words, is that an American Airlines plane was putting on an attention-getting exhibition to draw all eyes to itself. Then it flew towards the Pentagon while the missile was heading in the same direction—too close to the ground for most witnesses to see it even if they had not been distracted by the airliner. Then the airliner veered off at the last second, disappearing behind the immense cloud of smoke produced by the crash. It then landed unnoticed at Reagan National Airport, which was only a mile away in the direction it was headed.[57]

These four approaches are not mutually exclusive. Although Eastman and Holmgren take different approaches, they can actually be viewed as mutually supportive. That is, Holmgren's main point is that most of the eyewitnesses who seemed to claim that they saw an American Airlines passenger plane hit the Pentagon actually claimed only that they saw it come very close to the Pentagon just before the explosion. Eastman's two-aircraft hypothesis explains why this distinction may be important and also provides a reconciliation of all the testimony about an American airplane with the physical evidence that the Pentagon was not struck by any such airplane. Also, Meyssan's two approaches can be strengthened by combining them with Eastman's approach, Holmgren's approach, or an Eastman-Holmgren approach.[58]

For our present purposes, it is not necessary to decide what the truth of the matter is. The purpose of this discussion has been simply to show that the easy assumption that Meyssan's missile theory is disproved by eyewitness testimony is far from the truth. Having made this point, I now return to the list of reasons for believing that the aircraft that crashed into the Pentagon was not Flight 77. The first two reasons, to recall, were that the identification was based on dubious sources and that the physical evidence was incompatible with this identification.

Why Would Terrorists Have Struck the West Wing?

A third fact about the Pentagon crash suggesting that it was not caused by hijackers on Flight 77 was the location of the crash. Assuming that terrorists in control of a Boeing 757 would want to be certain of hitting their target, why would they aim at one of the facades, which are only 80 feet high, when they could have simply dived into the roof, which covers 29 acres? More important, one would assume that they would have wanted to cause as much damage to the Pentagon and kill as many of its employees as possible, and these aims would also have made the roof the logical target.[59] Furthermore, even if there were an answer to that question, why would they hit the *west* wing, which was the one part of the Pentagon that was being renovated? As the *Los Angeles Times* reported:

> It was the only area of the Pentagon with a sprinkler system, and it had been reconstructed with a web of steel columns and bars [and blast-resistant windows] to withstand bomb blasts.... While perhaps 4,500 people normally would have been working in the hardest-hit areas, because of the renovation work only about 800 were there.[60]

One would also assume that terrorists would be especially interested in killing the Pentagon's top civilian and military leaders, but the attack on the west wing killed none of them.[61] Most of the casualties were civilians, many of whom were working on the renovation, "and only one general was to be found among the military victims."[62] If the Pentagon was struck by terrorists flying a Boeing 757, why would they target the west wing, where the crash would have the least rather than the greatest impact? The force of this question is increased by the fact that according to the reported radar data, the aircraft, given its trajectory, was able to hit the west wing only by executing a very difficult downward spiral.[63] In other words, it was actually *technically difficult* to do as little damage to the Pentagon as was done.

Could an Inexperienced Pilot Have Flown the Aircraft?

This downward spiral was so difficult and so perfectly executed, in fact, that it raises a fourth argument against the official account. This argument is that no pilot with the minimal training the hijackers evidently had could have executed this maneuver.[64] On this issue, Ahmed quotes the military expert Stan Goff's description of what he considers "the real kicker" in the official account:

A pilot they want us to believe was trained at a Florida puddle-jumper school for Piper Cubs and Cessnas, conducts a well-controlled downward spiral, descending the last 7,000 feet in two-and-a-half minutes, brings the plane in so low and flat that it clips the electrical wires across the street from the Pentagon, and flies it with pinpoint accuracy into the side of this building at 460 nauts.... When the theory about learning to fly this well at the puddle-jumper school began to lose ground, it was added that they received further training on a flight simulator. This is like saying you prepared your teenager for her first drive on I-40 at rush hour by buying her a video driving game.[65]

This argument is made even stronger by the fact that the man who was supposed to be the pilot, Hani Hanjour, was reportedly not just an amateur but also an especially incompetent one. According to a story in the *New York Times*:

Staff members characterized Mr. Hanjour as polite, meek and very quiet. But most of all, [a] former employee said, they considered him a very bad pilot. "I'm still to this day amazed that he could have flown into the Pentagon," the former employee said. "He could not fly at all."

And according to a report on CBS News:

Months before Hani Hanjour is believed to have flown an American Airlines jet into the Pentagon, managers at an Arizona flight school reported him at least five times to the FAA. They reported him not because they feared he was a terrorist, but because his English and flying skills were so bad.... [T]hey didn't think he should keep his pilot's license. "I couldn't believe he had a commercial license of any kind with the skills that he had," said Peggy Chevrette, Arizona flight school manager.[66]

How could anyone believe that this pilot could have handled the perfect maneuver executed by the aircraft that hit the Pentagon?

Could Flight 77 Really Have Been Lost for Half an Hour?

A fifth problem that has been raised for the official account is that it entails Flight 77 having flown toward Washington for 29 minutes without being detected by any radar system. A Pentagon spokesman reportedly said: "The Pentagon was simply not aware that this aircraft was coming our way."[67] Thompson asks, rhetorically: "Is it conceivable that an airplane could be lost inside US air space for [that long]?"[68] Even if the local air controllers did not have the kind of radar system that can track a plane with its transponder off, as claimed,[69] the FAA system certainly would have been able track the flight path back to Washington.[70] Even more, Meyssan argues, the Pentagon possesses "several very sophisticated radar monitoring systems, incomparable with the civilian systems." The PAVE PAWS system, for example, "does not miss anything occurring in North American airspace." According to its website, it is "capable of detecting and monitoring a great number of targets that would be consistent with a massive SLBM [Submarine Launched Ballistic Missile] attack." Are we to believe that it can do all this, Meyssan wonders, while not being able to detect a single giant airliner headed toward the Pentagon itself?[71]

Why Was the Strike Not Prevented by Standard Operating Procedures?

Besides all these questions, which are specific to the strike on the Pentagon, the official account of the Pentagon strike is faced by the generic question: Assuming that the strike was made by Flight 77 under the control of hijackers, why was it not prevented by standard operating procedures? To critics, this question seems even more powerful in relation to this strike because it occurred over a half hour after the second WTC tower was hit, so that the National Military Command Center at the Pentagon should have been in the highest possible state of alert, and also because the Pentagon is probably the most well-defended building on the face of the planet.[72] How does the official account explain the fact that in this case it was not defended at all?

According to the first version, as we have seen, fighter jets were not even ordered until after the Pentagon had been struck. However, since US officials quickly gave up this story, we will move directly to criticisms of the second version. According to this account, given by NORAD, the FAA did not notify it that Flight 77 had been hijacked and was heading toward Washington until 9:24[73]—which would be 34 minutes after the FAA had, according to the official account, lost radio contact with the plane and 28 minutes after the plane disappeared from its radar. Then at 9:27, NORAD ordered planes scrambled from Langley Air Force Base. These planes are said not to have arrived until about 15 minutes after the Pentagon was struck at 9:38.[74]

Critics ask several questions about this account. Why was not the NMCC and hence NORAD, with its superior radar system, independently monitoring the flight path? Even if we ignore this question, how could the FAA have been so leisurely, especially given the fact that shortly after 9:03 everyone in the system would have known that two hijacked airplanes had been flown into the WTC? "Is such a long delay believable," Thompson asks, "or has that information been doctored to cover the lack of any scrambling of fighters?"[75] Also, why would it take NORAD, after finally hearing from the FAA, another three minutes to order planes scrambled? And why would it order those planes from Langley, which is 130 miles from Washington, rather than from Andrews Air Force Base, which is only 10 miles away and has the assignment to protect Washington?

In relation to this last question, *USA Today* reported that it was told by Pentagon sources that Andrews "had no fighters assigned to it." Another story in that newspaper the same day reported that Andrews did have fighters present "but those planes were not on alert."[76] Bykov and Israel argue that both stories, besides being inherently implausible, are contradicted by the US military information website. According to it, Andrews houses the 121st Fighter Squadron of the 113th Fighter Wing, which is equipped with F-16 fighters and "provides capable and ready response forces for the District of Columbia in the event of natural disaster or civil emergency." Andrews also has the Marine Fighter Attack Squadron 321, which "flies the sophisticated F/A-18 Hornet" and is supported by a reserve squadron that "provides maintenance and supply functions necessary to maintain a force in readiness."[77] Andrews also has the District of Columbia Air National Guard (DCANG), which said on its website that its "mission" was "to provide combat units in the highest possible state of readiness."[78] In addition to this evidence, the falsity of the claim that Andrews had no fighters on alert, say critics, is shown by the fact that, as widely reported, immediately after the attack on the Pentagon, F-16s from Andrews were flying over Washington.[79] One of the disturbing questions, therefore, is why the Pentagon would have put out disinformation.

Another question is why some of the websites were changed after 9/11. Thompson reports, for example, that the DCANG website was changed to say merely that it had a "vision" to "provide peacetime command and control and administrative mission oversight to support customers, DCANG units, and NGB in achieving the highest state of readiness."[80]

In any case, it remains a puzzle, these critics say, why officials at NORAD—or NMCC—would have ordered planes to come from Langley, unless they were simply inventing a story to explain why no planes appeared in time to stop the attack. If so, the critics add, even this story is inadequate. Thompson writes (from within the framework of the official account) that if F-16s from Langley were airborne by 9:30, as alleged, they

> would have to travel slightly over 700 mph to reach Washington before Flight 77 does. The maximum speed of an F-16 is 1,500 mph. Even at traveling 1,300 mph, these planes could have reached Washington in six minutes—well before any claim of when Flight 77 crashed.[81]

Given the fact that the planes were said to arrive 15 minutes too late, critics find this story absurd. As George Szamuely puts it: "If it took the F-16s half an hour to cover 150 miles, they could not have been traveling at more than 300 mph—at 20 percent capability."[82] In any case, had the jet fighters been ordered from Andrews, as they should have been, they would have had even more time.

A still deeper problem is why the fighters were not flying over Washington long before that. Captain Michael Jellinek, the command director of NORAD, reportedly said that at some point not long after the first attack on the WTC, telephone links were established with the NMCC, Strategic Command, theater commanders, and federal emergency-response agencies in order to have an Air Threat Conference Call. At one time or another, it was reported, the voices of President Bush, Vice President Cheney, key military officers, FAA and NORAD leaders, the White House, and Air Force One were heard on the open line. Brigadier General Montague Winfield, head of the NMCC, reportedly said: "All of the governmental agencies there that, that were involved in any activity that was going on in the United States at that point, were in that conference." The call reportedly continued right through the Pentagon explosion.[83] One implication of this admitted fact is that all of these individuals and agencies would have known since 8:56 that Flight 77 was presumed to be hijacked and also that all airplane takeoffs from Washington were stopped shortly after the crash of Flight 175 at 9:03. Thompson asks: "Why is the emergency considered important enough to stop all takeoffs from Washington at this time, but not important enough to scramble even a single plane to defend Washington?"[84]

Why Was the Pentagon Not Evacuated?

One of the disturbing questions raised by the crash of Flight 175 into the second tower of the WTC, as we saw, was why there was a public announcement telling people that the building was secure so they should return to their offices. A similar question is raised by the attack on the Pentagon, even if the official account is accepted. According to this account, Flight 77 was lost at 8:56, just after the radar allegedly showed it making a U-turn back towards Washington. Given the fact that the Pentagon was called by its staff "Ground Zero," even having a snack bar of that name,[85] why would its officials, knowing of the attacks on the WTC, not have ordered its immediate evacuation? Furthermore, even if they did not do so shortly after 8:56, why did they not do so immediately upon learning that the air traffic controllers had spotted an unidentified fast-flying aircraft heading in the direction of the Pentagon and the White House at 9:25? In the 13 minutes remaining before the Pentagon was hit, virtually everyone, presumably, could have been evacuated.

In explaining why this was not done, a Pentagon spokesman said: "The Pentagon was simply not aware that this aircraft was coming our way." Defense Secretary Rumsfeld and his top aides, in particular, were said to be unaware of any danger up to the moment of impact.[86] However, since the crash of the first plane into the WTC at 8:46, according to the *New York Times*, "military officials in [the National Military Command Center] on the east side of the [Pentagon] were urgently talking to law enforcement and air traffic control officials about what to do." And, according to the official story, the FAA had notified NORAD at 9:24 that Flight 77 appeared to be headed back towards Washington.[87] Having cited these reports, Thompson asks: "Is it believable that everyone in the Pentagon outside of that command center, even the Secretary of Defense, would remain uninformed?"[88] And if it is not believable, then why were those people in the west wing allowed to be killed?

Official Reaction to Meyssan's Theory

When Meyssan's theory was published, it was immediately denounced by U.S. officials. On April 2, 2002, the FBI issued a statement saying:

To even suggest that AA77 did not crash into the Pentagon on September 11 is the ultimate insult to the memory of the 59 men, women and children on AA77 and the 125 dedicated military and civilian workers in the Pentagon who were ruthlessly murdered by terrorists on September 11.

A similar statement was made later that month on behalf of the Department of Defense by Victoria Clarke, who said:

I think even the suggestion of it is ludicrous. And finally, it is just an incredible, incredible insult to the friends and the relatives and the family members of the almost 200 people that got killed here on September 11th and the thousands who were killed in New York.[89]

Meyssan agrees, of course, that the 125 Pentagon workers were ruthlessly murdered by terrorists. He simply disagrees with the official theory as to the identity of these ruthless terrorists. He also agrees that it would be an insult to the victims and their families and friends for anyone knowingly to perpetrate a false account of who was responsible. He simply disagrees on the question of who is guilty of this insult. These mutual recriminations, of course, settle nothing. What we need is a full investigation into the strike on the Pentagon, in conjunction with such an investigation into the attacks on the World Trade Center, in which all the disturbing questions raised by Meyssan and other critics of the official accounts can be thoroughly examined.

If the evidence related to the strike on the Pentagon is added, the third of the possible views discussed in the Introduction would seem to be ruled out. According to that view, no US officials participated in the planning for the attacks. But the evidence about the Pentagon strike presented by the critics of the official account, especially Meyssan, seems to require active planning by members of the US military, at least in this incident (because only an aircraft belonging to the US military would have had a transponder that signaled *friendly* to the Pentagon's antimissile batteries and thereby avoided being shot down). Although the evidence from this flight itself might allow these members to belong to some rogue outfit within the military, the evidence from the previous flights has already shown that the conspirators must have included NMCC officials in the Pentagon itself. Also, if the stories about Rumsfeld's prediction of the strike on the Pentagon as well as the strike on one of the WTC towers is true, the civilian head of the Pentagon would seem to have known when the attacks were to occur.

To summarize where we are with regard to the first three flights: From the point of view of the critics, a scrutiny of the official account of 9/11 in light of the actual facts leaves us only two possible conclusions: our government and military leaders were either incredibly incompetent or criminally complicit. And the problem with the incompetence theory, says Canada's award-winning journalist Barrie Zwicker, is that "[i]ncompetence usually earns reprimands" and yet "there have been no reports, to my knowledge, of reprimands." He then adds: "This causes me to ask—and other media need to ask—if there were 'stand down' orders."[90] Answering his own question, he says:

> In the almost two hours of the total drama not a single US Air Force interceptor turns a wheel until it's too late. Why? Was it total incompetence on the part of aircrews trained and equipped to scramble in minutes?... Simply to ask these few questions is to find the official narrative frankly implausible. The more questions you pursue, it becomes more plausible that there's a different explanation: Namely, that elements within the top US military, intelligence and political leadership...are complicit in what happened on September the 11th.[91]

Gore Vidal reaches the same conclusion. Reflecting on the official rejection of any inquiry "not limited to the assumption that the administration's inaction was solely a consequence of 'breakdowns among federal agencies,'" he concludes:

> So for reasons that we must never know, those "breakdowns" are to be the goat. That they were more likely to be not break but "stand-downs" is not for us to pry. Certainly the hour-twenty-minute failure to put fighter planes in the air could not have been due to a breakdown throughout the entire Air Force along the East Coast. Mandatory standard operating procedure had been told to cease and desist.[92]

Both Zwicker and Vidal conclude that complicity rather than incompetence—"stand down" rather than "break down"—is the more plausible explanation of how the attacks on the WTC could have succeeded.

Relevant to this discussion is Michael Parenti's observation that political leaders sometimes "seize upon incompetence as a cover"—that is, as a way to deny their active involvement in some illegal operation.

This admission of incompetence is then "eagerly embraced by various commentators," because they prefer to see their leaders as suffering from incompetence "rather than to see deliberate deception." Is that what is going on here? Ahmed, reflecting on Jared Israel's discussion, says that if there was as much incompetence on 9/11 as the official account implies, "then evidence of institutional incompetence within these emergency response services should have frequently surfaced during previous responses to routine emergencies, possible hijackings, and so on. *There is no such evidence.*"[93] Must not this question be pressed? How could a system that normally works flawlessly, according to all available evidence, suddenly, on the day that these attacks were scheduled to occur, suffer so many inexplicable breakdowns?

This question has not gone unasked by family members of the victims of 9/11. For example, Kristen Breitweiser, whose husband died in the WTC, said on Phil Donahue's television show:

> I don't understand how a plane could hit our Defense Department... an hour after the first plane hit the first tower. I don't understand how that is possible. I'm a reasonable person. But when you look at the fact that we spend a half trillion dollars on national defense and you're telling me that a plane is able to hit our Pentagon...an hour after the first tower is hit? There are procedures and protocols in place in this nation that are to be followed when transponders are disconnected, and they were not followed on September 11th.[94]

Do we not owe her an answer?

An interesting footnote to this chapter: While correcting page proofs, I learned of an interview with Secretary of Defense Rumsfeld in the Pentagon on October 12, 2001, in which he, in speaking of the various kinds of weapons used by the terrorists, referred to "the missile [used] to damage this building."[95] Was this a revealing slip?

CHAPTER THREE

FLIGHT 93: WAS IT THE ONE FLIGHT THAT WAS SHOT DOWN?

The main problem raised by the first three flights—aside from the question of the identity of the aircraft that hit the Pentagon—was the fact that aircraft that *should* have been shot down were *not*. The fate of UA Flight 93, say critics, presents us with the opposite problem: A plane that should *not* have been shot down *was*. Paul Thompson's timeline provides evidence from which he draws this conclusion.

The crucial items in the first part of this timeline are the following: Flight 93 departed from Newark 41 minutes late, at 8:42 AM. At 9:27, one passenger, Tom Burnett, called his wife, telling her that the plane had been hijacked and that she should call the FBI, which she did. At 9:28, ground flight controllers heard sounds of screaming and scuffling. At 9:34, Tom Burnett again called his wife, who told him about the attacks on the WTC, leading him to realize that his own plane was on "a suicide mission." At 9:36, the plane turned toward Washington. At 9:37, Jeremy Glick and two other passengers learned about the WTC attacks.[1] At 9:45, Tom Burnett told his wife that he did not think, contrary to the hijackers' claim, that they had a bomb, and that he and others were making a plan. By this time, which was 19 minutes before the plane went down, the FBI was monitoring these calls. At 9:45, with the FBI listening in, passenger Todd Beamer began a long phone conversation with a Verizon representative, describing the situation on board.[2] Shortly after 9:47, Jeremy Glick told his wife that all the men had voted to attack the hijackers, adding that the latter had only knives, no guns (which would, in combination with the conviction that the hijackers did not really have a bomb, have increased the passengers' belief that they could be successful).[3] At 9:54, Tom Burnett called his wife again. According to early reports, he said: "I know we're all going to die. There's three of us who are going to do something about it."[4] However, according to a later, more complete account, he sounded more optimistic, saying: "It's up to us. I think we can do it," adding that they were planning to gain control of the plane over a rural area.[5]

The following incidents in Thompson's timeline suggest to him that the plane was shot down after it became evident that the passengers—among whom were a professional pilot and a flight controller[6]—might gain control of the plane. At 9:57, one of the hijackers was heard saying that there was fighting outside the cockpit. A voice from outside said: "Let's get them." At 9:58, Todd Beamer ended his phone call by saying that the passengers planned "to jump" the hijacker in the back of the plane, then uttered his famous words: "Are you ready guys? Let's roll."[7] At 9:58, a passenger talking on the phone to her husband said: "I think they're going to do it. They're forcing their way into the cockpit." A little later, she exclaimed: "They're doing it! They're doing it! They're doing it!" But her husband then heard screaming in the background followed by a "whooshing sound, a sound like wind," then more screaming, after which he lost contact.[8] Another passenger, calling from a restroom, reportedly said just before contact was lost that he heard "some sort of explosion" and saw "white smoke coming from the plane."[9] (Months later, the FBI denied that the recording of this call contained any mention of smoke or an explosion, but the person who took this call was not allowed to speak to the media.[10]) The person listening to Jeremy Glick's open phone line reportedly said: "The silence lasted two minutes and then there was a mechanical sound, followed by more screams. Finally, there was a mechanical sound, followed by nothing."[11] According to one newspaper report, moreover: "Sources claim the last thing heard on the cockpit voice recorder is the sound of wind—suggesting the plane had been holed."[12] Thompson believes that this record shows that the plane was indeed "holed"—shot down by a missile or two—after it seemed that the passengers were gaining control of it.

Thompson is also suspicious about the tape of the cockpit recording and the official crash time. Relatives of victims have been allowed to listen to this tape. It begins at 9:31 and runs for 31 minutes, so that it ends at 10:02. This would be close to the time of the crash—*if* the crash occurred at 10:03, as the US government claims. However, a seismic study concluded that the crash occurred slightly after 10:06, leading the *Philadelphia Daily News* to print an article entitled "Three-Minute Discrepancy in Tape." Thompson asks: "What happened to the last three or four minutes of this tape?"[13] And this was not, Thompson reports, the only record of this flight that was missing. On October 16, the government released flight control transcripts of the airplanes—except for Flight 93.[14]

With regard to the suspicion that the plane was shot down, it is significant that according to news reports, it was shortly after 9:56 that fighter jets were finally given orders to intercept and shoot down any airplanes under the control of hijackers.[15] Shortly thereafter, a military aide reportedly said to Vice President Cheney: "There is a plane 80 miles out. There is a fighter in the area. Should we engage?", to which Cheney responded "Yes," after which an F-16 went in pursuit of Flight 93.[16] It was also reported that as the fighter got nearer to Flight 93, Cheney was asked two more times to confirm that the fighter should engage, which Cheney did.[17] Also, Brigadier General Winfield of the NMCC later said: "At some point, the closure time came and went, and nothing happened, so you can imagine everything was very tense at the NMCC."[18] Furthermore, when President Bush was told of the crash of Flyght 93 at 10:08, he reportedly asked: "Did we shoot it town or did it crash?"[19] These reports, which are contained in Thompson's timeline, suggest to him that the intention to shoot down Flight 93 was in several minds.

Reports of fighter jets in the area add to his suspicion that Flight 93 was indeed shot down. Shortly before the crash, CBS television reported that two F-16 fighters were tailing the flight. And a flight controller, ignoring an order to controllers not to talk to the media, reportedly said that "an F-16 fighter closely pursued Flight 93.... [T]he F-16 made 360-degree turns to remain close to the commercial jet."[20] The existence of a fighter plane in the area is supported, furthermore, by many witnesses on the ground. Accoring to a story in the *Independent*, "At least half a dozen named individuals...have reported seeing a second plane flying low...over the crash site within minutes of the United flight crashing. They describe the plane as a small, white jet with rear engines and no discernible markings."[21] The FBI claimed that the plane was a Fairchild Falcon 20 business jet.[22] But, said one woman:

It was white with no markings but it was definitely military.... It had two rear engines, a big fin on the back like a spoiler.... It definitely wasn't one of those executive jets. The FBI came and talked to me and said there was no plane around.... But I saw it and it was there before the crash and it was 40 feet above my head. They did not want my story.[23]

Her assertion, which is supported by the consensus reported by the *Independent*, is further supported by statements quoted by Thompson, in which several other people say that they had seen a white plane, with some of them adding the details about rear engines and the lack of discernible markings.

Even stronger evidence that the plane was shot down is provided by witnesses who heard sounds. One witness said that after she heard the plane's engine, she heard "a loud thump" and then "two more loud thumps and didn't hear the plane's engine anymore." Another witness heard "a loud bang." Another heard "two loud bangs" before watching the plane take a downward turn. Another heard a sound that "wasn't quite right," after which the plane "dropped all of a sudden, like a stone." Another heard a "loud bang" and then saw the plane's right wing dip, after which the plane plunged into the earth. And the mayor of Shanksville reportedly said that he knew of two people who "heard a missile," adding that one of them "served in Vietnam and he says he's heard them." Thompson concludes that while some of the accounts have conflicting elements, they "virtually all support a missile strike."[24]

This conclusion is undergirded still further by reports about the location of remnants from the plane. For one thing, a half-ton piece of one of the engines was reportedly found over a mile away. One newspaper story called this fact "intriguing" because "the heat-seeking, air-to-air Sidewinder missiles aboard an F-16 would likely target one of the Boeing 757's two large engines."[25] Also consistent with one or more missile strikes, Thompson points out, is the fact that witnesses reported seeing burning debris fall from the plane as far as eight miles away, with workers at Indian Lake Marina saying that they saw "a cloud of confetti-like debris descend on the lake and nearby farms minutes after hearing the explosion."[26] And debris, including what appeared to be human remains, was indeed reportedly found as far as eight miles from the crash site.[27]

The inference that Flight 93 was shot down is additionally supported by subsequent statements made by military and government officials. One F-15 pilot reportedly said that after returning from his assignment to patrol the skies over NYC in the early afternoon, he was told that a military F-16 had shot down a fourth airliner in Pennsylvania.[28] This rumor was sufficiently widespread that when General Myers was being interviewed by the Armed Services Committee on September 13, Senator Carl Levin, asking Myers whether the Defense Department took action against any aircraft, mentioned that "there have been statements that the aircraft that crashed in Pennsylvania was shot down," adding: "Those stories continue to exist." Although Myers declared that "the armed forces did not shoot down any aircraft,"[29] Paul Wolfowitz, Deputy Secretary of Defense, reportedly said that "the Air Force was tracking the hijacked plane that crashed in Pennsylvania...and had been in a position to bring it down if necessary."[30]

Thompson believes that the government decided that it *was* necessary—but *not* because the hijackers' mission was going to succeed. Thompson asks why fighter pilots were given authorization to shoot down hijacked airplanes only after Flight 93 was the only one left in the sky.[31] This is, of course, the disturbing question raised by the evidence Thompson presents about this flight. His implicit answer, given the evidence that the passengers were successfully wresting control of the plane away from the hijackers, is that this was the one plane that was likely to be landed safely—which would, among other things, mean that there might be live hijackers to be interrogated. Thus interpreted, the evidence about Flight 93 provides further reason to conclude that the failure to shoot down the previous three flights was *not* due to incompetence. This evidence suggests that when the authorities wanted a flight shot down, they were not hindered by lack of either competence or coordination.

The evidence from this flight suggests, like the previous ones, active involvement of US military leaders in planning the attacks. In this case, they apparently also had to take remedial action because of an unexpected development. With regard to the possible levels of official complicity listed in the Introduction: Insofar as the revisionary account of Flight 93 (and/or Flight 77) is accepted, all the possible views lower than the fifth one are ruled out.

An intriguing dimension of this story is that Flight 93's fate was evidently due to the fact that it was 41 minutes late departing from the airport. All four flights were scheduled to leave at about the same time and were hence probably intended to hit their respective targets at about the same time. The other three planes were fairly well synchronized, departing only between 10 and 16 minutes late. But because Flight 93's departure was 41 minutes late, by the time the hijackers took control of it the two planes headed toward the WTC had already hit their targets. Passengers making phone calls from Flight 93 learned, therefore, that their flight was on a suicide mission. Unlike the passengers on the two flights headed for the WTC, accordingly, the passengers on Flight 93, knowing that they were headed for certain death if they remained passive, decided to try to gain control of the plane.[32] Had the plane not been so late leaving, the passengers may not have tried this, so this plane might also have hit its target.

Had it hit its target, furthermore, we might well look back upon Flight 93's mission as in some respects the most devastating one. Evacuation of the US Capitol building did not begin until 9:48, which was 23 minutes after an unidentified aircraft had been spotted flying across Washington and 10 minutes after it had hit the Pentagon. What if Flight 93 had been more nearly on time? Thompson says: "It is later reported that the target for Flight 93 was the Capitol building, so had that flight not been delayed 40 minutes before takeoff, it is possible most senators and congresspeople would have been killed."[33] Thompson is perhaps trying to motivate them to undertake a more far-reaching investigation into the events of 9/11.

Also, given the fact that the other main hypothesis about Flight 93's intended target is that it was the White House, critics also wonder why it was not evacuated sooner. According to many news reports, both Vice President Cheney and National Security Advisor Rice were taken to the White House's underground bunker by the Secret Service at about 9:03.[34] However, it was over 40 minutes later, at 9:45, when a general evacuation of the White House was begun.[35] If it was thought at 9:03 that Cheney and Rice were in danger, why were not the other people told to leave at that time? At the very least, why was the White House not evacuated shortly after 9:25, when the air traffic controllers at Dulles reported a fast-flying plane headed toward the White House? This question is even more pressing insofar as the official account of Flight 77 is accepted, according to which the passengers were told that they were all going to die because the plane was going to crash into the White House.[36] Had that been true, people working in the White House, instead of people working in the Pentagon, would have been killed, since the evacuation of the White House did not begin until seven minutes after the Pentagon was struck. We have, accordingly, still another disturbing question: Was there a plan to have deaths in the White House or the US Capitol Building as well as the Pentagon and the World Trade Center?

CHAPTER FOUR

THE PRESIDENT'S BEHAVIOR: WHY DID HE ACT AS HE DID?

Disturbing questions about the official account have been raised not only by the four aircraft crashes of 9/11 but also by President Bush's behavior on that day. Although the questions that critics have raised about that behavior are legion, I will focus on those that seem most disturbing.

The president's schedule that day called for him to visit an elementary school in Sarasota, Florida, where he was to listen to students read as a "photo opportunity." He arrived at the school shortly before 9:00 AM, at which time, according to at least one version of the official account, he was told that a plane had flown into the WTC. Since it was by then known that this plane as well as two others had been hijacked, one would assume, critics point out, that the president would also know this. Allan Wood and Paul Thompson state the problem thus:

> The first media reports of Flight 11's crash into the World Trade Center began around 8:48, two minutes after the crash happened. CNN broke into its regular programming at that time.... So within minutes, millions were aware of the story, yet Bush supposedly remained unaware for about another ten minutes.[1]

Critics find this difficult to believe.

The members of the president's traveling staff, including the Secret Service, argues Barrie Zwicker, "have the best communications equipment in the world." Accordingly, says Zwicker, within a minute after the first airliner hit the World Trade Center, the Secret Service and the president would have known about it.[2] In fact, Thompson points out, Vice President Cheney evidently let the cat out of the bag. During his interview on "Meet the Press" on September 16, Cheney said: "The Secret Service has an arrangement with the FAA. They had open lines after the World Trade Center was..."—stopping himself, Thompson adds, before finishing the sentence.[3] So, the Secret Service personnel in the president's motorcade, including the ones in his own car, would have known about the first attack on the WTC before the motorcade arrived at the school at 9:00. Indeed, it is even part of the official account that Ari Fleischer, the White House press secretary, learned about the first attack on the way. Having cited that story, Thompson adds: "It would make sense that Bush is told about the crash immediately and at the same time that others hear about it. Yet Bush and others claim he isn't told until he arrives at the school." Thompson's implied question, of course, is that if President Bush knew about the crash before arriving at the school, why did he and others pretend otherwise?

The vice president's inadvertent revelation about the open lines between the Secret Service and the FAA creates an even greater difficulty, critics point out, for another part of the official account. Upon learning that a plane had hit the WTC, President Bush reportedly referred to the crash as a "horrible accident."[4] However, Zwicker's complete statement, only partially summarized above, includes the point that by that time, the Secret Service and the president would have known that several airliners had been hijacked. So how could President Bush have assumed that the first crash into the WTC was an accident? Giving voice to the disturbing question raised by this story, Thompson asks: "[Are] Bush and his aides putting on a charade to pretend he doesn't know there is a national emergency? If so, why?"[5]

In any case, the president was then reportedly updated on the situation via telephone by his National Security Advisor, Condoleezza Rice, who would presumably have made sure that he knew not only about all the hijackings but also that the Director of the CIA, George Tenet, had already concluded that the hijackings were orchestrated by Osama bin Laden to carry out terrorist attacks.[6] But the president reportedly told the school's principal that "a commercial plane has hit the World Trade Center and we're going to go ahead and...do the reading thing anyway."[7]

Critics find this incredible. If the hijackings were unanticipated occurrences, as claimed, with one of the hijacked airplanes having already completed its terrorist mission, the country was suffering the worst terrorist attack of its history. And yet the Commander in Chief, rather than making sure that his military was prepared to shoot down all hijacked planes, sticks to his planned schedule. The strangeness of this behavior is brought out well in a summary of the situation by Wood and Thompson:

> At approximately 8:48 AM...,the first pictures of the burning World Trade Center were broadcast on live television.... By that time, the Federal Aviation Administration (FAA), the North American Aerospace Defense Command (NORAD), the National Military Command Center, the Pentagon, the White House, the Secret Service, and Canada's Strategic Command all knew that three commercial airplanes had been hijacked. They knew that one plane had been flown deliberately into the World Trade Center's North Tower; a second plane was wildly off course and also heading toward Manhattan.... So why, at 9:03 AM—fifteen minutes after it was clear the United States was under terrorist attack—did President Bush sit down with a classroom of second-graders and begin a 20-minute pre-planned photo op?[8]

Bush's behavior is made even more astounding by the fact that his Secret Service would have had to assume that he was one of the intended targets. Indeed, one Secret Service agent, seeing the television coverage of the crash of the second airliner into the WTC, reportedly said: "We're out of here."[9] But if one of the agents actually said this, he was obviously overruled. At the same time, by contrast, Cheney and Rice were reportedly being rushed to bunkers under the White House.[10] And yet, "For some reason, Secret Service agents [do] not hustle [Bush] away," comments the *Globe and Mail*. "Why doesn't this happen to Bush at the same time?" Thompson asks. "Why doesn't the Secret Service move Bush away from his known location?"[11] The reason for pressing this question is that, as Wood and Thompson point out: "Hijackers could have crashed a plane into Bush's publicized location and his security would have been completely helpless to stop it."[12]

This apparently unconcerned behavior, critics point out, continued for almost an hour. The intelligence expert James Bamford has written:

> [H]aving just been told that the country was under attack, the Commander in Chief appeared uninterested in further details. He never asked if there had been any additional threats, where the attacks were coming from, how to best protect the country from further attacks.... Instead, in the middle of a modern-day Pearl Harbor, he simply turned back to the matter at hand: the day's photo op.[13]

This photo opportunity involved, as indicated above, the president's listening to second graders read a book about a pet goat. After Bush had been in the classroom a few minutes, his chief of staff, Andrew Card, came in and whispered in his ear, reportedly telling him about the second attack. But the president, after a brief pause, had the children go ahead with the reading demonstration. To emphasize the strangeness of this behavior, Bamford adds this reflection:

> As President Bush continued with his reading lesson, life within the burning towers of the World Trade Center was becoming ever more desperate.... Within minutes, people began jumping, preferring a quick death to burning alive or suffocating.[14]

While this was going on, the president was listening to the students read: "The-Pet-Goat. A-girl-got-a-pet-goat. But-the-goat-did-some-things-that-made-the-girl's-dad-mad." After listening to this for several minutes, President Bush made a joke, saying: "Really good readers, whew! These must be sixth graders!"[15]

Another person who has found the contrast between the president's behavior and what was happening in New York troubling is Lorie van Auken, whose husband was one of the victims of the attacks on the towers. Having obtained the video of the president's session with the children, she watched it over and over, saying later: "I couldn't stop watching the president sitting there, listening to second graders, while my husband was burning in a building." Also, noting that the president had just been told by an advisor that the country was under attack, she wondered how the president could make a joke.[16]

Besides joking, the president lingered, not at all acting like a commander in chief with an emergency on his hands. Indeed, according to a book called *Fighting Back* by the White House correspondent for the *Washington Times*, Bill Sammon—a book that presents the White House perspective on most issues and generally provides an extremely sympathetic account of the president[17]—Bush was "openly stretching out the moment." When the lesson was over, according to Sammon's account, Bush said:

> Hoo! These are great readers. Very impressive! Thank you all so much for showing me your reading skills. I bet they practice too. Don't you? Reading more than they watch TV? Anybody do that? Read more than you watch TV? [Hands go up] Oh that's great! Very good. Very important to practice! Thanks for having me. Very impressed.[18]

Bush then continued to talk, advising the children to stay in school and be good citizens. And in response to a question, he talked about his education policy.[19] Sammon describes Bush as smiling and chatting with the children "as if he didn't have a care in the world" and "in the most relaxed manner imaginable." After a reporter asked if the president had heard about what had happened in New York, Bush said, "I'll talk about it later," then, in Sammon's words, "stepped forward and shook hands with [the classroom teacher] Daniels, slipping his left hand behind her in another photo-op pose. He was taking his good old time.... Bush lingered until the press was gone." Sammon, in fact, refers to the president as "the dawdler in chief."[20]

Amazingly, perhaps stung by the criticisms of the president's behavior, the White House put out a different account a year later. Andrew Card, Bush's chief of staff, was quoted as saying that after he told the president about the second attack on the World Trade Center, Bush "excused himself very politely to the teacher and to the students" and left the classroom within "a matter of seconds."[21] In an alternative wording of the new story, Card said, "Not that many seconds later the president excused himself from the classroom."[22] Apparently, say critics, the White House was so confident that none of its lies about 9/11 would be challenged by the media that it felt safe telling this one even though it is flatly contradicted by Sammon's pro-Bush book and by the video tape produced that day, which, as Wood and Thompson put it, "shows these statements are lies—unless 'a matter of seconds' means over 700 seconds!"[23]

In any case, back to real history, the president finally left the classroom at 9:16 to meet with his advisors, reportedly to prepare his television address to the nation, which he delivered at 9:29. Thompson comments: "The talk occurs at exactly the time and place stated in his publicly announced advance schedule—making Bush a possible terrorist target."[24] And not only Bush. When Andrew Card and Karl Rove were later asked why the president had not left the classroom as soon as he had word of the second attack, their answer, Wood and Thompson point out, was that he did not want to upset the children. But, they ask, "why didn't Bush's concern for the children extend to not making them and the rest of the 200 or so people at the school terrorist targets?"[25] Might the answer be that Bush knew that there was really no danger?

In any case, the president and his people then went in their scheduled motorcade on their scheduled route to the airport, during which they reportedly learned that the Pentagon had been struck and also heard that the president's plane, Air Force One, was a terrorist target. Nevertheless, no military escort was ordered. "Amazingly," says Thompson, "his plane takes off without any fighters protecting it."[26] This seems especially surprising given the fact that there were still over 3,000 planes in the air over the United States and there was no way to know at that time how many airlines had been hijacked. For example, about an hour later, Thompson reports, the FAA had said that there were *six* missing aircraft— a figure that Cheney subsequently mentioned—and at one time *eleven* flights were suspected of having been hijacked.[27] According to Karl Rove, furthermore, the Secret Service had learned of "a specific threat made to Air Force One."[28] So, why had fighter jets not been ordered from one of the two nearby military bases, which have fighters on 24-hour alert?[29]

The strangeness of the president's behavior, given the apparent circumstances, has not gone unnoticed by family members of the victims of the attacks of 9/11. For example, Kristen Breitweiser, whose question about how a plane could have struck the Pentagon was quoted earlier, also said:

> It was clear that we were under attack. Why didn't the Secret Service whisk him out of that school? He was on live local television in Florida. The terrorists, you know, had been in Florida.... I want to know why he sat there for 25 minutes.[30]

Much attention at the time was given to the fact that once Air Force One became airborne at 9:55, President Bush remained away from Washington for a long time, perhaps, speculated some commentators, out of fear. Indeed, some reporters who criticized the president on that score lost their jobs[31]—which may account for why the White House could later be confident that the news media would not challenge any of its fabrications. In any case, the real question, the critics suggest, is why there was apparently no fear during the first hour. The implied question is, of course, a disturbing one: Did the president and at least the head of his Secret Service detail know that he was *not* a target?

The idea that the Bush administration had advance knowledge of the attacks is further suggested by a statement later made by Bush himself: "I was sitting outside the classroom waiting to go in," he claimed, "and I saw an airplane hit the tower—the TV was obviously on, and I used to fly myself, and I said, 'There's one terrible pilot.'"[32] Given the fact that according to the official story, Bush did not have access to a television set until at least 15 minutes later,[33] this statement raised questions. An article in the *Boston Herald* said:

> Think about that. Bush's remark implies he saw the first plane hit the tower. But we all know that video of the first plane hitting did not surface until the next day. Could Bush have meant he saw the second plane hit—which many Americans witnessed? No, because he said that he was in the classroom when Card whispered in his ear that a second plane hit.

Pointing out that Bush had told this story several times, the writer asked: "How could the commander-in-chief have seen the plane fly into the first building—as it happened?"[34]

This is an excellent question. But it is simply one of many excellent questions that have been raised by individual reporters and then allowed to die by the rest of the news media. They have not pressed for an answer.

Thierry Meyssan, however, has suggested a possible answer. Pointing out that "according to his own declaration, the President of the United States saw pictures of the first crash before the second had taken place," Meyssan emphasizes the fact that the pictures reportedly seen by Bush could *not* have been "those accidentally filmed by French documentary-makers Jules and Gédéon Naudet," because "their video was not released until thirteen hours later." On the morning of 9/11, therefore, Bush could not have seen the pictures of the first crash that we have all seen time and time again. Therefore, Meyssan suggests, the pictures must

> have been secret images transmitted to him without delay in the secure communications room that was installed in the elementary school in preparation for his visit. But if the US intelligence services could have filmed the first attack, that means they must have been informed beforehand.[35]

Meyssan's suggestion, in other words, is that although the president did not see the plane fly into the first building "as it happened," he did see it, as he claimed, before he went into the classroom.

According to critics of the official account, in sum, the behavior of President Bush on 9/11 reinforces the conclusion, inferable from the fate of the four crashed airliners, that government and military officials at the highest level had advance knowledge of, and conspired to allow, the traumatic events of that day.[36] With regard to our list of possible views, furthermore, the critical account of the president's behavior seems to eliminate the first five possible views, according to which the White House had no expectation of any attacks. The behavior of President Bush and his Secret Service seems to imply at least the sixth view, according to which the White House expected *some* sort of attacks. Furthermore, if we accept Meyssan's conjecture about Bush's statement that he saw the first WTC crash on television before entering the classroom, the seventh view—according to which the White House had foreknowledge of the targets and the timing of the attacks—is suggested. That view is also suggested by the evidence that President Bush and his Secret Service seemed to know that *they* would not be targets of the attack.

For the critics of the official account, this conclusion for some sort of official complicity is made even stronger when the events of 9/11 are seen in the larger context provided by information about relevant events both prior to and after 9/11. This larger context will be the subject of the second part of this book.

PART TWO

THE LARGER CONTEXT

CHAPTER FIVE

DID US OFFICIALS HAVE ADVANCE INFORMATION ABOUT 9/11?

The larger context for viewing the events of 9/11, according to critics of the official account, consists of four more types of evidence against that account. In this chapter, I explore the first type: evidence that US officials had information about the attacks before they happened.

Many leading officials in the Bush administration have claimed that the events of 9/11 were completely unanticipated. For example, Condoleezza Rice, Bush's National Security Advisor, said in May of 2002: "I don't think anybody could have predicted that these people would take an airplane and slam it into the World Trade Center, take another one and slam it into the Pentagon, that they would try to use...a hijacked airplane as a missile."[1] The next month, President Bush, in an address to the nation, said: "Based on everything I've seen, I do not believe anyone could have prevented the horror of September the 11th."[2] A further claim, endorsed in the summary of the final report of the Joint Inquiry conducted by the intelligence committees of the US Senate and House of Representatives, is that although there were some indications of plans for terrorist attacks within the United States, "it was the general view of the Intelligence Community, in the spring and summer of 2001, that the threatened bin Laden attacks would most likely occur against US interests overseas."[3] These general claims can be divided into two more particular ones, each of which has been challenged by critics of the official account.

Was the Very Possibility of Such Attacks not Envisioned?

One of these claims is that the very possibility that someone would use airplanes as weapons had not been imagined. For example, a defense official was quoted as saying: "I don't think any of us envisioned an internal air threat by big aircraft. I don't know of anybody that ever thought through that."[4] About a year later, White House Press Secretary Ari Fleischer said: "Until the attack took place, I think it's fair to say that no one envisioned that as a possibility."[5]

Critics say, however, that there is much evidence to the contrary. For example, in 1993 a panel of experts commissioned by the Pentagon suggested that airplanes could be used as missiles to bomb national landmarks. However, this notion was not published in its report, *Terror 2000*, because, said one of its authors: "We were told by the Department of Defense not to put it in." But in 1994, one of these experts wrote in the *Futurist* magazine:

> Targets such as the World Trade Center not only provide the requisite casualties but, because of their symbolic nature, provide more bang for the buck. In order to maximize their odds for success, terrorist groups will likely consider mounting multiple, simultaneous operations.[6]

In that same year, there were three airplanes hijacked with the intent to use them as weapons, including a highly publicized plan of a terrorist group linked with al-Qaeda to crash one into the Eiffel Tower. In 1995, Senator Sam Nunn, in *Time* magazine's cover story, described a scenario in which terrorists crash a radio-controlled airplane into the US Capitol building.[7]

The year 1995 also brought the most important discovery, which has been widely reported: Philippine police found an al-Qaeda computer with a plan called Project Bojinka, one version of which involved hijacking planes and flying them into targets such as the World Trade Center, the White House, CIA headquarters, and the Pentagon. This plan—which was evidently formulated by Khalid Shaikh Mohammed (later to be identified as the mastermind of 9/11) and his relative Ramsi Yousef[8]—resurfaced in the 1996 trial of the latter for masterminding the 1993 attack on the World Trade Center (in which Mohammed was also indicted).[9] Yousef's conviction, Ahmed points out, was on September 11, 1996, so that 9/11 was its fifth anniversary.[10] Furthermore, after the attacks, reports Thompson, a Philippine investigator said: "It's Bojinka.... We told the Americans everything about Bojinka. Why didn't they pay attention?"[11]

In 1999, the National Intelligence Council, which advises the President and US intelligence agencies on emerging threats, said in a special report on terrorism:

Al-Qaeda's expected retaliation for the US cruise missile attack [of 1998]...could take several forms of terrorist attack in the nation's capitol. Suicide bombers belonging to al-Qaeda's Martyrdom Battalion could crash-land an aircraft packed with high explosives...into the Pentagon, the headquarters of the Central Intelligence Agency (CIA), or the White House.[12]

With regard to the Pentagon in particular, officials in October of 2000 carried out an emergency drill to prepare for the possibility that a hijacked airliner might be crashed into the Pentagon.[13]

In sum, argue critics, the claim that the possibility of such attacks had not been envisioned is clearly untrue.

Were There No Specific Warnings about the Attacks?

A second, narrower claim is that although there were warnings about the possibility of this kind of attack, there were no specific warnings relating to 9/11. For example, three days afterwards, FBI Director Robert Mueller said: "There were no warning signs that I'm aware of that would indicate this type of operation in the country."[14] A year later, he still claimed: "To this day we have found no one in the United States except the actual hijackers who knew of the plot."[15]

Acceptance of this claim is reflected in the summary of the final report of the Joint Inquiry conducted by the House and Senate intelligence committees. The first "finding" reported in this summary reads:

While the Intelligence Community had amassed a great deal of valuable intelligence regarding Usama Bin Ladin and his terrorist activities, none of it identified the time, place, and specific nature of the attacks that were planned for September 11, 2001. [*Author's note: Spellings of his name shift due to different styles of transliterating the Arabic into English.*]

Indeed, as we saw earlier, this summary of the Joint Inquiry's final report said that the information led the intelligence community to expect the attacks to be directed "against US interests overseas."

But in fact, critics argue, there were evidently many quite specific warnings in the months leading up to 9/11 and, given the fact that by May of 2001, warnings of an attack against the US were reportedly higher than ever before, US intelligence agencies should have been especially on the alert.[16] This state of alert should have been increased still further, one would assume, given the fact that an intelligence summary for Condoleezza Rice from CIA Director George Tenet on June 28 said: "It is highly likely that a significant al-Qaeda attack is in the near future, within several weeks."[17] It was in such a context that the rather specific warnings came.

In late July, for example, the Taliban's Foreign Minister informed US officials that Osama bin Laden was planning a "huge attack" inside America that was imminent and would kill thousands.[18] That the information indicated that the attack was to involve commercial airlines is suggested by the fact that on July 26, CBS News reported that Attorney General Ashcroft had decided to quit using this mode of travel because of a threat assessment—although "neither the FBI nor the Justice Department...would identify what the threat was, when it was detected or who made it."[19] In May of 2002, it was claimed that the threat assessment had nothing to do with al-Qaeda, but Ashcroft, according to the Associated Press, walked out of his office rather than answer questions about it. The *San Francisco Chronicle* complained: "The FBI obviously knew something was in the wind.... The FBI did advise Ashcroft to stay off commercial aircraft. The rest of us just had to take our chances." CBS's Dan Rather later asked, with regard to this warning: "Why wasn't it shared with the public at large?"[20]

August and September brought more warnings. A Moroccan agent who had penetrated al-Qaeda was evidently brought to the United States to discuss his report that bin Laden, being disappointed that the 1993 bombing had not toppled the WTC, planned "large scale operations in New York in the summer or fall of 2001."[21] Former CIA agent Robert Baer reportedly told the CIA's Counter-Terrorism Center that he had learned from a military associate of a Persian Gulf prince that a "spectacular terrorist operation" was about to take place.[22] Some warnings, furthermore, were reportedly given by several foreign intelligence agencies. For example, Russian President Putin later stated that in August, "I ordered my intelligence to warn President Bush in the strongest terms that 25 terrorists were getting ready to attack the US, including important government buildings like the Pentagon." The head of Russian intelligence also said: "We had clearly warned them" on several occasions, but they "did not pay the necessary attention."[23] Warnings were also reportedly given by Jordan, Egypt, and Israel,[24] with the latter country warning, a few days before 9/11, that perhaps 200 terrorists linked to Osama bin Laden were "preparing a big operation."[25]

One of the official warnings during this period became widely known—a memo provided by Great Britain, which was included in the intelligence briefing for President Bush on August 6. This warning said that al-Qaeda had planned an attack in the United States involving multiple airplane hijackings. The White House kept this warning secret, with the president repeatedly claiming after 9/11 that he had received no warning of any kind. But on May 15, 2002, CBS Evening News revealed the existence of this memo from British intelligence. Condoleezza Rice tried to dismiss its significance by saying that it was "fuzzy and thin," consisting of only a page and a half. Newspaper accounts, however, said that it was 11 pages long.[26] Press Secretary Ari Fleischer said in no uncertain terms: "The president did not—not—receive information about the use of airplanes as missiles by suicide bombers."[27] A few days later, however, the *Guardian* reported that "the [August 6] memo left little doubt that the hijacked airliners were intended for use as missiles and that intended targets were to be inside the US."[28] Doubt about the administration's truthfulness is raised by the fact that it has refused to release the memo while claiming that there is nothing specific in it. As Michael Moore has asked: "If there is nothing specific, then why can't they release it?"[29]

In any case, if that information is still considered too general to have made the events of 9/11 preventable, even more specific information was provided by the stock market. Intelligence agencies monitor the stock market, critics point out, to watch for clues of impending catastrophes. And the days just before September 11 saw an extremely high volume of "put options" purchased for the stock of Morgan Stanley Dean Witter, which occupied 22 stories of the World Trade Center, and for United and American Airlines, the two airlines used in the attacks.[30] For these two airlines, and only these two, "the level of these trades was up by 1,200 percent in the three days prior to the World Trade Center attacks."[31] To buy a put option is to bet that the price of shares is going to go down, and in this case the bet was highly profitable. As the *San Francisco Chronicle* explained: "When the stock prices...dropped...in response to the terrorist attacks, the options multiplied a hundredfold in value, making millions of dollars in profit." If a single group of speculators purchased most of the thousands of put options for those three stocks, this group would have made over $10 million. This unusual set of purchases "raises suspicions that the investors...had advance knowledge of the strikes."[32]

Even more important here is the conclusion that any intelligence officer looking at this development, especially in light of all the warnings, would easily have concluded that someone with inside information knew that *in the near future both American and United airplanes were going to be used in attacks, quite likely on the World Trade Center.* And there can be no serious doubt, Ahmed adds, that intelligence officers monitor the market looking for such anomalies. He quotes investigative journalist Michael Ruppert, a former detective for the Los Angeles Police Department, who wrote: "It is well documented that the CIA has long monitored such trades—in real time—as potential warnings of terrorist attacks and other economic moves contrary to US interests." Ahmed adds that "[t]he UPI also reported that the US-sponsored ECHELON intelligence network closely monitors stock trading."[33]

An intriguing footnote to this story is that A. B. "Buzzy" Krongard, who in March of 2001 was promoted within the CIA by President Bush to become its executive director, had until 1998 been the manager of Deutsche Bank, one of the major banks through which put options on United Airlines were purchased.[34] The implication, of course, is that there might have been insider trading going on that dwarfed Martha Stewart's in size and significance.

In any case, further specific information, critics continue, was evidently obtained from electronic intercepts. Shortly before 9/11, the FBI reportedly intercepted messages such as "There is a big thing coming" and "They're going to pay the price."[35] On September 9, a foreign intelligence service reportedly passed on to US intelligence an intercepted message from bin Laden to his mother, in which he told her: "In two days you're going to hear big news, and you're not going to hear from me for a while."[36] And the next day, September 10, US intelligence reportedly obtained electronic intercepts of conversations in which al-Qaeda members said: "Tomorrow will be a great day for us."[37] One of those intercepts was reportedly made by the National Security Agency (NSA), which had monitored a call during the summer between Mohamed Atta and Khalid Shaikh Mohammed, believed to be one of the architects of Project Bojinka, the 1993 bombing of the WTC, and the bombing of the *USS Cole*.[38] In the intercept of September 10, 2001, Atta reportedly received final approval for the 9/11 attacks from Mohammed. According to the September 15, 2002 story in the *Independent* that reported this intercept, information as to when the intercept was translated had not been released.[39] But given the fact that US intelligence had learned in June of 2001 that Khalid Shaikh Mohammed was interested in "sending terrorists to the United States,"[40] one would assume that translating an intercepted message from him would have had the highest priority.

US intelligence agencies, however, would later claim that the highly specific messages received the two days before 9/11 were not translated until afterwards. In relation to this claim, it is significant, as Thompson points out, that Senator Orrin Hatch reported that US officials had overheard two bin Laden aides celebrating the successful terrorist attack. At a news briefing on September 12, Secretary of Defense Rumsfeld reportedly manifested chagrin at Hatch's breach, which revealed that the US government was, in fact, monitoring these communications electronically in real time.[41] The idea that specific information was not only received but also translated on September 10 is further suggested by *Newsweek's* report that on that day "a group of top Pentagon officials suddenly canceled travel plans for the next morning, apparently because of security concerns."[42]

With this information before us, we can better evaluate the Joint Inquiry's final report, as reflected in its summary, according to which none of the information available to the intelligence community "identified the time, place, and specific nature of the attacks that were planned for September 11, 2001." The Joint Inquiry evidently tried to reconcile this finding with the kind of very specific information reviewed above by saying: "In the period from September 8 to September 10, 2001, NSA intercepted, but did not translate or disseminate until after September 11, some communications that indicated possible impending terrorist activity."[43] It would be interesting to know, however, whether this conclusion was based on any evidence other than testimony by members of the NSA. It would also be interesting to know whether the Joint Inquiry tried to explain why on September 10 "a group of top Pentagon officials suddenly canceled travel plans for the next morning." And whether they asked why, given the many very specific reports *prior* to

September 8, the NSA was *not* translating and disseminating the warnings it intercepted from September 8 to 10—in other words, whether the claim that it did not do so is really believable.

In any case, Ahmed, referring to Condoleezza Rice's statement that US officials had no specific information about the attacks in advance, concludes that it is "patently false."[44] Michel Chossudovsky, referring to the discussion of whether members of the Bush administration knew about the attacks beforehand, says: "Of course they knew!"—adding that "the American people have been consciously and deliberately deceived."[45] Critics of the official account have certainly provided evidence that seems to support these conclusions. The material in this chapter provides, at the very least, further evidence against the first two of the possible views, according to which US intelligence agencies had no specific information about the attacks. Some of this evidence, furthermore, seems to rule out the first six views, according to which at least the White House had no specific knowledge about the impending attacks. All the views except the seventh and the eighth, accordingly, would seem to be ruled out insofar as the evidence summarized in this chapter stands up to further scrutiny.

The cumulative evidence of government complicity becomes even more compelling, critics of the official account of 9/11 believe, when it includes evidence that US officials actively obstructed investigations that might have uncovered the plot.

CHAPTER SIX

DID US OFFICIALS OBSTRUCT INVESTIGATIONS PRIOR TO 9/11?

When information of some of the warnings discussed in the previous chapter leaked out, US officials dismissed the importance of these warnings by claiming that there is always so much intelligence coming in that it is often difficult to distinguish the significant information from the "noise," meaning all the reports that turn out to be false or insignificant. After a catastrophe such as 9/11 happens, they say, it is unfair to pick out those few bits of information related to it and claim, with 20/20 hindsight, that officials should have been able to "connect the dots." However, say critics, even if that argument could legitimately be used to dismiss the warnings discussed in the previous chapter (which, they maintain, it could not), the fact of official complicity would be strongly suggested if there is evidence that governmental agencies had purposely prevented investigations of al-Qaeda and individuals thought to be connected to it. And, they claim, such evidence does exist.

The Anti-Hunt for Osama bin Laden and al-Qaeda

One of the main reasons for doubting the official story about 9/11, say critics, is evidence that, far from doing everything it could to kill or capture bin Laden, US government officials repeatedly failed to do so when they had opportunities. I will summarize a few of the episodes that have been dug up by Ahmed and Thompson.

In December of 1998, CIA Director George Tenet reportedly circulated a memorandum in the intelligence community that said: "We are at war," and added: "I want no resources or people spared in this effort, either inside CIA or the [larger intelligence] community." But the Congressional Joint Inquiry would later learn that there was no significant shift in budget or personnel and that few FBI agents had ever heard of the declaration.[1]

On December 20 of 2000, Richard Clarke, a counter-terrorism expert, submitted a plan to "roll back" al-Qaeda in response to the bombing of the *USS Cole* (which had occurred in October). The main component of Clarke's plan was a dramatic increase in covert action in Afghanistan to "eliminate the sanctuary" for bin Laden. The Clinton administration, on the grounds that the Bush administration would be taking over in only a few weeks, passed the plan on to it. In January, however, the Bush administration rejected the plan and took no action.[2]

According to a story reported by ABC News, Julie Sirrs, an agent for the Defense Intelligence Agency (DIA), traveled to Afghanistan twice in 2001. On her first trip, she met with Northern Alliance leader Ahmad Masood.[3] On her second trip, she returned home with what she later called "a treasure trove of information," including evidence that bin Laden was planning to assassinate Masood (and Masood would indeed be assassinated on September 9, as discussed in Chapter 8). But she was met at the airport by a security officer, who confiscated her material, after which the DIA and the FBI investigated her. However, she said, no higher intelligence officials wanted to hear what she had learned in Afghanistan. Finally, her security clearance was pulled and she resigned from the DIA.[4]

In March of 2001, the Russian Permanent Mission at the United Nations secretly submitted "an unprecedentedly detailed report" to the UN Security Council about bin Laden and his whereabouts, including "a listing of all bin Laden's bases, his government contacts and foreign advisors"—enough information, they said, to kill him. But the Bush administration took no action. Alex Standish, the editor of *Jane's Intelligence Review*, would later conclude that the attacks of 9/11 were not an intelligence failure but the result of "a political decision not to act against bin Laden."[5]

By the summer of 2001, Osama bin Laden was America's "most wanted" criminal, for whom it was offering a $5 million bounty, and the US government had supposedly tried to kill him. And yet in July, according to reports by several of Europe's most respected news sources, bin Laden spent two weeks in the American hospital in Dubai (of the United Arab Emirates). Besides being treated by an American surgeon, Dr. Terry Callaway, he was also reportedly visited by the head of Saudi intelligence and, on July 12, by the local CIA agent, Larry Mitchell. Although the reports were denied by the CIA, the hospital, and bin

Laden himself, Dr. Callaway reportedly simply refused comment, and the news agencies stood by their story.[6]

"The explosive story," comments Thompson, was "widely reported in Europe, but barely at all in the US."[7] After this story broke in November, Chossudovsky, quoting Secretary of Defense Rumsfeld's comment that finding bid Laden would be like "searching for a needle in a stack of hay," said: "But the US could have ordered his arrest and extradition in Dubai last July. But then they would not have had a pretext for waging a war."[8]

Hidden Connections between Bush, bin Laden, and Saudi Royals

One of the disturbing questions that has been raised by critics of the official account is whether the actual relations between the Bush administration, Osama bin Laden, and the Saudi Royal family are not rather different from the public portrayal of these relations. There are several grounds for suspicion. First, the bin Laden family—one of the wealthiest and most influential families in Saudi Arabia—and the Bush family had business relations for over 20 years.[9] Second, although Osama bin Laden has been portrayed as the black sheep of the family who was disowned for his terrorist ways—so that the "good bin Ladens" could be radically distinguished from the "bad bin Laden"—there is much evidence that Osama's close ties with his family continued.[10] Third, there is evidence that Osama bin Laden continued to receive covert aid from America's close ally, Saudi Arabia.[11] A fourth ground for suspicion is the report that immediately after 9/11, the US government, working with the Saudi government, helped many members of the bin Laden family depart from the United States, even allowing their jets to fly before the national air ban was lifted.[12] A fifth cause for suspicion is the fact that when the final report of the Joint Inquiry into 9/11 carried out by the House and Senate intelligence committees was finally released in 2003, the administration had insisted on blocking out some 28 pages, which reportedly dealt primarily with Saudi Arabia. There is, finally, the simple fact that most of the alleged hijackers were from Saudi Arabia.

These grounds for suspicion are, furthermore, supported by reports from credible people about continuing ties between the Saudi government, Osama bin Laden, and al-Qaeda.

On August 22, 2001, John O'Neill, a counter-terrorism expert who was said to be the US government's "most committed tracker of Osama bin Laden and his al-Qaeda network of terrorists," resigned from the FBI, citing repeated obstruction of his investigations into al-Qaeda.[13] The previous month, O'Neill, who held one of the top positions in the FBI, had reportedly complained of obstruction by the White House, saying that the main obstacles to investigating al-Qaeda were "US oil corporate interests and the role played by Saudi Arabia." He then added: "All the answers, everything needed to dismantle Osama bin Laden's organization, can be found in Saudi Arabia."[14] O'Neill's assessment, Ahmed comments, was given support by Tariq Ali, who wrote: "Bin Laden and his gang are just the tentacles [of the Wahhabi octopus]; the head lies safely in Saudi Arabia, protected by US forces."[15]

The idea that any serious investigation would need to focus on Saudi Arabia has, interestingly, been supported more recently by Gerald Posner, an author who on most points supports the official account of 9/11.[16] On the basis of information provided anonymously but independently by two sources in the US government, Possner reports on the US interrogation of the Saudi Arabian Abu Zubaydah, one of al-Qaeda's top operatives, who was captured in Pakistan late in March of 2002. The interrogation, aided by thiopental sodium (Sodium Pentothal), was carried out by two Arab-Americans pretending to be Saudi Arabians. Relieved to be in the presence of men he believed to be fellow countrymen, Zubaydah became very talkative.[17]

Hoping to save himself, Zubaydah claimed that he, as a member of al-Qaeda, had been working on behalf of senior Saudi officials. Encouraging his interrogators to confirm his claim, he told them to call one of King Fahd's nephews, Prince Ahmed bin Salman bin Abdul-Aziz (chairman of a huge publishing empire and founder of the Thoroughbred Corporation, which produced Kentucky Derby winner War Emblem). Zubaydah even gave them Prince Ahmed's telephone numbers from memory. When his interrogators said that 9/11 had surely changed everything, so that Prince Ahmed would no longer be supportive of al-Qaeda, Zubaydah told them that it would not have changed anything, *because Prince Ahmed had known in advance that America would be attacked on 9/11.* Zubaydah also gave from memory the phone numbers of two other relatives of King Fahd's who could confirm his claims: Prince Sultan bin Faisal bin Turki al-Saud and Prince Fahd bin Turki bin Saud al-Kabir.

Less than four months later, events occurred that suggested to Posner that Zubaydah's testimony may have been true. Within an eight-day period, all three of the named Saudis died. On July 22, Prince Ahmed, who was 43, reportedly died of a heart attack. The next day, Prince Sultan bin Faisal, who was 41, reportedly died in a single-car accident. And a week later, Prince Fahd bin Turki, who was 21, "died of thirst."[18]

Zubaydah also said that he had been present at several meetings between Osama bin Laden and Prince Turki bin Faisal, the chief of Saudi intelligence, including a meeting in Kandahar in 1998 at which Prince Turki promised that Saudis would continue to support the Taliban and would not ask for Osama's extradition as long as al-Qaeda kept its promise not to attack the Saudi kingdom. But Prince Turki—who had been dismissed as head of Saudi intelligence ten days before 9/11, after which he became the Saudi ambassador to Great Britain—survived the testimony about him.[19]

In any case, the accounts of these interconnections between Saudi royals, Osama bin Laden, and al-Qaeda suggest that the American failure to capture bin Laden may be connected with the close relations between the Saudi royals, the bin Laden family, and the Bush administration. According to a story by investigative reporters Gregory Palast and David Pallister, US intelligence agents, having long complained that they had been "prevented for political reasons from carrying out full investigations into members of the bin Laden family," said that after the Bush administration took over, things had become worse—that they "had been told to 'back off' from investigations involving other members of the Bin Laden family [and] the Saudi royals."[20] Palast, elaborating on this point in an interview, stated: "There is no question we had what looked like the biggest failure of the intelligence community since Pearl Harbor but what we are learning now is it wasn't a failure, it was a directive."[21] This conclusion is supported by an American intelligence agent, who said: "There were particular investigations [of the bin Laden family] that were effectively killed."[22]

It was not, however, only with regard to bin Laden and his family that investigations were reportedly stifled. Ahmed and Thompson point to several cases in which investigations of other promising leads were apparently either obstructed or not even initiated. These cases are especially pertinent to the Joint Inquiry's conclusion that the attacks of 9/11 were due to intelligence failures that were regrettable but understandable. While pointing out that the intelligence agencies had received more warnings than they had admitted, the Joint Inquiry partly let them off the hook by saying that although they had missed some important clues, "They are the kinds of misses that happen when people...are simply overwhelmed."[23] In some of the following cases, agents in the field were evidently less overwhelmed than overruled.

Ignoring the FBI in Phoenix

On July 10, 2001, Phoenix FBI agent Ken Williams sent a now well-known memorandum to the counterterrorism division at FBI headquarters, warning about suspicious activities involving a group of Middle Eastern men who were taking flight training lessons. Williams had begun investigating them in 2000, but early in 2001 he was reassigned to an arson case—leading a retired agent in Phoenix to write FBI Director Mueller after 9/11, asking: "Why take your best terrorism investigator and put him on an arson case?" Williams had been back on the flight-school case for only a month when he wrote his memo. Suggesting that bin Laden's followers might be taking flying lessons for terrorist purposes, he recommended a national program to track suspicious flight-school students. FBI headquarters, however, did not institute such a program.[24]

Blocking the FBI in Minneapolis

In mid-August of 2001, the staff at a flight school in Minneapolis called the local FBI to report their suspicion that Zacarias Moussaoui, who had paid to train on a Boeing 747 simulator, was planning to use a real 747 "as a weapon."[25] After the Minneapolis FBI agents arrested Moussaoui and discovered many suspicious things about him, they asked FBI headquarters for a warrant to search his laptop computer and other possessions. However, even though FBI headquarters received additional information about Moussaoui from France—which according to French officials clearly showed that he posed a threat[26]— senior FBI officials said that the information "was too sketchy to justify a search warrant for his computer."[27] But the Minneapolis agents, having seen the French intelligence report, were "in a frenzy," with one agent speculating that Moussaoui might "fly something into the World Trade Center."[28] Becoming "desperate to search the computer lap top," the Minneapolis agents sent a request through FBI headquarters for a search warrant under the Foreign Intelligence Surveillance Act (FISA), which would be certain to grant it, because in the past its officials had granted virtually all requests.[29]

At FBI headquarters, however, the request was given to the Radical Fundamentalist Unit (RFU), one of whose agents criticized the Minneapolis FBI supervisor for getting people "spun up" over Moussaoui—but without telling this supervisor about the memo from Ken Williams in Phoenix, which the head of the RFU had received.[30] The Minneapolis request was then given to RFU agent Marion "Spike" Bowman, who lived up to his nickname by proceeding to remove the evidence that Moussaoui was connected to al-Qaeda through a rebel group in Chechnya. Then the FBI Deputy General Counsel, on the basis of this edited request, said that there was insufficient connection to al-Qaeda for a search warrant and did not even forward the request to FISA.[31] Minneapolis FBI legal officer Coleen Rowley asked: "Why would an FBI agent deliberately sabotage a case?" Other agents in the Minneapolis office joked that those at headquarters who blocked the request "had to be spies or moles...working for Osama bin Laden," while one agent concluded that FBI headquarters was "setting this up for failure."[32]

It is interesting to compare this account of what happened with the "finding" in the Joint Inquiry's summary of its final report, which says that "personnel at FBI Headquarters, including the Radical Fundamentalist Unit and the National Security Law Unit, as well as agents in the Minneapolis field office, misunderstood the legal standard for obtaining an order under FISA," having "the perception...that the FISA process was lengthy and fraught with peril." According to this finding, there was no sabotage, just misunderstanding all around, even in Minneapolis. Given the fact that this report was published many months after Coleen Rowley's blistering memo, discussed below, became part of the public record, it is puzzling how the Joint Inquiry could have thought that the agents in Minneapolis were confused.

In any case, the Minneapolis FBI agents were unable to examine Moussaoui's computer and other personal effects until after the 9/11 attacks.[33] Following that search, the former FBI Deputy Director said that the computer contained "nothing significant...pertaining to 9/11," but the *Washington Post* cited congressional investigators as saying that "the evidence that lay unexamined in Zacarias Moussaoui's possession was even more valuable than previously believed," as it connected him "to the main hijacking cell in Hamburg" and to "an al-Qaeda associate in Malaysia whose activities [had been] monitored by the CIA."[34] The *New York Times* concluded that the Moussaoui case "raised new questions about why the Federal Bureau of Investigation and other agencies did not prevent the hijackings."[35]

Three days after 9/11, FBI Director Mueller, who had only recently been appointed to this position, made his previously quoted statement: "There were no warning signs that I'm aware of that would indicate this type of operation in the country." Coleen Rowley and other Minneapolis agents tried to reach his office to make him aware of the Moussaoui case so that his "public statements could be accordingly modified," yet Mueller continued to make similar comments, including his testimony in a Senate hearing on May 8, 2002, that "there was nothing the agency could have done to anticipate and prevent the attacks."[36] According to reports of this hearing, however, Mueller finally had to admit that a month before 9/11, one FBI agent had speculated "at a high-level meeting that Moussaoui might have been taking lessons to enable him to crash an aircraft into the World Trade Center in New York."[37] Two weeks later, Rowley released a long memo she had written about the FBI's handling of the Moussaoui case, which *Time* magazine called a "colossal indictment of our chief law-enforcement agency's neglect."[38] After this memo became publicized, Mueller modified his public stance slightly, saying: "I cannot say for sure that there wasn't a possibility we could have come across some lead that would have led us to the hijackers."[39]

Blocking the FBI in Chicago

In 1998, FBI agent Robert Wright had begun tracking a terrorist cell in Chicago, suspecting that money used for the 1998 bombings of US embassies came from a Saudi multimillionaire living in Chicago. In January of 2001, in spite of his belief that his case was growing stronger, he was told that it was being closed. In June, he wrote an internal memo charging that the FBI, rather than trying to prevent a terrorist attack, "was merely gathering intelligence so they would know who to arrest when a terrorist attack occurred."[40] In May of 2002, Wright announced that he was suing the FBI for refusing to allow him to publish a book he had written about the affair. Included in his description of the actions of his superiors in curtailing his investigations were words such as "prevented," "thwarted," "obstructed," "threatened," "intimidated," and "retaliation."[41] In a later interview, reporting that he had been told that his case was being closed because it was "better to let sleeping dogs lie," he said: "Those dogs weren't sleeping, they were training, they were getting ready.... September the 11th is a direct result of the incompetence of the FBI's International Terrorism Unit." Chicago federal prosecutor Mark Flessner, who also worked on the case, evidently thought that something other than incompetence was involved, saying that there "were powers bigger than I was in the Justice Department and within the FBI that simply were not going to let [the building of a criminal case] happen."[42]

Blocking the FBI in New York

On August 28, 2001, the FBI office in New York, believing Khalid Almihdhar—who would later be named as one of the hijackers—had been involved in the bombing of the USS Cole, tried to convince FBI headquarters to open a criminal investigation. But the New York request was turned down on the grounds that Almihdhar could not be tied to the Cole investigation without the inclusion of sensitive intelligence information. One New York agent expressed his frustration in an e-mail letter, saying, "Whatever has happened to this—someday someone will die—and...the public will not understand why we were not more effective.... Let's hope the [FBI's] National Security Law Unit will stand behind their decisions then, especially since the biggest threat to us now, UBL [Usama bin Laden], is getting the most 'protection.'"[43]

Justice for a Spy

Sibel Edmonds and Can Dickerson were both hired by the FBI as translators after the 9/11 attacks. Edmonds soon informed her superiors that Dickerson had previously worked for a particular foreign organization, which was being investigated by the FBI, and that Dickerson was mistranslating, or even not translating at all, sensitive information regarding this organization. Edmonds informed her superiors, furthermore, that Dickerson had threatened her for refusing to work as a spy for this organization. But, Edmonds reported, the FBI failed to respond to her complaints, which she had made more than once, so in March she wrote a letter to the Inspector General of the Department of Justice, soon after which she was fired. Claiming that she was fired for whistleblowing, she sued. In October, at FBI Director Mueller's request, Attorney General Ashcroft, appealing to the privilege of state secrets "to protect the foreign policy and national security interests of the United States," asked a judge to throw out Edmonds' lawsuit.[44] Critics wonder, of course, why the national security of the United States would be protected by ignoring a claim that a spy for a foreign organization being investigated by the FBI was sabotaging that investigation.

Schippers and FBI Agents Versus the US Government

On September 13, 2001, Attorney David Schippers—who was the Chief Investigative Counsel for the US House of Representatives' Judiciary Committee in 1998 and its chief prosecutor for the impeachment of President Clinton in 1999—publicly stated that he had attempted to warn Attorney General Ashcroft about attacks planned for "lower Manhattan" six weeks beforehand, based on information he had received from FBI agents. In this and subsequent statements, Schippers said that *the dates and targets* of the attacks as well as the names and funding sources of the hijackers were known by these agents months in advance. Schippers claimed further that the FBI curtailed these investigations, then threatened the agents with prosecution if they went public with their information. At that time, Schippers further stated, the agents asked him to try to use his influence to get the government to take action to prevent the attacks. Having failed in that effort, Schippers agreed to represent some of the agents in a suit against the federal government, during which, if subpoenaed, they would be able to tell their story without fear of prosecution.[45]

Because of this suit, Schippers—like the public interest law firm Judicial Watch, which joined forces with him on this case—is not a disinterested witness. But Schippers' allegations have been corroborated,

Ahmed points out, in a story by William Norman Grigg in a conservative magazine, *The New American.* Grigg, having interviewed three FBI agents, reported that they had confirmed "that the information provided to Schippers was widely known within the Bureau before September 11th." One of them reportedly said that some of the FBI field agents—who were some of the "most experienced guys"—"predicted, almost precisely, what happened on September 11th." He also said that it was widely known "all over the Bureau, how these [warnings] were ignored by Washington."[46]

These reports make even more puzzling how the Joint Inquiry could have concluded, as mentioned in the previous chapter, that none of the information available to the intelligence community "identified the time, place, and specific nature of the attacks that were planned for September 11, 2001." It seems that at least one US intelligence agency had this kind of very specific advance knowledge.

Visa and Watch List Violations

Immediately after 9/11, a number of irregularities regarding the alleged hijackers became known. It was learned, for example, that Mohamed Atta, considered the ringleader, was allowed back in the United States three times in 2001, in spite of the fact that he had let his visa expire in 2000, had violated his visa by taking flying lessons, was known to have terrorist connections, and was under FBI surveillance. It was reported, furthermore, that evidently over 50 people were involved in planning 9/11. These facts led to this criticism in a review by Accuracy in Media (AIM):

> Yet the conspirators proceeded unmolested. What is striking is how safe these people apparently felt, how unthreatened by law enforcement.... They left and entered the country unimpeded. Some were reportedly on the so-called "watch list".... Yet this apparently caused them no problems.[47]

The critics suspect, of course, that something other than incompetence might account for this pattern.

The Question of the True Identity of the Hijackers

Although this issue does not, strictly speaking, belong in this chapter, I should explain why I have been qualifying "hijackers" with the adjective "alleged." One of the unanswered questions about 9/11 is whether the hijackings were really carried out by any of the men later named. Shortly after the attacks, stories appeared in newspapers suggesting that at least five of the men identified by the FBI as 9/11 hijackers were still alive, and these stories were supported by reports of "stolen identities."[48] The Saudi embassy in Washington, reports Meyssan, said that Abdulaziz al-Omari (supposedly the pilot of Flight 11, which crashed into the North Tower of the WTC), Mohand al-Shehri, Salem al-Hazmi, and Saeed al-Bhamdi were all alive and living in Saudi Arabia. Meyssan also says that a fifth alleged hijacker, Waleed M. al-Shehri, "gave an interview to the Arab-language daily, *Al-Quds al-Arabi*, based in London."[49] One report even said that "investigators are studying the possibility that the entire suicide squad consisted of impostors."[50] FBI Director Mueller, however, later claimed: "We at this point definitely know the 19 hijackers who were responsible."[51] "Yet many of the names and photos are known to be wrong," says Thompson. "Perhaps embarrassing facts would come out if we knew their real names."[52]

Another report that creates suspicion regarding the official story, according to which the hijackers were "fundamentalist" Muslims, is that between May and August of 2001, several of the alleged hijackers, including Mohamed Atta, reportedly made at least six visits to Las Vegas, during which they drank alcohol, gambled, and frequented strip clubs, where they had lap dances performed for them.[53] Is this something that true believers would do shortly before going on a suicide mission to meet their maker?

There are also grounds for suspicion that evidence was planted to connect some of the alleged hijackers to the flights. On 9/11, for example, authorities found two of Atta's bags, which failed to get loaded onto Flight 11. These bags contained various items, including flight simulation manuals for Boeing airplanes, a copy of the Koran, a religious cassette tape, a note to other hijackers about mental preparation, and Atta's will, passport, and international driver's license. A reporter for the *New Yorker* later wrote:

> many of the investigators believe that some of the initial clues that were uncovered about the terrorists' identities and preparations, such as flight manuals, were meant to be found. A former high-level intelligence official told me, "Whatever trail was left was left deliberately—for the FBI to chase."

As Thompson asks, why would Atta have planned to bring his will "onto a plane he knew would be destroyed?"[54] Also suspicious was the discovery, a few blocks from the WTC on the day after 9/11, of the passport of alleged hijacker Satam al-Suqami.[55] One newspaper—reflecting the fact that it was widely but mistakenly reported that the passport belonged to Atta—said "the idea that Atta's passport had escaped from that inferno unsinged [strains] credulity."[56]

These stories suggest that the truth about what happened on 9/11 may be even further from the official account than suggested by the evidence I have cited prior to this section. Meyssan, for example, proposes that "the FBI invented a list of hijackers from which it drew an identikit portrait of the enemies of the West."[57] I will, however, not pursue this question further.

This chapter obviously provides additional evidence against any position weaker than the third possible view, because it suggests that at least one US agency—the FBI—had specific advance knowledge of the plot and took deliberate steps to prevent this plot from being uncovered.

Tyrone Powers, a former FBI special agent, is quoted by Ahmed as saying that within the intelligence community, "on occasion, [damaging] acts are allowed if in the minds of the decision makers, they will lead to 'greater good.'" One of the FBI agents interviewed by Grigg for *The New American* said: "There's got to be more to this than we can see.... Obviously, people had to know.... It's terrible to think this, but this must have been allowed to happen as part of some other agenda."[58] The critics of the official account have some suggestions as to what this agenda might have been.

CHAPTER SEVEN

DID US OFFICIALS HAVE REASONS FOR ALLOWING 9/11?

The wars waged by the US government in Afghanistan and Iraq have been portrayed as part of its "war on terrorism." These wars have been, in other words, justified as *responses* to the terrorist attacks of 9/11. However, say critics of the official account, these wars were actually on the agenda of the Bush administration long before the attacks. Furthermore, they claim, these wars were part of an even larger agenda.

Pre-9/11 Plans to Attack Afghanistan

With regard to Afghanistan, Ahmed, drawing on various sources,[1] calls it a matter of public record that "corresponding with the growing shift in US policy against the Taliban, a military invasion of Afghanistan was planned long before 11th September."[2] Ahmed and Thompson both suggest that at least one of the fundamental purposes behind this plan was to facilitate a huge project of a consortium of oil companies known as CentGas (Central Asia Gas Pipeline). This consortium, which includes Delta Oil of Saudi Arabia, was formed by Unocal, one of the oil giants of the United States, to build pipelines through Afghanistan and Pakistan for transporting oil and gas from Turkmenistan to the Indian Ocean. In September of 2000, a year before 9/11, an Energy Information Fact Sheet, published by the US government, said:

> Afghanistan's significance from an energy standpoint stems from its geographic position as a potential transit route for oil and natural gas exports from Central Asia to the Arabian Sea. This potential includes proposed multibillion dollar oil and gas export pipelines through Afghanistan.[3]

At one time, Unocal and Washington had hoped that the Taliban would provide sufficient stability for their project to move forward, but they had lost this hope.

Providing some background, Ahmed and Thompson explain that the Taliban was originally created by the CIA, working in conjunction with Pakistan's ISI (Inter-Services Intelligence), with additional financial support from Saudi Arabia.[4] According to Ahmed Rashid's well-known book *Taliban*, the pipeline project was central to this support:

> Impressed by the ruthlessness and willingness of the then-emerging Taliban to cut a pipeline deal, the State Department and Pakistan's Inter-Services Intelligence agency agreed to funnel arms and funding to the Taliban.[5]

When the Taliban, with this financial support from Saudi Arabia and the CIA funneled through the ISI, conquered Kabul in 1996, Unocal was hopeful that it would provide enough stability to allow its pipelines to be built and protected. Indeed, it was reported, "preliminary agreement [on the pipeline project] was reached between the [Taliban and Unocal] long before the fall of Kabul."[6] Unocal even reportedly provided some of the financial support for the Taliban.[7] The fact that the Taliban continued to serve the purposes of the ISI is illustrated, Thompson points out, by the fact that when Taliban troops were about to conquer the major city in northern Afghanistan in 1998, an ISI officer sent a message saying: "My boys and I are riding into Mazar-i-Sharif."[8] In any case, after the Taliban conquered this city, it had control of most of Afghanistan, including the entire pipeline route. CentGas then announced that it was "ready to proceed."[9]

Later that year, however, Unocal, having become dubious about the Taliban's ability to provide sufficient stability, pulled out of CentGas. From then on, says Ahmed, "the US grew progressively more hostile toward the Taliban, and began exploring other possibilities to secure its regional supremacy, while maintaining basic ties with the regime, to negotiate a non-military solution."[10]

The final attempt to find a non-military solution reportedly occurred at a four-day meeting in Berlin in July of 2001. The Bush administration tried to get the Taliban to share power, thereby creating a joint government of "national unity." According to the Pakistani representative at the meeting, Niaz Naik, one of the Americans said "either the Taliban behave as they ought to...or we will use another option...a military operation." Another American reportedly told the Taliban: "Either you accept our offer of a carpet of gold, or we bury you under a carpet of bombs."[11] Although one of the Americans later denied that such a threat was made, one of them confirmed it, saying: "I think there was some discussion of the fact that the United States was so disgusted with the Taliban that they might be considering some military action."[12]

According to a BBC report, furthermore, Naik said that he was told by senior American officials that "military action against Afghanistan would go ahead by the middle of October"—that it would take place "before the snows started falling in Afghanistan, by the middle of October at the latest."[13] Thompson, noting that the United States started bombing Afghanistan on October 7, asks: "Is it coincidence that the attacks begin exactly when the US said they would, months before 9/11?"[14] The supposition that it was *not* simply a coincidence is supported by an account from a former member of the South Carolina National Guard, who later declared:

> My unit reported for drill in July 2001 and we were suddenly and unexpectedly informed that all activities planned for the next two months would be suspended in order to prepare for a mobilization exercise to be held on Sept. 14, 2001. We worked diligently for two weekends and even came in on an unscheduled day in August to prepare for the exercise. By the end of August all we needed was a phone call, which we were to expect, and we could hop into a fully prepared convoy with our bags and equipment packed.[15]

If this report is true, it suggests that it was known in July that the attacks would occur shortly before September 14. In any case, Niaz Naik also did not think that mere coincidence was involved. The BBC report quoted him as saying that he "was in no doubt that after the World Trade Center bombings, this pre-existing US plan had been built upon and would be implemented within two or three weeks."

Naik also said it was doubtful that Washington would drop its plan even if bin Laden were to be surrendered immediately by the Taliban, because "the wider objective was to topple the Taleban [sic] regime and install a transitional government."[16] Ahmed and Thompson find this assessment of the wider objective, along with the view that included facilitating the pipeline project, to be confirmed by subsequent events, such as the fact commented upon in the following statement by a writer in an Israeli newspaper:

> If one looks at the map of the big American bases created, one is struck by the fact that they are completely identical to the route of the projected oil pipeline to the Indian Ocean.... If I were a believer in conspiracy theory, I would think that bin Laden is an American agent.[17]

Thompson and Ahmed also point out that both the new Afghani prime minister, Hamid Karzai, and President Bush's special envoy to Afghanistan, Zalamy Khalilzad, were previously on Unocal's payroll. These appointments, Ahmed adds, "illustrate the fundamental interests behind US military intervention in Afghanistan."[18] As early as October 10, Ahmed further notes, the US Department of State had informed the Pakistani Minister of Oil that "in view of recent geopolitical developments," Unocal was ready to go ahead with the pipeline project.[19]

In light of this background, Ahmed concludes that 9/11 was more the "trigger" than the reason for the US war in Afghanistan.[20]

Pre-9/11 Plans to Attack Iraq

In a statement in early March of 2002, President Bush, after saying that he was not very concerned about Osama bin Laden, added: "I am deeply concerned about Iraq."[21] Thompson and Ahmed believe that this was not a recent concern, that the war against Iraq, like the war against Afghanistan, had already been planned by US officials prior to 9/11.

Part of the evidence for this claim is found in the document *Rebuilding America's Defenses: Strategy, Forces, and Resources for a New Century*, which I briefly mentioned in the Introduction. This document was published in September of 2000 by the Project for the New American Century (PNAC), a neo-conservative think tank that was formed by many people who went on to become insiders in the Bush administration, including Dick Cheney, Donald Rumsfeld, Paul Wolfowitz (Rumsfeld's deputy at the Defense Department), and Lewis "Scooter" Libby (Cheney's chief of staff).[22] With regard to the question of whether the 2003 war against Iraq was really motivated by the perceived need to eliminate Saddam, as these men would then claim, the following passage in *Rebuilding America's Defenses* (quoted by Thompson) is relevant:

The United States has for decades sought to play a more permanent role in Gulf regional security. While the unresolved conflict with Iraq provides the immediate justification, the need for a substantial American force presence in the Gulf transcends the issue of the regime of Saddam Hussein.[23]

The main thing, in other words, was getting a "substantial American force presence in the Gulf," with Saddam providing the "immediate justification." Edward Herman also points to the importance of this document for assessing the sincerity of the public rationale given for the war: "Key members of the Bush administration," points out Herman, "had announced an aim of 'toppling Saddam Hussein' back in 2000 in the publication of the Project for the New American Century."[24]

This group made an even earlier statement of this aim in a letter to President Clinton in January of 1998, urging him to adopt a strategy aimed at "the removal of Saddam Hussein's regime from power." This letter, signed by Donald Rumsfeld, Paul Wolfowitz, and Richard Perle, among others, urged Clinton "to take the necessary steps, including military steps, to protect our vital interests in the Gulf," adding that "American policy cannot continue to be crippled by a misguided insistence on unanimity in the UN Security Council."[25]

In supporting the contention that 9/11 was more a pretext than a reason for the attack on Iraq, Thompson quotes a report that Secretary of Defense Rumsfeld, only a few hours after the Pentagon had been struck, wrote a memo saying that he wanted the "best info fast. Judge whether good enough hit S.H. [Saddam Hussein] at same time. Not only UBL [Usama bin Laden]. Go massive. Sweep it all up. Things related and not."[26] Thompson's contention is given additional support by John Pilger, who cites Bob Woodward's report that the next day at the meeting of the National Security Council, Rumsfeld said that Saddam's Iraq should be targeted in the first round of the war on terrorism.[27]

Critics can, furthermore, point to both actions and statements during and after the war that support their contention that the war had much more to do with oil and regional control than it did with the announced purposes for the war. Whereas the Bush and Blair administrations claimed that the war was to remove weapons of mass destruction, through which Saddam Hussein posed a threat to his neighbors and even the United Kingdom and the United States, the intelligence behind this assessment has been widely reported to have been distorted, even invented. Sir Jonathan Porritt, head of the Sustainable Development Commission, which advises Blair's government on ecological issues, publicly stated that the prospect of winning access to Iraqi oil was "a very large factor" in the allies' decision to attack Iraq in March, adding: "I don't think the war would have happened if Iraq didn't have the second-largest oil reserves in the world." Paul O'Neill, Bush's former Treasury Secretary, has said that the Bush administration had from the outset planned to attack Iraq, in large part for its oil.[28]

The fact that oil was of preeminent importance was demonstrated, Stephen Gowans says, by the fact that

> the top item on the Pentagon's agenda, once it gave the order for jackboots to begin marching on Baghdad, was to secure the oil fields in southern Iraq. And when chaos broke out in Baghdad, US forces let gangs of looters and arsonists run riot through "the Ministry of Planning, the Ministry of Education, the Ministry of Irrigation, the Ministry of Trade, the Ministry of Industry, the Ministry of Foreign Affairs, the Ministry of Culture and the Ministry of Information." ...But at the Ministry of Oil, where archives and files related to all the oil wealth Washington has been itching to get its hands on, all was calm, for ringing the Ministry was a phalanx of tanks and armoured personnel carriers.[29]

The suspicion that Iraq was not attacked primarily for the publicly stated reasons is also suggested by the evidence that the Bush administration planned to use its post-9/11 "war on terrorism" as a pretext for attacks on still other countries. A report in *Newsweek*, for example, said that prior to the attack on Iraq, some of Bush's advisors advocated also attacking Saudi Arabia, Iran, North Korea, Syria, and Egypt. One senior British official was quoted as saying: "Everyone wants to go to Baghdad. Real men want to go to Tehran."[30]

One of those "real men" was Richard Perle, a founding member of PNAC, who has been quoted as describing America's "war on terrorism" in these words:

> This is total war. We are fighting a variety of enemies. There are lots of them out there. All this talk about first we are going to do Afghanistan, then we will do Iraq.... [T]his is entirely the wrong way to go about it. If we just let our vision of the world go forth, and...just wage a total war...our children will sing great songs about us years from now.[31]

This kind of vision could give fanaticism a bad name.

It is now increasingly recognized that insofar as the United States is waging a war on terrorism, "terrorism" is being defined in a very selective, self-serving way. "For Bush," Meyssan says, "terrorism seems to be defined as any form of violent opposition to American leadership."[32] Richard Falk likewise says that it soon became clear that the "war on terrorism was being waged against all non-state revolutionary forces perceived as hostile to American global interests." What is really going on, in other words, is "an empire-building project undertaken behind the smokescreen of the war on global terror."[33] Phyllis Bennis agrees, saying that "the war [on terrorism] was never about bringing anyone to justice; it was about conquest and the mushrooming of US global power, all in the name of righteous vengeance."[34] Chossudovsky, Mahajan, and countless other critics have made the same point.

In any case, it is now widely agreed that the Bush administration (as well as Blair's government) lied about the reasons for attacking Iraq. Is it not time to expand this question to whether it also lied about the event itself, 9/11, that was used as the primary justification for the wars against Afghanistan and Iraq and the even larger agenda of the Bush administration?

A New Pearl Harbor Would Help

With regard to this larger agenda, both Ahmed and Thompson refer to the 1997 book by former National Security Advisor Zbigniew Brzezinski, *The Grand Chessboard: American Primacy and its Geostrategic Imperatives.* Besides portraying the Eurasian landmass as the key to world power, Brzezinski portrayed Central Asia, with its vast oil reserves, as the key to the domination of Eurasia. Having summarized this argument, Ahmed and Thompson point to Brzezinski's statement that ensuring continued "American primacy" by getting control of this region will require "a consensus on foreign policy issues" within the American public. Getting such consensus, however, will be difficult, because "America is too democratic at home to be autocratic abroad," a fact that "limits the use of America's power, especially its capacity for military intimidation." Continuing his analysis of the defects in the American character, Brzezinski explained that "the pursuit of power is not a goal that commands popular passion, except in conditions of a sudden threat or challenge to the public's sense of domestic well being."[35] Therefore, he counseled, the needed consensus on foreign policy issues will be difficult to obtain "except in the circumstance of a truly massive and widely perceived direct external threat."[36] Ahmed connects this passage to an earlier one, in which Brzezinski said that the American public, which is ambivalent about "the external projection of American power," had "supported America's engagement in World War II largely because of the shock effect of the Japanese attack on Pearl Harbor."[37]

Ahmed's point is that if those two passages are read together, the kind of "widely perceived direct external threat" said to be needed would be a Pearl Harbor type of event. Brzezinski's book, authored by a former national security advisor, cannot be considered simply one book among hundreds offering advice to the government. Although Brzezinski advised a Democratic president (Jimmy Carter), he is a hard liner who has reportedly been highly regarded by the Bush administration.

It is perhaps not merely coincidental, therefore, that three years after Brzezinski's apparent wish for a Pearl-Harbor-type event was published, the aforementioned publication of the Project for the New American Century would contain a similar passage. Although this passage has previously been cited, it is important to emphasize that it comes in the context of a call for the completion of the "revolution in military affairs," through which a *Pax Americana*, or "American Peace," can be more efficiently established. Unfortunately, according to this document's authors, the needed transformation would probably come about slowly "absent some catastrophic and catalyzing event—like a new Pearl Harbor."[38] If a new Pearl Harbor were to occur, in other words, this completion of the revolution in military affairs could be brought about more quickly, because the massive funding needed could be obtained. It was in response to this prediction that John Pilger made the assertion, quoted in the Introduction, that "[t]he attacks of 11 September 2001 provided the 'new Pearl Harbor.'"[39] What kind of changes did these advocates of American dominance outline, and has the New Pearl Harbor helped bring them about?

Missile Defense and a Space Pearl Harbor

It is important to realize that the centerpiece of the "revolution in military affairs" is a program to weaponize and hence dominate space. This program will require much of the massive increase in funding for "defense" for which Brzezinski and the Project for the New American

Century have called. The purpose of this program is spelled out quite explicitly in a document called "Vision for 2020," which begins with this mission statement: "US Space Command—dominating the space dimension of military operations to protect US interests and investment."[40] Its primary purpose, in other words, is not to protect the American homeland, but to protect American investments abroad. It makes this point even more explicit by comparing the importance of the Space Command today with the fact that in previous times "nations built navies to protect and enhance their commercial interests." It is to dominate space to protect the commercial interests of America's elite class that, according to current projections, over $1 trillion will be required from American taxpayers.[41]

The "Vision for 2020" document engages in no sentimental propaganda about the need for the United States to dominate space for the sake of promoting democracy or otherwise serving humanity. Rather, it says candidly, if indiscreetly: "The globalization of the world economy...will continue with a widening between 'haves' and 'have-nots.'" In other words, as America's domination of the world economy increases, the poor will get still poorer while the rich get still richer, and this will make the "have-nots" hate America all the more, so we need to be able to keep them in line. We can do this through what the advocates of this program originally called "Global Battlespace Dominance." Because some people found this term too explicit, the preferred term today is "Full Spectrum Dominance" (which provided the title for a previously quoted book by Rahul Mahajan). This term means not only being dominant on land, on the sea, and in the air, as the US military is already, but also having control of space. Discussing this "American project of global domination associated with the weaponization of space," Richard Falk says: "The empire-building quest for such awesome power is an unprecedented exhibition of geopolitical greed at its worst, and needs to be exposed and abandoned before it is too late."[42]

The only part of this program that has received much public discussion is the defensive aspect of it, which in the Reagan Administration was called the Strategic Defensive Initiative and is today called the Missile Defense Shield. Although these names suggest that America's goal in space is purely defensive, this so-called shield is only one part of a three-part program. One of the other parts is putting surveillance technology in space, with the goal of being able to zero in on any part of the planet with such precision that every enemy of US forces can be identified. This part is already well on the way to realization.[43] The third part of the program—which shows that the informal name for this program, "Star Wars," is more accurate than its technical name—is putting actual weapons in space, including laser cannons. These laser cannons have the offensive potential, as one writer put it, to "make a cruise missile look like a firecracker."[44] With laser weapons on our satellites, the United States will be able to destroy the military satellites any adversarial country would try to send up, and this is, indeed, part of the announced intention: "to deny others the use of space." The US Space Command could thereby maintain total and permanent dominance. The aggressive purpose of the US Space Command's program is announced in the logo of one of its divisions: "In Your Face from Outer Space."[45]

It is not only in this document that such aggressive aims are frankly stated. As Mahajan points out, the Project for the New American Century's document makes the following "remarkable admission":

> In the post-Cold-War era, America and its allies...have become the primary objects of deterrence and it is states like Iraq, Iran and North Korea who most wish to develop deterrent capabilities. Projecting conventional military forces...will be far more complex and constrained when the American homeland...is subject to attack by otherwise weak rogue regimes capable of cobbling together a minuscule ballistic missile force. Building an effective...system of missile defenses is a prerequisite for maintaining American preeminence.[46]

In other words, although the name "missile defense shield" suggests that the system is designed to shield America from attacks, its real purpose is to prevent other nations from deterring America from attacking *them*. This statement further suggests that Iran, Iraq, and North Korea were later determined by President Bush to deserve the title "axis of evil" because of their perverse wish to develop the capacity to deter the United States from projecting military force against them. The Project's description of the US military's role in these offensive terms is fully in accord with the Bush administration's *National Security Strategy*, published in 2002, which, besides embodying most of the recommendations of *Rebuilding America's Defenses*, says that "our best defense is a good offense."[47] The most important new component of this offense is to be the "full spectrum dominance" afforded by complementing America's land, air, and sea forces with a full-fledged Space Force.

Shortly before becoming Secretary of Defense in January of 2001, Donald Rumsfeld completed his work as chairman of the Commission to Assess US National Security Space Management and Organization. This "Rumsfeld Commission," as it was informally known, published its report in the second week of January.[48] The aim of its proposals, it said, was to "increase the asymmetry between US forces and those of other military powers." Besides advocating the termination of the 1972 ABM Treaty (which the Bush administration acted on promptly), this report recommended substantial changes, including the subordination of all the other armed forces and the intelligence agencies to the Space Force. Recognizing that such a drastic reorganization of the armed forces and intelligence agencies would normally evoke great resistance, the report added:

> History is replete with instances in which warning signs were ignored and change resisted until an external, "improbable" event forced resistant bureaucracies to take action. The question is whether the US will be wise enough to act responsibly and soon enough to reduce US space vulnerability. Or whether, as in the past, a disabling attack against the country and its people—a "Space Pearl Harbor"—will be the only event able to galvanize the nation and cause the US Government to act.[49]

We have, accordingly, yet another suggestion by a central figure in the Bush administration that another "Pearl Harbor" may be necessary to "galvanize the nation."

This report was released on January 11, 2001, exactly nine months before the US suffered *attacks from the air that our defenses appeared to be helpless to prevent.* And the primary response evoked by these attacks was a sense of America's *vulnerability.* The chairman of the commission that issued the above report was, furthermore, well placed to take advantage of those attacks and the resulting sense of "US space vulnerability." As Meyssan points out, at a press conference that began at 6:42 PM on 9/11 itself, Rumsfeld, now Secretary of Defense, used the attacks to browbeat Democratic Senator Carl Levin, who was then chair of the Senate Armed Services Committee (during the brief period of the Bush administration during which Democrats had control of the

Senate). Before live cameras, Rumsfeld said:

> Senator Levin, you and other Democrats in Congress have voiced
> fear that you simply don't have enough money for the large increase
> in defense that the Pentagon is seeking, especially for missile
> defense, and you fear that you'll have to dip into the Social Security
> funds to pay for it. Does this sort of thing convince you that an
> emergency exists in this country to increase defense spending, to dip
> into Social Security, if necessary, to pay for defense spending—
> increase defense spending?[50]

It does appear that the attacks of 9/11 provided Rumsfeld with what he
thought could pass for "a Space Pearl Harbor," and he seemed remarkably
prepared to take advantage of it.

Furthermore, if US officials were involved in facilitating the attacks
of 9/11, Rumsfeld was not the only one with great interest in the Space
Command. Its other primary advocate was its current commander,
General Ralph E. Eberhart, who in his role as commander of NORAD
was in charge of air traffic control on 9/11.[51] Also, General Richard
Myers, who was in the process of becoming the new chairman of the
Joint Chiefs of Staff and was the Acting Chairman on 9/11, had
previously been head of the US Space Command. Known by some as
"General Starwars," he was in charge during the writing of "Vision for
2020," with its quite explicit expression of the intent to get absolute
control of space so that the Pentagon can protect American commercial
interests while they are increasing the gap between the "haves" and the
"have-nots" of the world. Accordingly, the three men who have been
most identified with advocacy of the US Space Force are also the three
figures who would have been most directly involved in promulgating
and overseeing a "stand down" order on 9/11, if such was given.

The evidence summarized in this chapter shows that officials of the
Pentagon and the Bush administration would have had many reasons—
from their plans for Afghanistan and Iraq to their desire for massive
funding to weaponize space—for allowing, if not planning, the attacks
of 9/11. Some of this evidence points to the truth of at least the seventh
possible view—that the White House had specific knowledge of the

attacks in advance, knowing that they would occur, for example, in time to launch a war against Afghanistan before the winter snows started. Some of the evidence even suggests the eighth view, according to which the White House was involved in the planning. It is possible, of course, that although central figures of the Bush administration evidently desired "a new Pearl Harbor," they did not plan the attacks but simply learned that they had been planned by others, so that all they had to do was to make sure that the attacks were not prevented. Yet with all that was apparently riding on the occurrence of a new Pearl Harbor, reasonable people could conclude that the White House would not have left this occurrence to chance.

A Precedent: Operation Northwoods

All the information summarized so far arguably presents strong evidence pointing to US complicity in the attacks of 9/11 involving US intelligence agencies, the Pentagon, and the White House. But regardless of how strong this evidence may be considered, many and perhaps most Americans will resist the idea that this "attack on America" could have been an inside job, staged by America's own leaders. The primary responsibility of the president and vice president, their cabinet, US intelligence agencies, and US military leaders is to protect America and its citizens. Even if the official account of 9/11 leaves dozens of unanswered questions, the true account cannot, many Americans will assume, be that American political and military leaders colluded to allow, much less stage, the attacks of 9/11. Regardless of the benefits that may have been foreseen if a "new Pearl Harbor" were to occur, our military and political leaders would not have participated in a plan to bring about such an event. We feel that we know *a priori* that all conspiracy theories of this type are false, because American military and political leaders simply would not do such a thing.

In 1962, however, a plan was formulated that provides a partial precedent, a plan about which we now know because of recently declassified documents. The background to this plan was President Eisenhower's request to the CIA, near the end of his administration, to come up with a pretext to invade Cuba. The CIA formulated "A Program of Covert Operations Against the Castro Regime," the goal of which was "the replacement of the Castro regime with one more devoted to the true interests of the Cuban people and more acceptable to the US, in such a manner to avoid any appearance of US intervention."[52] Eisenhower had approved this plan. But after the next president, John Kennedy, accepted a CIA plan that led to the Bay of Pigs fiasco, he had responsibility for Cuba taken away from the CIA and assigned it to the Department of Defense. Early in 1962, the Chairman of the Joint Chiefs of Staff, General Lyman Lemnitzer, brought Kennedy a plan called Operation Northwoods.[53]

According to the covering "Memorandum for the Secretary of Defense," signed by all the Joint Chiefs, this plan, marked Top Secret, described "pretexts which would provide justification for US military intervention in Cuba."[54] According to the "Memorandum for Chief of Operations, Cuba Project," a decision to intervene "will result from a period of heightened US–Cuban tensions which place the United States in the position of suffering justifiable grievances." It was important, the memorandum said, "to camouflage the ultimate objective." Part of the idea was to influence world opinion in general and the United Nations in particular "by developing the image of the Cuban government as rash and irresponsible, and as an alarming and unpredictable threat to the peace of the Western Hemisphere."[55]

The plan then listed a series of possible actions to create this image. For example: "We could develop a Communist Cuban terror campaign in the Miami area, in other Florida cities and even in Washington...We could sink a boatload of Cubans enroute to Florida (real or simulated)."[56] Particularly interesting, in light of some of the proposed scenarios as to "what really happened" on 9/11 (see Ch. 1, n. 32), is the following idea:

> It is possible to create an incident which will demonstrate convincingly that a Cuban aircraft has attacked and shot down a chartered civil airliner.... The destination would be chosen only to cause the flight plan route to cross Cuba. The passengers could be a group of college students off on a holiday....
>
> a. An aircraft at Eglin AFB would be painted and numbered as an exact duplication for a civil registered aircraft belonging to a CIA proprietary organization in the Miami area. At a designated time the duplication would be substituted for the actual civil aircraft and would be loaded with the selected passengers, all boarded under carefully prepared aliases. The actual registered aircraft would be converted to a drone.

b. Take off times of the drone aircraft and the actual aircraft will be scheduled to allow a rendezvous south of Florida. From the rendezvous point the passenger-carrying aircraft will descend to minimum altitude and go directly into an auxiliary field at Eglin AFB where arrangements will have been made to evacuate the passengers and return the aircraft to its original status. The drone aircraft meanwhile will continue to fly the filed flight plan. When over Cuba the drone will being [sic] transmitting on the international distress frequency a "MAY DAY" message stating he is under attack by Cuban MIG aircraft. The transmission will be interrupted by destruction of the aircraft which will be triggered by radio signal.[57]

In this and some of the other plans, although casualty lists would be placed in US newspapers to "cause a wave of national indignation,"[58] the subterfuge would not actually result in the loss of life. But this was not true of all of the plans, such as the plan to "sink a boatload of Cubans." At least one plan, furthermore, would have taken the lives of Americans. According to this idea, called a "Remember the Maine" incident: "We could blow up a US ship in Guantánamo Bay and blame Cuba."[59]

Kennedy rejected this plan, even though it was endorsed by all the joint chiefs. Those who say that, although military leaders might formulate such plans, an American president would never agree to such a despicable plan can point to this rejection as evidence. However, different presidents, in different circumstances, make different decisions. For example, in the early 1890s, a plan to annex Hawaii was rejected by President Grover Cleveland, whose secretary of state considered the plan "a selfish and dishonourable scheme of a lot of adventurers." But this scheme was accepted by the next president, William McKinley[60] (who was also the one who used the *Maine* incident to justify entering the war against Spain in order to take control of Cuba, Puerto Rico, and the Philippines). Accordingly, the fact that Kennedy turned down that particular plan at that particular time—shortly after the Bay of Pigs embarrassment—does not necessarily mean that all American presidents in all circumstances would turn down plans to achieve geopolitical goals through "incidents" involving the taking of innocent lives, even innocent American lives.[61]

The evidence in this chapter, in any case, provides further support for the conclusion of Michel Chossudovsky, only partially quoted earlier, that the post-9/11 American war "is not a 'campaign against international terrorism'. It is a war of conquest...[a]nd the American people have been consciously and deliberately deceived by their government."[62] The next chapter will provide one more kind of evidence presented by the critics for this conclusion.

CHAPTER EIGHT

DID US OFFICIALS BLOCK CAPTURES AND INVESTIGATIONS AFTER 9/11?

Having suggested that the "new Pearl Harbor" that occurred on 9/11 served as a pretext for a pre-established agenda, the critics then argue that US behavior *after* 9/11 supports this view. Portions of this behavior—namely, the wars against both Afghanistan and Iraq—were mentioned in the previous chapter. The present chapter summarizes evidence pointing to other examples of US behavior after 9/11 that point, according to critics, to the falsity of the official account.

Continuing the Anti-Hunt for Osama bin Laden and al-Qaeda

Ahmed and Thompson provide considerable evidence that although the war in Afghanistan was supposedly to root out al-Qaeda and bin Laden—taking him, in President Bush's language, "dead or alive"—the actual objective must have been something else, since there were several instances in which the government and its military commanders seemed at pains to allow bin Laden and al-Qaeda to escape.

For example, according to many residents of Kabul, a convoy of al-Qaeda forces, thought to include its top leaders, made a remarkable escape during one night in early November of 2001. A local businessman said:

> We don't understand how they weren't all killed the night before because they came in a convoy of at least 1,000 cars and trucks. It was a very dark night, but it must have been easy for the American pilots to see the headlights. The main road was jammed from eight in the evening until three in the morning.

Thompson comments: "With all of the satellite imagery and intense focus on the Kabul area at the time, how could such a force have escaped the city unobserved by the US?"[1]

Also early in November, US intelligence agencies, having watched al-Qaeda fighters and leaders move into the area of Jalalabad, reported that bin Laden himself had arrived. According to Knight-Ridder newspapers, this is what happened next:

> American intelligence analysts concluded that bin Laden and his retreating fighters were preparing to flee across the border. But the US Central Command, which was running the war, made no move to block their escape. "It was obvious from at least early November that this area was to be the base for an exodus into Pakistan," said one intelligence official, who spoke only on condition of anonymity. "All of this was known, and frankly we were amazed that nothing was done to prepare for it."[2]

Shortly thereafter, on November 14, the Northern Alliance captured Jalalabad. That night, a convoy of "several hundred cars" holding 1,000 or more al-Qaeda and Taliban fighters, evidently including bin Laden, escaped from Jalalabad and reached the fortress of Tora Bora. US forces bombed the nearby Jalalabad airport, but apparently not the convoy.[3]

On November 16, approximately 600 al-Qaeda and Taliban fighters, including many senior leaders, reportedly escaped from Afghanistan, by taking a long trek to escape the bombing in the Tora Bora region. Although there are two main routes from the Tora Bora region to Pakistan, US planes bombed only one of these routes, so that the 600 men were able to escape unharmed by using the other one. Hundreds more reportedly continued to use this escape route over the next weeks, generally not bothered by US bombing or Pakistani border guards.[4] One Afghan intelligence officer reportedly said that he was astounded that the Americans did not station troops to block the most obvious exit routes. The *Telegraph* later said: "In retrospect, and with the benefit of dozens of accounts from the participants, the battle for Tora Bora looks more like a grand charade." Eyewitnesses expressed shock, it said, that US forces pinned in Taliban and al-Qaeda forces, thought to contain many high leaders, on three sides only, leaving the route to Pakistan open. An intelligence chief in Afghanistan's new government was quoted as saying: "The border with Pakistan was the key, but no one paid any attention to it."[5]

A Special Forces soldier stationed in Fayetteville, North Carolina, later stated that on November 28, US forces had bin Laden pinned in a

Tora Bora cave but failed to act. While Special Forces soldiers were waiting for orders, he said, they watched two helicopters fly into the area where bin Laden was believed to be, load up passengers, and fly toward Pakistan. This statement, made on condition of anonymity, is given more credibility, Thompson points out, by the fact that *Newsweek* separately reported that many Tora Bora locals claimed that "mysterious black helicopters swept in, flying low over the mountains at night, and scooped up al-Qaeda's top leaders."[6] "Perhaps just coincidentally," Thompson adds, the same day that this story was reported there was also a story reporting that five soldiers at Fayetteville—at least three of whom were Special Forces soldiers who had recently returned from Afghanistan—and their wives had died since June in apparent murder-suicides.[7]

In late December of 2001, the new Afghan interior minister, Younis Qanooni, claimed that the ISI had helped bin Laden escape from Afghanistan.[8] For critics of the official account, this claim is significant given the fact that the Bush administration has considered Pakistan a partner in its post-9/11 efforts.

In March of 2002, this apparent lack of interest in killing or capturing bin Laden was put into words by the president himself, who said of bin Laden: "He's a person who's now been marginalized...I just don't spend that much time on him...I truly am not that concerned about him." The suspicion that the war was never about bin Laden, which Bush's statement could be taken to imply, was explicitly stated, Thompson points out, a month later by General Richard Myers, who said that "the goal has never been to get bin Laden."[9] Another American official was quoted as making an even more revealing statement, saying that "casting our objectives too narrowly" risked "a premature collapse of the international effort if by some lucky chance Mr. bin Laden was captured."[10] A way of making sense of all this was provided by George Monbiot, who wrote a week after 9/11:

> If Osama bin Laden did not exist, it would be necessary to invent him. For the past four years, his name has been invoked whenever a US president has sought to increase the defence budget or wriggle out of arms control treaties. He has been used to justify even President Bush's missile defence programme.... Now he has become the personification of evil required to launch a crusade for good: the face behind the faceless terror.... [H]is usefulness to western governments

lies in his power to terrify. When billions of pounds of military spending are at stake, rogue states and terrorist warlords become assets precisely because they are liabilities.[11]

Monbiot's statement, in conjunction with the American official's concern about a "premature collapse of the international effort," provides a possible explanation as to why the "hunt for bin Laden" was unsuccessful.

Concealing the Role of Pakistan's ISI

As we saw earlier, the CIA and its counterpart in Pakistan, the ISI, worked together in the late 1990s to create the Taliban and ensure its victory. This point is reinforced by Chossudovsky, who says: "Without US support channeled through the Pakistani ISI, the Taliban would not have been able to form a government in 1996."[12] Furthermore, he says, just as without the ISI there would have been no Taliban government in Kabul, "without the unbending support of the US government, there would be no powerful military-intelligence apparatus in Pakistan."[13]

This close relationship between the CIA and the ISI goes back to the 1980s, during which the ISI was the local agency through which the CIA conducted its covert operation in Afghanistan, which began in 1979. The CIA and the ISI recruited radical Muslims from around the world to form the Mujaheddin to fight against Soviet forces.[14] Osama bin Laden was originally brought to Pakistan to help with this effort. Although he was under contract to the CIA, "the CIA gave Usama free rein in Afghanistan, as did Pakistan's intelligence generals"—Ahmed quotes John Cooley as saying—and bin Laden used that free rein and his accumulated wealth to begin organizing al-Qaeda in 1985.[15] In the late 1980s, Pakistan's President Benazir Bhutto, seeing how strong the Mujaheddin movement was becoming, told President Bush: "You are creating a Frankenstein."[16] Then in the late 1990s, after the CIA had worked with the ISI to create the Taliban, South East Asia specialist Selig Harrison, who knew CIA agents, reports that he warned them that they "were creating a monster."[17]

And if both al-Qaeda and the Taliban were reportedly becoming monstrous, the same was said of the ISI itself. After the withdrawal of the Soviet Union from Afghanistan, the ISI, which had at the instigation of the CIA begun producing heroin in order to turn Soviet soldiers into addicts, began smuggling its heroin into Western countries, using the huge profits to build itself up. As a result, said one analyst, the ISI became a "parallel structure wielding enormous power over all aspects of government." *Time* magazine later confirmed this analysis, saying that the "notorious" ISI "is commonly branded 'a state within the state,' or Pakistan's 'invisible government,'" and a story in the *New Yorker* called the ISI "a parallel government of its own."[18]

This history of the ISI, with its links to the CIA on the one hand and al-Qaeda and the Taliban on the other, is important in light of evidence that these links were never broken. Chossudovsky, rejecting the view that the "Osama-CIA links belong to the 'bygone era' of the Soviet-Afghan war," asserts: "The CIA has never severed its ties to the 'Islamic Militant Network.'"[19] And Ahmed quotes Selig Harrison's statement, made in March of 2001, that "[t]he CIA still has close links with the ISI."[20]

These links are also supported by an investigator with a very different political perspective from Ahmed's and Chossudovky's, Gerald Posner. I cited earlier Posner's report on the interrogation of Abu Zubaydah insofar as it dealt with Zubaydah's claim that his al-Qaeda activities were carried out on behalf of Saudi officials. Zubaydah also reportedly said that it was on behalf of Pakistani officials. "According to Zubaydah," reports Posner,

> he was present in 1996, in Pakistan, when bin Laden struck a deal with Mushaf Ali Mir, a highly placed military officer with close ties to some of the most pro-Islamist elements in ISI. It was a relationship that was still active and provided bin Laden and al-Qaeda protection, arms, and supplies.[21]

Posner also reports that, just as three of the Saudis identified by Zubaydah died within four months, the same fate befell Mushaf Ali Mir seven months later. On February 20, 2003, he, his wife, and many of his closest confidants were killed when their air force plane—which had recently passed inspection—went down in good weather.[22] Accordingly, although Posner accepts the official American position on most issues, he here presents evidence against the US attempt to distance the Pakistanis, portrayed as good, from bin Laden and al-Qaeda, portrayed as evil.

In any case, the importance of the fact that the ISI continued to be closely linked with both the CIA and al-Qaeda may have been made manifest by a discovery coming shortly after 9/11. This was the discovery that an ISI agent, Saeed Sheikh, had made a wire transfer of $100,000 to Mohamed Atta's bank accounts in Florida, and that he had done this at the instruction of none other than General Mahmoud Ahmad, the Director of the ISI.[23] Accordingly, the ISI, which had continued to work closely with the CIA, was discovered to have secretly sent money to the man considered to be the ringleader of the 9/11 terrorists. This "damning link," as Agence France-Press called it, was reportedly first revealed to the US government by the Indian government.[24]

The discovery of this transfer took on even more potential significance when it was learned that General Mahmoud Ahmad had been in Washington on 9/11—having, in fact, been there from September 4 until several days after 9/11. During this period, he reportedly met with CIA Director George Tenet until September 9, then met with officials in the Pentagon, the National Security Council, and the State Department, as well as with the chairmen of the House and Senate Intelligence committees. The *News*, a leading newspaper in Pakistan, made this significant comment on September 10: "What added interest to [General Ahmad's] visit is the history of such visits. Last time [his] predecessor was [in Washington], the domestic [Pakistani] politics turned topsy-turvy within days." The reference, Thompson points out, is to the coup of October 12, 1999, when General Musharraf took over the government—after which he made General Ahmad, who had been instrumental to the success of the coup, the Director of the ISI.[25]

Big things also happened on the occasion of this visit, and not only the attacks of 9/11 itself. On September 9, the leader of the Northern Alliance, Ahmad Masood, was the victim of an assassination, which the Northern Alliance declared to be the work of the ISI. That this assassination followed immediately upon extended conversations between the head of the ISI and the head of the CIA is especially significant, suggests Chossudovsky, in light of the fact that the United States had long been seeking to "weaken Masood, who was perceived as a nationalist reformer." Suggesting that this assassination "served US interests," Chossudovsky adds that after Masood was dead, "the Northern Alliance became fragmented into different factions. Had Masood not been assassinated, he would have become the head of the post-Taliban government formed in the wake of the US bombings of Afghanistan."[26] These reflections provide a possible explanation of the treatment of Julie Sirrs by the Defense Intelligence Agency, discussed in Chapter 6 (see page 76).

The significance of Masood's assassination was perhaps alluded to by John O'Neill, the investigator who had resigned from the FBI after having his attempts to investigate al-Qaeda obstructed. On September 10, the day after Masood's assassination, O'Neill moved into his new office in the North Tower of the WTC, where he had become director of security, and on 9/11 he was one of the people killed. On the night of September 10, he had reportedly told a colleague: "We're due for something big. I don't like the way things are lining up in Afghanistan."[27]

From the perspective of the critics of the official account of 9/11, the fact that Masood was assassinated while the ISI chief was visiting Washington might have been one of the reasons Washington tried to keep this visit quiet. In any case, a comparison of transcripts of Condoleezza Rice's press conference on May 16, 2002, suggests, believes Chossudovsky, that the Bush administration did want to keep General Ahmad's presence in Washington from being widely known. The transcript from the Federal News Service shows that the following interchange occurred:

> QUESTION: Are you aware of the reports at the time that the ISI chief was in Washington on September 11th, and on September 10th, $100,000 was wired from Pakistan to these groups in this area? And why he was here? Was he meeting with you or anybody in the administration?
>
> MS. RICE: I have not seen that report, and he was certainly not meeting with me.

Besides the question whether it is credible that the head of Pakistan's intelligence agency would meet with the National Security Council but not with the president's National Security Advisor, the other suspicious thing is that, as pointed out by Chossudovsky, the White House version of this transcript begins thus:

> QUESTION: Dr. Rice, are you aware of the reports at the time that (inaudible) was in Washington on September 11th...?

This version of the transcript, which—unlike the transcript from the Federal News Service—does not contain the information that the person being discussed was "the ISI chief," was the one reported on the CNN show "Inside Politics" later that day.[28]

The suspicion that US officials wanted to conceal the ISI connection is also suggested by the evidence, raised by Chossudovsky, that the FBI, in reporting on the connection with Pakistan, did not specifically mention General Ahmad, Saeed Sheikh, or the ISI. For example, Brian Ross of ABC News reported that he had been told by federal authorities that they had "tracked more than $100,000 from banks in Pakistan." Ross also reported that according to *Time* magazine, "some of that money...can be traced directly to people connected to Osama bin Laden."[29] The FBI's way of reporting the story, saying that the money came from "people connected to Osama bin Laden," diverted attention from General Ahmad, Saeed Sheikh, and the ISI. Indeed, thus laundered, the potentially embarrassing discovery about the transfer of money was used to confirm the official account—that primary responsibility for the attacks belonged to Osama bin Laden.

Later evidence suggested that Saeed Sheikh had transferred even more money to Atta. Thompson says that evidently $100,000 was transferred in 2000 and another $100,000 on August 11 of 2001, and that it is not clear to which of these transfers the story that broke in October referred.[30] Also, the *New York Times* suggested that a total of about $325,000 was transferred to Atta's Florida accounts by one "Mustafa Ahmed," and this name was thought by some, including the *Guardian* and CNN, to be an alias for Saeed Sheikh.[31] This individual's final transfers to Atta's account occurred on September 8 and 9.[32] "These last-minute transfers," Thompson reports, "are touted as the 'smoking gun' proving al-Qaeda involvement in the 9/11 attacks, since Saeed is a known financial manager for bin Laden." However, Thompson asks, "since Saeed also works for the ISI, aren't these transfers equally a smoking gun of ISI involvement in the 9/11 attacks?"[33]

Chossudovsky takes this thought a step further, calling the story of the ISI's transfer of money to Atta, in conjunction with the presence of the ISI chief in Washington during the week, "the missing link behind 9-11." According to his summary statement:

> The 9-11 terrorists did not act on their own volition. The suicide hijackers were instruments in a carefully planned intelligence operation. The evidence confirms that al-Qaeda is supported by Pakistan's ISI [and it is amply documented that] the ISI owes its existence to the CIA.[34]

Chossudovsky, accordingly, believes that this evidence suggests possible complicity by "key individuals within the US military-intelligence establishment," adding: "Whether this amounts to complicity on the part of the Bush administration remains to be firmly established. The least one can expect at this stage is an inquiry."[35]

Chossudovsky is not alone in his musings on the possibility that the money transfer might point to direct US involvement in the planning of 9/11. Ahmed and Jared Israel both ask whether the long-time connection between the CIA and the ISI might mean that US financial aid was funneled to al-Qaeda through the ISI.[36] This possibility is also suggested by a story in the *Pittsburgh Tribune-Review*, which said: "There are many in Musharraf's government who believe that Saeed Sheikh's power comes not from the ISI, but from his connections with our own CIA. The theory is that...Saeed Sheikh was bought and paid for."[37]

Ahmed, realizing that the suggestion of CIA financing is speculative, believes that what happened next at least demonstrated that Washington did not want the continuing relationship between al-Qaeda and the ISI explored. On October 8, just before the beginning of the bombing campaign in Afghanistan, General Ahmad gave up his position with the ISI. Although it was publicly announced that he had decided it was time to retire, a story in the *Times of India* said: "the truth is more shocking." This more shocking truth was that after India had given US officials evidence of the money transfer ordered by General Ahmad, he had been quietly dismissed after "US authorities sought his removal."[38] For Ahmed, this behavior suggests a cover-up:

> The US, which one would think would be spearheading a full-scale investigation into the role of the ISI, actually prevented one from going ahead by asking from behind the scenes for the ISI chief...to quietly resign....
>
> By pressuring the then ISI Director-General to resign without scandal on the pretext of reshuffling, while avoiding any publicity with respect to his siphoning of funds to alleged lead hijacker Mohamed Atta, the US had effectively blocked any sort of investigation into the matter. It prevented wide publicity of these facts, and allowed the ISI chief, who was clearly complicit in the terrorist attacks of 11th September, to walk away free.

Whatever the motivations behind such a cynical policy, it is indisputable that the US response at least suggests a significant degree of indirect complicity on the part of the US government, which appears more interested in protecting, rather than investigating and prosecuting, a military intelligence agency that funded the lead hijacker in the WTC and Pentagon attacks.[39]

Chossudovsky likewise finds it disturbing that "the Bush administration refuses to investigate these ISI links."[40]

Another possible connection between the ISI and 9/11 is Khalid Shaikh Mohammed, identified by the US government as the mastermind of the 9/11 attacks (as well as one of the planners of Project Bojinka, the 1993 bombing of the WTC, and the bombing of the *USS Cole*). In 1999, according to reports, he repeatedly visited Atta's apartment in Hamburg.[41] As we saw earlier, the day before 9/11 he evidently gave Atta final approval during a telephone call intercepted by the NSA. All this is generally known (with the proviso that, according to the NSA, it did not translate the content of that call until after 9/11). What has rarely been mentioned, however, is evidence that Mohammed, a Pakistani, had links to the ISI. One of the few exceptions to this silence was Josef Bodansky, the director of the Congressional Task Force on Terrorism and Unconventional Warfare, who stated in 2002 that Mohammed was related to the ISI, which had acted to shield him.[42] If this is correct, then *the day before 9/11, Mohamed Atta was given money by one ISI agent (Saeed Sheikh) and final authorization by another ISI agent (Khalid Shaikh Mohammed).* We will see below, furthermore, that there is evidence that Saeed and Mohammed worked closely together on another ISI-related operation.

Further Evidence that the ISI Should Be Investigated

Critics of the official account of 9/11 report that in addition to the fact that US officials evidently tried to cover up the connection between the ISI and the al-Qaeda operatives in the United States, there have been still other stories about the ISI suggesting that any real attempt to understand 9/11 would need to focus on it. Some of these stories have involved investigative reporters.

In November of 2001, Christina Lamb was in Pakistan investigating the connections between the ISI and the Taliban, but the ISI had her arrested and expelled from the country.[43]

In late January of 2002, *Wall Street Journal* reporter Daniel Pearl was kidnapped while in Pakistan investigating, according to a story in the *Washington Post*, "links between Pakistani extremists and Richard C. Reid, the British man accused of trying to blow up an American airliner with explosives hidden in his sneakers." Pearl, who had read a story in the *Boston Globe* suggesting that Reid may have had ties to a religious group called al-Fuqra, was evidently going to see its leader, Ali Gilani, when he was kidnapped. Gilani reportedly had links with Saeed Sheikh and the ISI. The story in the *Washington Post* continued: "As part of that probe, Pearl may have strayed into areas involving Pakistan's secret intelligence organizations."[44] The US press suspected early on, therefore, that the ISI was responsible for Pearl's fate.

That the kidnappers were not just ordinary terrorists was suggested by their demands, especially their demand that the United States sell F-16 fighters to Pakistan. As Thompson comments: "No terrorist group had ever shown interest in the F-16's, but this demand and the others reflect the desires of Pakistan's military and the ISI."[45] It was reported by UPI at the end of January, in fact, that US intelligence believed the kidnappers to be connected to the ISI.[46] After this, stories about Pearl would only seldom mention the ISI.

After it was learned that Pearl had been murdered, it was also learned that Saeed, the ISI agent who had wired $100,000 to Mohamed Atta, had been involved in the kidnapping. The ISI picked him up and held him secretly for a week, after which neither Saeed nor the ISI would discuss what had transpired that week. The Pakistani police then attributed Pearl's murder to him. Saeed at first confessed, but, after he was sentenced to hang, he recanted. Thompson asks: "Did Saeed work out a secret deal during his 'missing week' in ISI custody to get a light sentence, a deal that is later broken?"[47] In any case, between Saeed's arrest and his conviction, Thompson reports, some news stories mentioned his links to al-Qaeda, some mentioned his links to ISI, and a few mentioned that he might have been related to both groups, but many stories failed to mention either connection. By the time of Saeed's conviction in July of 2002, moreover, "not a single US newspaper is connecting Saeed to either al-Qaeda or the ISI." Thompson asks: "Is the media afraid of reporting any news that could imply a connection between the ISI and the 9/11 attacks?"[48]

The same question could be asked, furthermore, with regard to the reporting about Khalid Shaikh Mohammed's involvement in the Pearl case. In 1997, former CIA agent Robert Baer was told by a former police chief in Qatar—to which Mohammed had fled after the exposure of the Bojinka plot in the Philippines—that Mohammed was one of bin Laden's key aides.[49] Baer then told Pearl about Mohammed, so Pearl may have been looking into the connection between Reid and Mohammed. Investigators later came to believe, in any case, that Reid operated under Mohammed's supervision.[50] They also came to believe that Mohammed was the mastermind behind the kidnapping.[51] Furthermore, Josef Bodansky, the man who claimed in 2002 that Mohammed had ties to the ISI, also claimed then that Mohammed was the one who ordered Pearl's murder,[52] and in October of 2003, reporter John Lupkin said that US officials "now have new information that leads them to believe [Mohammed] killed Pearl."[53] In this story, however, there is no mention of a possible ISI connection. Pearl is said to have been working on "a story on Islamic militants." And the only organization to which Mohammed is connected is al-Qaeda.

In any case, Khalid Shaikh Mohammed, thought to be the mastermind behind 9/11, is also thought to be behind the kidnapping and murder of Daniel Pearl. If that is so, it would not be a big leap to infer that Pearl may have been killed out of fear that he was uncovering the truth about 9/11. And if Mohammed was indeed connected with ISI, this would be further reason to suspect ISI involvement in 9/11.

Yet another story involving the ISI and reporters began when Pakistan's government failed in February of 2002 to prevent the *News* from publishing a story about Saeed's connections to the ISI. Saeed had not only admitted his involvement in attacks on the Indian parliament, the story revealed, but had also said that the ISI had helped him finance, plan, and execute the attacks. Shortly thereafter, the ISI pressured the *News* to fire the four journalists who worked on the story and also demanded an apology from the newspaper's editor. The journalists were fired and the editor fled the country.[54] After summarizing these reports, Thompson adds: "This information comes from an article titled, 'There's Much More To Daniel Pearl's Murder Than Meets the Eye,' and that certainly seems to be the case."[55]

The fact that the ISI apparently has so much to hide, combined with the fact that an American journalist was reportedly kidnapped and perhaps murdered by the same ISI agent who had sent money to Mohamed Atta, should, one would think, make US intelligence agencies very anxious to interview Saeed to learn all they could about the ISI. The *Washington Post*, for example, said: "The [ISI] is a house of horrors waiting to break open. Saeed has tales to tell."[56] However, in late February of 2002, *Time* magazine stated that the second highest Taliban official in US custody, Mullah Haji Abdul Samat Khaksar, had after several months still been waiting to talk to the CIA, even though he had reportedly volunteered the information that "ISI agents are still mixed up with the Taliban and al-Qaeda." Many months later, the *Indian Express* was wondering why Saeed, sitting in a Pakistani prison, still had not been interviewed by US intelligence agencies.[57] This lack of curiosity suggests to critics of the official account that US intelligence agencies assumed that these men had nothing to tell them that they did not already know.

Far from pursuing the ISI connections, in fact, Washington seemed intent on denying that there were any. In March of 2002, Secretary of State Powell declared that there were no links between Pearl's murder and "elements of the ISI." In light of the overwhelming evidence that the main suspect, Saeed Sheikh, worked for the ISI, said the *Guardian*, Powell's denial was "shocking."[58] Shortly thereafter, when Attorney General Ashcroft announced a criminal indictment against Saeed, there was no mention of his financing of the 9/11 attacks.[59]

These incidents suggesting an official desire to cover up ISI involvement, furthermore, reportedly had a startling precedent in 1999. According to later reports, an informant for the US government, Randy Glass, made a wire-recording of a conversation at a dinner involving himself, some illegal arms dealers, and an ISI agent named Rajaa Gulum Abbas. This dinner, which took place on July 14, 1999, and was observed by FBI agents at nearby tables pretending to be customers, was at a restaurant within view of the WTC. Abbas, besides saying that he wanted to buy a shipload of stolen US military weapons to give to bin Laden, pointed to the WTC and said: "Those towers are coming down."[60] In June of 2002, Abbas was secretly indicted for attempting to buy US military weapons illegally. But when the indictment was finally revealed in March of 2003, it made "no mention of Pakistan, any ties to Afghanistan's former Taliban regime or the ultimate destination of the weapons."[61]

If the part of this story about the towers is true, it suggests, obviously, that the plan to attack the WTC was discussed long before the Bush

administration took office, and even before September of 2000, when the
Project for the New American Century published its manifesto with its
reference to the good that could come out of "a new Pearl Harbor." And
if true, moreover, it makes the circumstantial case for ISI involvement in
the planning for 9/11 even stronger, adding further interest to the fact
that the Bush administration has been so intent to keep the ISI's name
out of all stories about 9/11.

FBI Flight from Flight School Investigations

Further lack of curiosity about the background to the attacks was shown
by the FBI in relation to a story, which broke four days after 9/11, that
many of the alleged hijackers had received flight training at US military
installations. These installations included the Naval Air Station in
Pensacola, Brooks Air Force Base in San Antonio, Maxwell Air Force Base
in Alabama, and the Defense Language Institute in Monterey,
California.[62] The Pensacola station was even listed on the driver's licenses
of three of the men as their permanent address.[63] When asked about this
report, a spokesperson for the US Air Force said that while the names
were similar, "we are probably not talking about the same people."[64]

TV producer, book author, and investigative journalist Daniel
Hopsicker reports that when he asked a major in the Air Force's Public
Affairs Office about this story, she said: "Biographically, they're not the
same people. Some of the ages are 20 years off." But when Hopsicker,
replying that he was interested only in Mohamed Atta, asked if she was
"saying that the age of the Mohamed Atta who attended the Air Force's
International Officer's School at Maxwell Air Force Base was different
from the terrorist Atta's age as reported," she replied: "Um, er, no." Then
when Hopsicker said that he would like information about the Mohamed
Atta who had attended the school at Maxwell, so that he could contact
him, the major reportedly said that she did not think he was going to get
that information. On September 16, news reports said that, with regard
to Atta and two other men who had reportedly attended US military
schools: "Officials would not release ages, country of origin or any other
specific details of the three individuals."[65]

Even US senators evidently got stonewalled. When Florida's Senator
Bill Nelson learned that three of the hijackers had been trained at
Pensacola Naval Station, he sent a letter to Attorney General Ashcroft

asking if this was true. Hopsicker reports that when a spokesman for Senator Nelson was asked about this, he said: "we never got a definitive answer from the Justice Department. So we asked the FBI for an answer.... Their response to date has been that they are trying to sort through something complicated and difficult."

Nevertheless, on October 10, with this "complicated and difficult" problem unsolved and dozens of other facts seeming to scream out for an extensive and intensive investigation, FBI Director Mueller, calling the FBI's month-long investigation of 9/11 "the most exhaustive in its history," declared it over. Officials reportedly said that Mueller's attitude was that his agents now had "a broad understanding of the events of September 11" and that it "was now time to move on."[66] Mueller, according to the *Washington Post*, "described reports that several of the hijackers had received flight training in the United States as 'news, quite obviously.'" But he had the agents who were investigating this news reassigned.[67] "The investigative staff has to be made to understand," one law enforcement official was quoted as saying, "that we're not trying to solve a crime now."[68]

To critics of the official account, a cover-up is suggested not only by the FBI's refusal to investigate this story but also by evidence that it had earlier tried to conceal the training received by some of the hijackers at two flight schools in Venice, Florida. Hopsicker, reporting that many of the men had trained at these two schools, also reports that just 18 hours after the 9/11 attacks—at 2 AM—FBI agents came to both schools and removed student files.[69] This story, like the one about the FBI confiscating the film from the gas station across from the Pentagon immediately after the crash there, lends additional support to the charge that the FBI had rather specific advance knowledge.

The FBI's Quick Release of Omar al-Bayoumi

One fact about post-9/11 investigations that the critics of the official account find significant is that whereas many people with no apparent connections to the hijackers were arrested and held for long periods, some people with seemingly obvious connections were, if arrested at all, quickly released. For example, reports Thompson, back in 1999, when Nawaf Alhazmi and Khalid Almihdhar—who would later be named as two of the hijackers—first entered the country, they were met at the airport in Los Angeles by a Saudi named Omar al-Bayoumi. He drove them to San Diego and provided an apartment for them. He also helped them open a bank account, obtain car insurance, get Social Security cards, and call flight schools in Florida.[70] As the Congressional Joint Inquiry would later learn, "One of the FBI's best sources in San Diego informed the bureau that he thought that al-Bayoumi," who seemed to have access to large sums of money, "must be an intelligence officer for Saudi Arabia."[71] Two months before 9/11, al-Bayoumi moved to England. After 9/11, he was arrested by British agents working with the FBI. However, the FBI, ostensibly accepting his story that he had met Alhazmi and Almihdhar by coincidence, angered British agents by releasing him "after a week without charge." Thompson comments: "Al-Bayoumi's quick release is in sharp contrast to that of hundreds of US Muslims who are held anonymously for many months after 9/11 despite having no connections to terrorism of any kind."[72]

A Cover-Up at the NSA?

In late October of 2001, the *Boston Globe* reported that some government intelligence officials were furious because, they said, information pertinent to the 9/11 investigation was being destroyed by the National Security Agency (NSA). They also claimed that possible leads were not being followed because of lack of cooperation by the NSA.[73] In a story that Thompson evidently thinks might be related, investigative reporter James Bamford, an authority on the NSA, reported that at least six of the identified hijackers, including all of those that boarded Flight 77 from Washington, had from August until 9/11 been "living, working, planning and developing all their activities in Laurel, Maryland, which happens to be the home of the NSA. So they were actually living alongside NSA employees as they were plotting all these things."[74] This fact might be simply a coincidence, but the accusations of a cover-up by NSA officials could make one wonder.

Later Developments Involving Moussaoui

On July 2, 2002, motions from Zacarias Moussaoui were unsealed in federal court. Claiming to have information showing the US government wanted the attacks of September to happen, Moussaoui indicated that he wanted to testify before both a grand jury and Congress.[75] Thus far what he has to say has not been made public.

In September of 2002, investigative reporter Seymour Hersh revealed that federal prosecutors had not discussed a plea bargain with Moussaoui since he had been indicted the previous November. Reporting that "Moussaoui's lawyers, and some FBI officials, remain bewildered at the government's failure to pursue a plea bargain," Hersh quoted a federal public defender as saying: "I've never been in a conspiracy case where the government wasn't interested in knowing if the defendant had any information—to see if there wasn't more to the conspiracy."[76]

On July of 2003, an Associated Press story contained the following statements:

Defying a court order, the Justice Department said Monday it would not make an al-Qaeda witness available to terrorism suspect Zacarias Moussaoui—even though prosecutors understood this could mean dismissal of the charges.

The only US case to arise from the September 11 attacks could be sent to a military tribunal if US District Judge Leonie Brinkema dismissed the case....

The government said it recognizes that its objection means the deposition of suspected September 11 organizer Ramzi Binalshibh cannot go forward. The Justice Department's decision also "obligates the court now to dismiss the indictment unless the court finds that the interests of justice can be served by another action," the prosecution filing said....

Brinkema has ruled that Moussaoui, who is representing himself, should be allowed to question Binalshibh via a satellite hookup. The exchange, which the government is desperately trying to stop, could be played to jurors if Moussaoui's case goes to trial....

Repeating earlier arguments, the government said Monday: "The deposition, which would involve an admitted and unrepentant terrorist (the defendant) questioning one of his al-Qaeda confederates, would necessarily result in the unauthorized disclosure of classified information. Such a scenario is unacceptable to the government, which not only carries the responsibility for prosecuting the defendant, but also of protecting this nation's security at a time of war with an enemy who already murdered thousands of our citizens."[77]

From the point of view of critics of the official account of 9/11, these stories suggest that the Justice Department's primary concern is not to find out what really happened, nor to prosecute the man who has been known as "the 20th hijacker," but to keep him from speaking in public.

Promotions Instead of Punishment

The two major theories to account for the failure to prevent the attacks of 9/11, as we have seen, are the complicity theory and the incompetence theory. As Barrie Zwicker pointed out, "Incompetence usually earns reprimands," so the incompetence theory is weakened in the eyes of critics by the absence of reprimands. Thompson reports, for example, that over a year after 9/11, the directors of the CIA, the FBI, and the NSA all admitted before a congressional committee that no individuals in their agencies had been fired or even punished for missteps connected to 9/11.[78]

To the contrary, Thompson adds, some of them were promoted. For example, Marion "Spike" Bowman—the agent at FBI headquarters who altered the Minneapolis FBI's request for the warrant to search Moussaoui's belongings—was in December of 2002 given an FBI award for "exceptional performance." This award came, furthermore, after a congressional report said that Bowman's RFU unit had given Minneapolis FBI agents "inexcusably confused and inaccurate information" that was "patently false."[79]

Reflecting on this and other promotions, a former Justice Department official said that FBI Director Mueller had "promoted the exact same people who have presided over the...failure."[80] Such actions, of course, give critics support for their contention that from the point of the FBI and the Bush administration more generally, the events of 9/11 represented not a failure but a spectacular success.

⁓⁓

For the critics of the official account, the evidence summarized in this chapter, which concerns official US behavior after 9/11, further strengthens the case for concluding not only that the official account is false but also that the true account would point to US complicity. For one thing, the evidence that American forces did not really try to capture

Osama bin Laden suggests that his long-term relationship with US agencies had not really, as the official account says, come to an end. As to exactly which US institutions were involved in the conspiracy, evidence in this chapter, more than that in previous ones, suggests CIA involvement. This chapter also provides further evidence of complicity by the White House, at least in the attempt to cover up the ISI's—and thereby the CIA's—involvement. With regard to White House involvement in the planning: If the prediction about the WTC towers made by an ISI agent in 1999 really occurred and reflected a joint ISI–CIA plan, then that plan must have been formulated long before it was certain that George W. Bush would become president. If he was involved in the planning, he would most likely have been brought in after the basic plan had already been formulated.

PART THREE

CONCLUSION

CHAPTER NINE

IS COMPLICITY BY US OFFICIALS THE BEST EXPLANATION FOR 9/11?

T hose who are *critics* of the official account of 9/11 believe that that account is, as the English title of Meyssan's first book says, "a big lie." At least most of these critics are also *revisionists* about 9/11, who believe, in Ahmed's words, that "the best explanation of [the facts on record] is one that points directly to US state responsibility for the events of 11th September 2001."[1] The most important question before the American people at this moment is whether we find the overall argument for this revisionist conclusion convincing enough, or at least disturbing enough, to undertake a thorough investigation of the various considerations used to support it.

Who Benefits?

At the center of these considerations is the fact that huge benefits from the attacks of 9/11 were reaped by the institutions that are suspected, by critics of the official account, of complicity in those attacks. Ahmed introduces the discussion of this issue by quoting a statement from investigative journalist Patrick Martin:

> In examining any crime, a central question must be "who benefits?" The principal beneficiaries of the destruction of the World Trade Center are in the United States: the Bush administration, the Pentagon, the CIA and FBI, the weapons industry, the oil industry. It is reasonable to ask whether those who have profited to such an extent from this tragedy contributed to bringing it about.[2]

To flesh out one of these examples: CIA Director George Tenet wanted authorization and funding for a plan to expand covert operations around the world. Called "Worldwide Attack Matrix," Tenet's plan, Bob Woodward has reported, "described covert operations in 80 countries that were either underway or that he was now recommending." At a meeting at Camp David four days after 9/11, Tenet received authorization.[3] Shortly afterwards, points out Meyssan, "the agency's funding was increased by 42 percent to successfully carry out the 'Worldwide Attack Matrix.'"[4]

With regard to the Pentagon and the weapons industry: The president, having asserted that US military capacity would be increased sufficiently to win this new war "whatever it costs," was able to push through the biggest increase for military spending since the end of the Cold War. Without 9/11, such an increase would have been highly unlikely. As Phyllis Bennis points out: "The $48 billion addition to the Pentagon budget requested by the Bush administration in January 2002 by itself was more money than any other country spent on its military."[5] In a calmer atmosphere, in other words, Congress might have decided that we were already spending more than enough.

The attacks of 9/11 allowed, in particular, greatly increased funding for the Space Force, championed by Donald Rumsfeld, General Eberhart, and General Myers. For these men, new support for the "missile defense system" may have been the most important benefit to come out of 9/11. Whereas in July of 2001, a Gallup Poll showed that only 53 percent of the population supported this system, a poll released on October 21 showed that support had jumped to 70 percent.[6]

With regard to benefits to the Bush administration as such, Ahmed reminds us that prior to 9/11 it was widely perceived to be in a crisis. Many Americans believed Bush to have gained the presidency fraudulently; there was a growing economic crisis, both domestic and globally; "the Bush administration was becoming increasingly isolated due to its foreign policies...and was consequently failing to push through resolutions via the United Nations Security Council and other international bodies"; there were massive "anti-globalization" demonstrations; "Bush approval ratings—both personal and political— were plummeting," so it was probably going to be "extremely difficult for the Bush administration to maintain its already uncomfortably slim majority in the House for the midterm elections in 2002; and "the strategic and military planning outlined in Brzezinski's [*The Great Chessboard*] would have been impossible to implement at this time."[7] However, "handed the public mood of shock and revulsion over the shocking tragedy of 11th September, the Bush administration was able to exploit these sentiments to advance long-standing global economic and strategic aims" and "to avert the crisis of legitimacy it had previously faced."[8]

With regard to implementing its strategic and military plans, the Bush administration and its advisors seemed well prepared to use this attack by *non-state terrorists* as a basis for going to war against *states* on its attack list. In his address to the nation on the evening of 9/11, President Bush said: "We will make no distinction between the terrorists who committed these acts and those who harbor them." Then, as mentioned in the Introduction, as soon as the president's address was completed, Henry Kissinger had an opinion piece ready to publish on the Internet. In that piece, he in effect supported Bush's "no distinction" point, saying:

> The government should be charged with a systematic response that, one hopes, will end the way that the attack on Pearl Harbor ended— with the destruction of the system that is responsible for it. That system is a network of terrorist organizations sheltered in capitals of certain countries.... [A]ny government that shelters groups capable of this kind of attack, whether or not they can be shown to have been involved in this attack, must pay an exorbitant price.[9]

A week later, Richard Perle made the same point in an editorial entitled "State Sponsors of Terrorism Should Be Wiped Out Too," in which he said:

> Those countries that harbour terrorists—that provide the means with which they would destroy innocent civilians—must themselves be destroyed. The war against terrorism is about the war against those regimes.[10]

It does appear that the administration and its advisors were ready to hit the ground running with this message.

And it worked. After the president announced his intention to "rally the world" in support of America's worldwide war on terrorism, says Phyllis Bennis:

> The world's leaders and the world's governments did not object. To the contrary. Before September 11, outrage had been rising among French intellectuals over whether the US hyperpower was behaving like a sovereign of an empire. Before September 11, Russia was audibly objecting to US threats to abandon the ABM treaty. Before September 11, Europeans and others had begun cautious efforts to punish Washington's lack of accountability to the international community.... But by 10 AM on that September Tuesday, all those already hesitant

moves came to an abrupt stop. Instead, governments cheered and much of the world stood by as the US asserted the rights of empire.[11]

With regard to the planned operation in Afghanistan in particular, Meyssan observes: "The attacks of September 11 allowed what was nothing more than a classic colonial expedition to be disguised as a legitimate operation."[12]

The fact that this *tragedy* for the country provided a tremendous *opportunity* for the administration was widely understood. For example, John Pilger, after saying that "[t]he attacks of 11 September 2001 provided the 'new Pearl Harbor,'" added that these attacks have been "described as 'the opportunity of ages.'"[13] They were described in those terms by the Bush administration itself. At the meeting of the National Security Council on the night of 9/11, President Bush reportedly said that the attacks provided "a great opportunity."[14] A month later, Donald Rumsfeld told the *New York Times* that 9/11 created "the kind of opportunities that World War II offered, to refashion the world."[15] Condoleezza Rice told senior members of the National Security Council to "think about 'how do you capitalize on these opportunities.'"[16] This point was even put in *The National Security Strategy of the United States of America*, issued by the Bush administration in September of 2002. "The events of September 11, 2001," it candidly declared, "opened vast, new opportunities."[17]

"Time and again," observers Pilger, "11 September is described as an 'opportunity.'" The opportunity provided by the attacks has been commented upon by many others. A story in *US News and World Report* said:

> Then came 9/11. Worldwide revulsion and the shared sense of threat handed Washington a once-in-a-generation chance to shake up international politics. Ten days after the attacks, State Department experts catalogued for [Colin] Powell a dozen "silver linings."[18]

Walden Bello, one of the major third-world critics of the US-led global economy, likewise said:

> The Al Qaeda New York mission was the best possible gift to the US and the global establishment.... As for the crisis of political governance in the US, September 11 has turned George W. Bush from a minority president whose party lost control of the Senate into arguably the most powerful US president in recent times.[19]

A statement by Karen Talbot, Director of the International Center for Peace and Justice, suggests that she had read Brzezinski's book:

> [T]he September 11th terrorist attacks have provided a qualitatively new opportunity for the US, acting particularly on behalf of giant oil companies, to permanently entrench its military in the former Soviet Republics of Central Asia, and the Transcaucusus where there are vast oil reserves—the second largest in the world. The way is now open to jump start projects for oil and gas pipelines through Afghanistan and Pakistan.... The big payoff for the US is the golden opportunity to establish a permanent military presence in oil-rich Central Asia.[20]

The well-known political commentator William Pfaff wrote:

> It seems to many Americans and others that the United States is already potentially head of a modern version of universal empire...The fundamental issue of the next two to three decades will inevitably be how the United States employs the amazing power it now exercises. Before September 11, the country...lacked the political will to impose itself. September 11 supplied that will.[21]

Ahmed quotes a statement by social philosopher John McMurtry that sums up the argument:

> [T]he forensic principle of "who most benefits from the crime?" clearly points in the direction of the Bush administration. One would be naive to think the Bush Jr. faction and its oil, military-industrial and Wall Street backers...do not benefit astronomically from this mass-kill explosion. If there was a wish-list, it is all granted by this numbing turn of events. Americans are diverted from a free-falling economy to attack another foreign Satan, while the Bush regime's popularity climbs. The military, the CIA, and every satellite armed security apparatus have more money and power than ever, and become as dominant as they can over civilians in "the whole new era" already being declared by the White House.[22]

Accordingly, given the principle that in general when crimes are committed, those who most benefit from them are to be considered the prime suspects, there is a *prima facie* case for assuming that the Bush administration was involved in this particular crime. Or, to repeat Patrick Martin's careful phrasing: "It is reasonable to ask whether those who have profited to such an extent from this tragedy contributed to bringing it about."

Having argued, along with others, that the principle "who most benefits?" should lead us to suspect complicity by the Bush administration, Ahmed then summarizes his evidence for this suspicion.

The Evidence for Official Complicity: A Summary

Ahmed's summary of his evidence,[23] supplemented with points contributed by Chossudovsky, Thompson, Meyssan, and other researchers, contains the following elements:

1. Evidence that the wars in Afghanistan and Iraq were already planned for geopolitical reasons, so that 9/11 provided not the reason for the wars but merely the pretext.

2. Evidence that men with connections to al-Qaeda were allowed into the United States in spite of regulations that should have kept them out.

3. Evidence that men with connections to al-Qaeda were allowed to train in US flight schools.

4. Evidence that the attacks of 9/11 could not have succeeded without an order from the highest level of government to suspend normal operating procedures for responding to hijackings.

5. Evidence that US political and military leaders made misleading and even false statements about their response to the hijackings.

6. Evidence in particular that the presently accepted official account, according to which jet fighter planes were scrambled but arrived too late, was invented some days after 9/11.

7. Evidence that the collapse of the WTC buildings was brought about by explosives, so that participation by the US government in the prevention of an adequate examination of the debris, especially the steel, constitutes evidence of its participation in a cover-up.

8. Evidence that someone in authority sought to ensure that there would be deaths in the attacks on the second WTC tower and the Pentagon by not having these buildings evacuated.

9. Evidence that what hit the Pentagon was not a Boeing 757 but a much smaller aircraft, such as a guided missile.

10. Evidence that Flight 93 was shot down after authorities learned that the passengers were gaining control of it.

11. Evidence that Secretary of Defense Rumsfeld revealed advance knowledge of two of the attacks.

12. Evidence that President Bush on 9/11 feigned ignorance of the occurrence and seriousness of the attacks.

13. Evidence that President Bush and his Secret Service knew on 9/11 that he would not be a target of attacks.

14. Evidence that the FBI had specific knowledge of the time and targets of the attacks at least a month in advance.

15. Evidence that the CIA and other intelligence agencies would have had very specific advance knowledge of the attacks by means of the put options purchased shortly before 9/11.

16. Evidence that the Bush administration lied about not having had specific warnings about the attacks.

17. Evidence that the FBI and other federal agencies prevented investigations prior to 9/11 that might have uncovered the plot.

18. Evidence that US officials sought to conceal evidence of involvement by Pakistan's ISI in the planning of 9/11.

19. Evidence that US officials sought to conceal the presence of the ISI chief in Washington during the week of 9/11.

20. Evidence that the FBI and other federal agencies blocked investigations after the attacks that might have revealed the true perpetrators.

21. Evidence that the United States did not really seek to kill or capture Osama bin Laden either before or after the attacks.

22. Evidence that figures central to the Bush administration had desired a "new Pearl Harbor" because of various benefits it would bring.

23. Evidence of motive provided by the predictable benefits that this event, called by Bush himself "the Pearl Harbor of the 21st century," did bestow on the Bush administration.

24. Evidence against the alternative explanation—the incompetence theory—provided by the fact that those who were allegedly guilty of incompetence were not fired but, in some cases, promoted.

In summarizing his argument for complicity (which contains many but not of all of these 24 points), Ahmed adds that he does not pretend to have presented a conclusive case. Rather, he considers his conclusions to be "merely the best available inferences from the available facts that have been so far unearthed."[24]

Possible Problems for a Complicity Theory

Ahmed is right to put it that way, because there well may be other facts that would cast the facts discussed by the revisionists in a different light. Also, some of the items they have presented as "facts" may not be such; only further investigations can decide. Moreover, the judgment that a case for some thesis is "conclusive" is always in part a subjective judgment, depending upon the biases of those making the judgment. The question, accordingly, is not whether the case for official complicity—the best case that can be constructed from the writings of Ahmed, Chossudovsky, Meyssan, Thompson, and other researchers—is conclusive. The question is whether it is likely to be widely *perceived* as conclusive. And for this to be so, critics of this revisionist theory could well claim, these revisionists must do more than show that the official account is implausible. They must also present an alternative account of what happened that incorporates all the relevant facts now available in a plausible way. Furthermore, these counter-critics could continue, insofar as an alternative account is already contained, at least implicitly, in the writings of the revisionists, it could be subjected to a great number of rhetorical questions, to which easy answers do not appear to be at hand.

One such question, for example, might be: If officials in the Bush administration wanted a new Pearl Harbor, why would they choose the set of events that occurred on 9/11, which required a massive conspiracy, involving at least members of the White House, the Justice Department, the FBI, the CIA, and the Pentagon? ("Choosing" here need not imply participation in planning the attacks; it can simply mean "choosing to allow.") Given standard procedures for dealing with hijacked planes, furthermore, allowing such planes to strike the WTC and the Pentagon required such obvious violations of standard procedures that the conspirators could hardly have expected not to be found out. They could, to be sure, have assumed that the shock of the attacks and the outburst of uncritical patriotism to follow would allow them to get away with the scheme for a while. But how could they have believed that the absurdities in their story would not eventually lead to their exposure? So why would they have concocted such a complex scheme, requiring such absurdities, when virtually the same effects could have been achieved with a much simpler hoax, such as an attack by chemical or biological weapons, which could have been carried out by a very small number of perpetrators? After all, the new Pearl Harbor did not need to mimic the original one to the extent of being an attack by airplanes.

Furthermore, even supposing that there was some rational reason for the administration to choose the kind of attacks that occurred on 9/11, why would they have risked exposure of the fact that the attack on the WTC was an inside job by having the buildings collapsed by explosives? Was ensuring the occurrence of several thousand deaths worth this additional risk of exposure? And why, in any case, would they have demolished WTC-7, thereby undermining the claim that the Twin Towers collapsed because of the impact of the airliners combined with the heat from the jet-fuel-fed fires?

Also, assuming for the sake of argument the revisionists' conspiracy theory, there are many features of the alleged conspirators' resulting behavior that suggest incompetence beyond belief. For example, given the fact that if no planes were scrambled until after the Pentagon had been hit, this would obviously have required an order to cancel standard procedures, why would the conspirators first tell this story? And then, when they realized that that story would likely implicate them, why would they concoct a second version almost equally absurd—with planes ordered from distant air bases and with travel times implying that they were flying only a few hundred miles per hour? Given the massive planning that must have gone into the whole operation, why was there not a carefully formulated, plausible cover story that would be told by everyone from the outset?

Moreover, critics can ask, why would the conspirators then raise additional doubts with needless lies and foolish statements? Why, for example, would they suggest that it required a presidential order merely to have hijacked planes intercepted, when any cub reporter could find out otherwise? Why would they claim that they had received no advance warnings of the attacks, when the falsity of this claim would surely be discovered? Why would they have President Bush appear to be ignorant of the fact that the country was (apparently) under attack, when it is well known that he would be informed of such events immediately? Why would the president then, after officially knowing that a modern-day Pearl Harbor was unfolding, continue to do "the reading thing"? And why would the president remain in his publicly known location, thereby appearing to demonstrate that he and his staff knew that no suicide missions were coming their way? Would not the conspirators have orchestrated a scene that made the Secret Service appear genuinely concerned and the president genuinely presidential? Furthermore, if Cheney, Rumsfeld, Wolfowitz, and Libby had been planning this incident when their Project for the New American Century produced its 2000 document, why would they have allowed what could be read as a call for a "new Pearl Harbor" to be included in this public document, which anyone could read? And why would Rumsfeld (assuming the truth of Representative Cox's report) predict the occurrence of more terrorist attacks on America just before the first attack on the WTC and again just before the attack on the Pentagon, thereby giving a basis for suspicion that he had foreknowledge of the fact and even the timing of the attacks?

Another set of rhetorical questions could be raised by the revisionist account of the attack on the Pentagon. One such question might be: Given the well-known fact that the Pentagon is defended by missiles, along with the more general assumption that it must be the most well-protected place on earth, why would the conspirators have it included among the targets? Or, if they did not choose the targets but merely allowed them to be hit, why—assuming that the original plan was for a hijacked airliner to strike the Pentagon—would the conspirators have planned to allow the Pentagon actually to be hit, especially since shooting down an attacking airplane would have provided evidence of their intent to defend? Or, if the theory is that the plan all along was to have the Pentagon struck by a military aircraft and then claim that it was a hijacked 757, why would they use a much smaller aircraft, perhaps a winged missile, which many people would see and which would neither create a big enough hole in the Pentagon nor leave enough big pieces of metal to be seen? (Nowadays airplanes, not just guided missiles, can fly without pilots.) Or, if the alternative theory is that the use of this much smaller aircraft was an improvisation, necessitated by the fact that Flight 77 crashed unexpectedly (perhaps because the passengers resisted the hijackers), why was there not a better back-up plan? Or better yet, why did the conspirators not simply let this part of the plan go rather than improvise a scenario the absurdity of which would be visible to someone from as far away as France? Why in any case did they make the totally ridiculous claim that the bodies of the victims were still identifiable, after they had claimed that the fire was so hot that it vaporized the plane's steel and aluminum? Furthermore, what plausible account can be given of the role of Ted Olson? Are we to believe that upon learning that his wife had just been killed in an operation overseen by his superiors, he willingly told a lie to help them out? Or that the whole story was a hoax—that Barbara Olson was not really killed, which would mean that she would have to spend the rest of her life incognito? And, in any case, why manufacture this implausible story—in which all the passengers are encouraged to call home but she is the only one to do so? There surely could have been some better way to convey the impression that Flight 77 had not crashed and might be headed back to Washington. Finally, if the Boeing 757 that was Flight 77 crashed somewhere, perhaps in Ohio or Kentucky, why have there been no reports of its discovery?

Still more rhetorical questions would doubtless be evoked by the account of Flight 93 implicit in the revisionist hypothesis, according to which government officials, after realizing that the passengers were gaining control of the plane, had it shot down. For example, why would not the conspirators, who could draw upon the best military and CIA minds with experience in covert operations, have not come up with a better back-up plan, such as installing a bomb that could be electronically detonated? Why risk a method of disposal that would likely provide so many tell-tale signs, especially the sightings of the jet fighter?

Finally, critics of the complicity theory might believe that the most damaging rhetorical question arises precisely from the fact, emphasized by critics of the incompetence theory, that there have been no known punishments. If 9/11 resulted from a conspiracy, critics of this view could ask, why were there no scapegoats? The official account involves, even if only implicitly, perhaps the most extensive incompetence theory in history, because this story implies that incredible incompetence was manifested by FBI agents, FAA flight controllers, NMCC officials, NORAD officials, and jet fighter pilots, among others. There were potential scapegoats galore, a few of whom could have been sacrificed to protect the actual conspirators from suspicion. Contrary to virtually all past experience, however, this was not done. Indeed, of all the people who must have manifested gross incompetence if the official account be true, evidently not one was fired or even publicly reprimanded, and some of them were even promoted—thereby increasing the suspicion that they had acted as their superiors wished. But would such behavior not be too arrogant, attributing too much stupidity or willing blindness to the press, to be believable? Must we not assume that if leading figures in the Bush administration were complicit in 9/11, they would have made a big show of punishing at least a few people for gross incompetence?

These are, at least, the rhetorical questions that have occurred to me as I have tried imaginatively to flesh out the complicity theory that seems to be implicit in the critiques of the official account. When all these rhetorical questions are taken together, it seems that we are faced not simply with a choice between an incompetence theory and a complicity theory. Rather, the choice seems to be between a theory involving subordinates who momentarily became incredibly incompetent, on the one hand, and a theory involving high-level officials who manifested incredible incompetence in creating a conspiracy, on the other. And to call this incompetence "incredible" is to suggest that it is difficult to believe. Critics of the complicity theory, therefore, can say that acceptance of this theory would require excessive credulity.

Those who accept the theory of high-level conspirators could, to be sure, explain the apparent incompetence of the plan by the theory of the "big lie," according to which the masses are more likely to believe a big lie than a little one, precisely because they cannot imagine that someone would try to get a way with such an audacious story. Gore Vidal, for example, says: "It would seem that the Hitler team got it about right when it comes to human credulity: the greater the lie, the more apt it is to be believed."[25] It is unlikely, however, that this explanation will serve to overcome many people's doubt that officials who had risen to the top in political, intelligence, and military circles would have devised a plan involving such an obviously implausible cover story.

In suggesting that it would be difficult to construct an account of official complicity that could be found widely plausible, at least on the basis of presently known facts, I am simply enlarging on Ahmed's admission that he does not claim to have presented a conclusive case. At this point, however, Ahmed, Chossudovsky, Meyssan, Thompson, and other critics of the official account might wish to interject a word of caution. The fact that there are questions that they cannot answer, they might add, should not be taken to mean that we are simply left with a toss-up between two hypotheses, each of which is subject to equally serious questions. Instead, the questions they have raised about the official account are based on conflicts between this account and known facts, whereas the questions just now raised about the complicity theory are rhetorical questions, implying that no answers could be given to any of them. But perhaps answers *can* be given to at least some of them.

For example, as to why the attacks involved attacks by airplanes, rather than some other form of terrorist attack that could have been more easily arranged, an answer has already been implied. If one of the motives for the attack was to garner support for spending tens of billions of dollars on the Missile Defense Shield, the attacks had to come from the air, being perceivable as a "Space Pearl Harbor." Although chemical and biological attacks would have been much simpler, requiring far fewer people to be in on the conspiracy, they would not have produced the desired effect.

With regard to the question of whether it is plausible that so many conspirators would have kept silent, the revisionists could reply, people raising this question have probably never experienced the kind of intimidation that can be brought to bear on individuals by threats of prosecution and worse.

Furthermore, the revisionists could add, some of the rhetorical questions depend on the fact that there are many things about 9/11 that we do not presently know. These questions might be answered through a full investigation. One cannot expect that the revisionists, being independent researchers with limited budgets and no power to subpoena testimony, could answer all the questions raised by their alternative scenario. Meyssan, for example, says that although in some instances the facts he has uncovered allow us to see the truth of what happened, in other cases "our questions remain for the moment unanswered." Pointing to one set of such questions to which he himself would most like answers, he asks: "What became of American Airlines flight 77? Are the passengers dead? If so, who killed them and why? If not, where are they?" While fully admitting he does not yet have all the answers, he adds that "this is no reason to go on believing the lies put forward by officials."[26] We will not get an account of what really happened on 9/11, in other words, until our awareness that they *are* lies leads us to demand full-scale investigations.

The remainder of the rhetorical questions simply suggest that to accept the complicity theory would be to attribute a degree of incompetence to the conspirators that is beyond belief. But the truth may be that they really were terribly incompetent. With regard to the occupation of Iraq, the incompetence of the Bush administration's plans—for everything except winning the initial military victory and securing the oil fields and ministries—has been becoming increasingly obvious. Perhaps their formulation of the plan for 9/11, with its cover story, involved comparable incompetence. Perhaps this fact is not yet widely recognized only because the news media have failed to inform the American public about the many tensions between the official account and the relevant facts. For example, the mass media have not educated the public about standard operating procedures for intercepting hijacked airliners. They have not emphasized the fact that what now passes for the official account of the government's response to the hijackings is very different from what was said the first few days after 9/11. They have not emphasized the fact that the explanations for why the fighter jets arrived too late to prevent the attacks do not make sense. Nor have they informed the public about the many physical facts that contradict the official account of the strike on the Pentagon. Once these and other relevant facts are well known, critics of the official theory can argue, it will become widely evident that, as the name of Jared Israel's website suggests, the emperor has no clothes.[27]

Problems for a Coincidence Theory

Even more important, critics of the official account could point out, rejection of the conspiracy theory exacts a high price. A conspiracy theory usually depends upon the perception of a pattern, plus a claim that the existence of this pattern is best explained by supposing that it was brought about through the combined efforts of two or more people. To reject a particular conspiracy theory of this nature requires either a denial that the alleged pattern exists or the assertion that the existence of the pattern could be purely coincidental. It would be hard to deny that the critics of the official account have discerned a pattern. They have shown that many otherwise puzzling events—before, during, and after 9/11—can be explained by the theory that high-level officials in the US government conspired to allow the attacks to occur and then to cover up this fact. Given that pattern, the price for rejecting this conspiracy theory is to accept a *coincidence* theory. And, critics of the official account can point out, the number of coincidences that would need to be accepted is enormous. A complete list would include the following coincidences:

1. Several FAA flight controllers exhibited extreme incompetence on 9/11, and evidently on that day only.

2. The officials in charge at both NMCC and NORAD also acted incompetently on 9/11, and evidently on that day only.

3. In particular, when NMCC-NORAD officials did finally order jet fighters to be scrambled to protect New York and Washington, they ordered them in each case from more distant bases, rather than from McGuire and Andrews, respectively.

4. After public statements saying that Andrews Air Force Base had no jet fighters on alert to protect Washington, its website, which had previously said that many jets were always on alert, was altered.

5. Several pilots who normally are airborne and going full speed in under three minutes all took much longer to get up on 9/11.

6. These same pilots, flying planes capable of going 1,500 to 1,850 miles per hour, on that day were all evidently able to get their planes to fly only 300 to 700 miles per hour.

7. The collapse of the buildings of the World Trade Center, besides occurring at almost free-fall speed, exhibited other signs of being controlled demolitions: molten steel, seismic shocks, and fine dust were all produced.

8. The video and physical evidence suggesting that controlled demolition was the cause of the collapse of the Twin Towers co-exists with testimony from people in these buildings that they heard, felt, and saw the effects of explosions.

9. The collapse of WTC-1 and WTC-2 had some of the same features as the collapse of WTC-7, even though the latter collapse could not be attributed to the impact and jet fuel of an airplane.

10. Both the North Tower and the South Tower collapsed just as their respective fires were dying down, even though this meant that the South Tower, which had been hit second, collapsed first.

11. Governmental agencies had the debris, including the steel, from the collapsed WTC buildings removed without investigation, which is what would be expected if the government wanted to prevent evidence of explosives from being discovered.

12. Physical evidence suggesting that what hit the Pentagon could not have been a Boeing 757 co-exists with testimony of several witnesses that the aircraft that did hit the Pentagon was far smaller than a 757.

13. This evidence about the aircraft that hit the Pentagon co-exists with reports that Flight 77 crashed in Kentucky or Ohio.

14. This evidence co-exists with the fact that the only evidence that Flight 77 did *not* crash was supplied by an attorney closely associated with the Bush administration.

15. Evidence that Flight 77 did not return to Washington to hit the Pentagon co-exists with the fact that when the flight control transcript was released, the final 20 minutes were missing.

16. The fact that the aircraft that hit the Pentagon did so only after executing a very difficult maneuver co-exists with the fact that it struck a section of the Pentagon that, besides containing none of its leaders, was the section in which the strike would cause the least death and destruction.

17. On the same day in which jet fighters were unable to protect the Pentagon from an attack by a single airplane, the missiles that normally protect the Pentagon also failed to do so.

18. Sounds from cell phones inside Flight 93 suggesting that the plane had been hit by a missile were matched by many reports to this effect from witnesses on the ground.

19. This evidence that Flight 93 was shot down co-exists with reports from both civilian and military leaders that there was intent to shoot this flight down.

20. The only plane that was evidently shot down, Flight 93, was the only one in which it appeared that passengers were going to gain control.

21. The evidence that Flight 93 was shot down after the passengers were about to gain control co-exists with the fact that the flight control transcript for this flight was not released.

22. That coincidence co-exists with the fact that when the cockpit recording of Flight 93 was released, the final three minutes were missing.

23. Evidence showing that the US government had far more specific evidence of what was to occur on 9/11 than it has admitted co-exists with evidence that it actively blocked investigations that might have prevented the attacks.

24. Reports of obstructions from FBI agents in Minneapolis co-exist with similar reports from Chicago and New York.

25. Reports of such obstructions prior to 9/11 co-exist with reports that investigations after 9/11 were also obstructed.

26. These reports of obstructionism co-exist with multiple reports suggesting that the US government did not really try to capture or kill Osama bin Laden either prior to or after 9/11, with the result that several people independently suggested that the US government must be working for bin Laden—or vice versa.

27. All these reports co-exist with reports of hijackers being allowed in the country in spite of known terrorist connections or visa violations.

28. These reports about immigration violations co-exist with evidence that some of these same men were allowed to train at US flight schools, some on military bases.

29. This evidence of training at various American flight schools co-exists with reports that US officials tried to conceal this evidence.

30. The traumatic events of 9/11 occurred just a year after a document published by the Project for the New American Century, an organization whose founders included several men who became central figures in the Bush administration, referred to benefits that could come from "a new Pearl Harbor."

31. The "unifying Pearl Harbor sort of purple American fury" produced by the 9/11 attacks did benefit the Bush administration in many ways.

32. A credible report that spokespersons for the Bush administration had earlier announced that the US government was planning a war on Afghanistan, which would begin before the middle of October, co-exists with the fact that the attacks of 9/11, by occurring on that date, gave US military forces time to be ready to attack Afghanistan on October 7.

33. Ahmad Masood, whose continued existence would have posed problems for US plans in Afghanistan, was assassinated, reportedly by ISI operatives, just after the head of the ISI, General Mahmoud Ahmad, had been meeting in Washington for several days with the head of the CIA.

34. In the White House's version of the recording of Condoleezza Rice's press briefing on May 16, the only portion that was inaudible was the portion in which the person under discussion, mentioned as having been in Washington on 9/11, was identified as "the ISI chief."

35. Evidence of official efforts to conceal General Ahmad's presence in Washington co-exists with evidence that, after it became known that General Ahmad had ordered $100,000 wired to Mohamed Atta, US leaders exerted pressure on the ISI to dismiss him from his post quietly.

36. Evidence of these attempts to conceal General Ahmad's involvement in 9/11 co-exists with evidence that the FBI and other federal agencies sought to obscure the fact that Saeed Sheikh, the man who wired the money to Atta, was an ISI agent.

37. The fact that agents in FBI headquarters who presided over the alleged intelligence failure that allowed 9/11 to happen, widely called the biggest intelligence failure since Pearl Harbor, were promoted instead of fired or otherwise punished co-exists with the fact that other intelligence agencies also reported that there had been no punishments for incompetence related to 9/11.

38. This evidence of lack of punishment for poor performance co-exists with reports that intelligence officers who were diligently trying to pursue investigations related to 9/11 suffered negative treatment from superiors.

As can be seen, what some critics call the *incompetence* theory can be understood as simply part of a larger *coincidence* theory, because it entails that FAA agents, NMCC and NORAD officials, pilots, immigration agents, US military leaders in Afghanistan, and numerous US intelligence agencies all coincidentally acted with extreme and unusual incompetence when dealing with matters related to 9/11.

But the coincidence theory requires even greater credulity. To accept it requires holding not only that each conjunction of events on the above list—which a conspiracy theory could explain by regarding each one as part of a pattern of events that had been planned—was purely coincidental. It also requires holding that the fact that there are *so many* events related to 9/11 that involve coincidences—at least 38 such events—is itself purely coincidental.

Seen in this light, the fact that a complicity theory may not at this time be able to answer all the questions it evokes, revisionists can say, is a relatively trivial problem. Once the relevant facts are put before us, the official account involves a coincidence theory that would require far greater credulity than that of which "conspiracy theorists" are accused.

Furthermore, the fact that the revisionists cannot yet answer all questions would be important only if they were claiming to have presented a fully conclusive case. But they are not. Meyssan, for example, tells readers that he is not asking them to accept his argument "as the definitive truth," but instead hopes that his readers will use his references to examine the evidence for themselves.[28] Ahmed says that the purpose of his book is not to provide a definitive account but merely "to clarify the dire need for an in-depth investigation into the events of 11th September."[29]

My book is an attempt to show, in relatively brief form, that he and the others have done just this.

CHAPTER TEN

THE NEED FOR A FULL INVESTIGATION

I have argued that our Fourth Estate needs to carry out a thorough investigation of the kind of information summarized in this book. It is usually only when the press leads the way that an official investigation is undertaken. But finally it will be the official investigation that is decisive. In considering the kind of investigation that is now needed, it will be helpful to review the official investigations that have been authorized thus far and the obstacles they have faced from the Bush administration.

The Joint Inquiry

As we have seen, the intelligence committees of the US Senate and House of Representatives carried out a Joint Inquiry in 2002. As we have also seen, however, there are many reasons to consider the report issued by this inquiry inadequate. For example, it concludes that US intelligence agencies, besides not having specific information about imminent attacks, did not even expect attacks to occur within the United States. The report does suggest that federal agencies were at fault. Indeed, the report was described by the press as a "scathing indictment" of the intelligence agencies. But the named problems—such as inadequate communication between agencies, failure to make rather obvious inferences, and failure to take warnings with sufficient seriousness—all fit under the incompetence and coincidence theories.

In light of the evidence summarized in this book, the underlying weakness of the Joint Inquiry is that its members apparently simply assumed from the outset that no deliberate complicity was involved, as illustrated by the fact that the testimony of the various witnesses was evidently accepted at face value. For example, if NSA officials said that they had not translated the specific warnings that had been intercepted between September 8 and 10 until after the attacks, that testimony was simply accepted as the truth. If agents at FBI headquarters said that they misunderstood the standards under FISA for issuing a warrant, that testimony was accepted as the truth, in spite of evidence of deliberate sabotage.

There are several possible explanations for the inadequacy of the Joint Inquiry. One is simply that a thorough investigation of the many questions raised by critics of the official account would have taken far more time and resources than were devoted to this inquiry, which reportedly involved only nine public hearings and thirteen closed sessions.

But there is also reason to believe that intimidation may have dampened some of the members' investigative zeal. Thompson cites a report that on August of 2002, FBI agents had questioned nearly all 37 members of the Senate and House intelligence committees about 9/11-related information leaks. The agents even demanded that these senators and representatives submit to lie detector tests and turn over phone records and appointment calendars. A law professor, commenting on this demand, said: "It creates a great chilling effect on those who would be critical of the FBI."[1] Some senators and representatives expressed grave concern about the violation of the separation of powers, with Senator John McCain saying: "What you have here is an organization compiling dossiers on people who are investigating the same organization." The FBI, said one senator, is "trying to put a damper on our activities and I think they will be successful."[2]

Beyond the problems with the Joint Inquiry, the larger question is why Congress did not immediately undertake a full-scale investigation into 9/11. Assigning the task simply to the intelligence committees implied that the success of the attacks of 9/11 was already known to be the result of nothing other than intelligence failures. A more sweeping investigation was evidently not undertaken because the congressional leaders acceded to requests from the White House that the scope of their investigation be limited. Both President Bush and Vice President Cheney, in personal appeals to Senate Majority Leader Tom Daschle, reportedly "asked that only the House and Senate intelligence committees look into the potential breakdowns among federal agencies that could have allowed the terrorist attacks to occur, rather than a broader inquiry that some lawmakers have proposed." Bush and Cheney were making this request, they said, because a broader inquiry would take resources and personnel "away from the war on terrorism."[3] In light of the fact that Bush and Cheney must now be included among the prime suspects, it would obviously be problematic if they had been allowed to determine the cause of the 9/11 attacks—that it was "breakdown" rather than "complicity"— and hence to limit the scope of the investigation carried out by the people's representatives. We normally do not allow the suspects in an investigation to make such decisions.

Nevertheless, in spite of all these problems, the work of the Joint Inquiry was not in vain. It provided enough damaging revelations to leave President Bush, after having long opposed the creation of any special investigating body, little choice but to support the creation of The National Commission on Terrorist Attacks upon the United States, informally known as the 9/11 Independent Commission.[4]

The 9/11 Independent Commission

Although it was good that this commission was finally created, it has also been riddled with problems. One problem is that the Bush administration placed obstacles in front of it from the outset. An immediate obstacle was the very small sum of money allocated by the administration to fund the commission's work. As of January 2003, the commission had been given only $3 million—whereas in 1996, by contrast, a federal commission to study legalized gambling was given $5 million.[5] In March of 2003, *Time* magazine reported that the commission had asked the Bush administration for an additional $11 million but had been turned down. One commissioner, pointing out that the request was hardly excessive, noted that the commission on the Columbia shuttle disaster, by contrast, had $50 million. Stephen Push, one of the leaders of families of the victims, said that this refusal suggested that the Bush administration saw this "as a convenient way for allowing the commission to fail. They've never wanted the commission and I feel the White House has always been looking for a way to kill it without having their finger on the murder weapon."[6] After more time passed, the additional funding was finally approved.

Yet another obstacle was that although the commission's mandate dictated that it must complete its work by May 2004, the Bush administration was very slow in issuing the needed security clearances to the commission's personnel. For example, even Slade Gorton, a former

Republican US senator with much experience with intelligence issues, still had not received a security clearance by March 12, 2003, leading the commission's vice chairman, former Democratic congressman Lee Hamilton, to say: "It's kind of astounding that someone like Senator Gorton can't get immediate clearance."[7] As a result of these delays, by the time the commission was finally able to begin work in the middle of 2003, it had less than a year to carry out its work.

Another obstacle was difficulty in obtaining needed documents and witnesses. For one thing, although this commission was supposed to use the final report of the Joint Inquiry as a point of departure, the Bush administration did not allow this report to be released until late in July of 2003. Also, shortly before this report was released, the commission's chairman, Thomas H. Kean, complained that the Justice Department and other federal agencies were withholding documents—which they obviously would not have done if they had been ordered by the White House to turn them over. Kean also complained that federal agencies were insisting on having "minders" present when any of their employees were called to give testimony, which Kean (reasonably) interpreted as an attempt to intimidate these employees. The White House also indicated that the president himself would not give testimony, at least under oath.

In light of the enormous number of questions that have been raised about 9/11, these obstacles were probably by themselves sufficient to prevent the commission from providing definitive answers to most of the questions, even if the commission carried out the most independent, aggressive investigation possible in the time remaining. Indeed, in October of 2003, one member of the commission, former senator Max Cleland, told *New York Times* reporter Philip Shenon that the commission could not complete its work by May of 2004, adding: "It's obvious that the White House wants to run out the clock here.... [W]e're still in negotiations with some assistant White House counsel about getting these documents—it's disgusting." Although Cleland is a Democrat, this attitude, reported Shenon, was bipartisan, with Slade Gorton also complaining that the "lack of cooperation" would make it "very difficult" for the commission to complete its work by the deadline.[8]

The obstacles created by the Bush administration, however, were not the only problem. Another reason to doubt that the commission's report would answer many questions was that its leaders adopted a very limited understanding of its task: "The focus of the commission will be on the future," said Vice Chairman Hamilton. "We're not interested in trying to assess blame, we do not consider that part of the commission's responsibility."[9] The commission, in other words, evidently approached its task by simply taking for granted the truth of the incompetence theory, so that the question of official complicity would not even be explored. Hamilton's words seemed, in fact, to imply that the commission would not even assess blame in the sense of incompetence. In saying that the commission's focus "will be on the future," Hamilton was apparently indicating that it would limit itself strictly to the question of how to make sure that a "breakdown" does not happen again.

Now that we have before us the questions raised by critics of the official account, along with the alternative theory implicit therein, we can see the absurdity of such a limited mandate. Any explanation of how the attacks on 9/11 could have occurred requires that there was either complicity at the highest level of the U.S. government or an unprecedented system-wide breakdown in this country's ability to protect itself from a very crude form of attack—and this despite the fact that a huge portion of our nation's trillion-dollar budget goes annually for "defense" and "intelligence." In the face of a seemingly forced choice between these two explanations, the commission's failure to assess blame would be an enormous dereliction of duty. We need an investigation that will seek to place blame where it belongs. We also need one that will not shrink from asking whether 9/11 resulted from official complicity rather than merely massive incompetence.

To be fair to Hamilton and the other members, it must be added that the commission's limited scope was perhaps imposed upon it. I have read reports that President Bush agreed to authorize the 9/11 Independent Commission only on condition that its scope would be limited to the question of how to prevent similar breakdowns in the future—in other words, only on condition that the commission would be independent in name only, not free to determine for itself the nature and scope of its investigation.

In any case, whatever be the facts with regard to the commission's mandate, the president clearly did make it a condition of his authorization of such a commission that he would appoint its chairman.[10] Bush's first choice, which many observers found incredible, was Henry

Kissinger. There was widespread scepticism about Kissinger's ability to guide the commission in an independent and impartial way.[11] "Indeed," said the *New York Times*, "it is tempting to wonder if the choice of Mr. Kissinger is not a clever maneuver by the White House to contain an investigation it long opposed."[12] Skepticism about Kissinger's capacity for independence was based in part on reports of possible conflicts of interest, about which he evidently had not been interrogated by the White House. Kissinger, for one thing, was getting huge consulting fees from corporations with heavy investments in Saudi Arabia.[13] And, of course, besides reportedly supplying many of the hijackers for 9/11, Saudi Arabia has been, according to John O'Neill and other intelligence agents, the primary continuing source of support for al-Qaeda. Kissinger's relationship with Unocal—the oil company with plans to build a pipeline through Afghanistan—was also reported.[14] The obvious problem here is that the attacks of 9/11 provided the basis for a war in Afghanistan, after which the United States installed a puppet government headed by a former Unocal employee and placed military bases along the proposed route for the pipeline. The fact that Bush would appoint someone reputed to be financially connected with Unocal as well as Saudi Arabia suggested, to say the least, that the impartiality of the commission's chairman was not his chief concern. Bush declared, in fact, that Kissinger was not required to reveal his business clients. The Congressional Research Service said otherwise, however, and Kissinger resigned rather than do so.[15]

It was after this debacle that Thomas Kean became the chairman. Kean, formerly the governor of New Jersey, was the president of Drew University at the time of his appointment. Because he was to continue as Drew's president, Kean would have only limited time to devote to the commission. Critics also complained about possible conflicts of interest, with the main problem being his membership on the Board of Directors for another oil company, Amerada Hess, with extensive investments in Central Asia. Amerada Hess had, furthermore, joined with Delta Oil of Saudi Arabia—one of the companies in the CentGas consortium—to form Hess-Delta.[16] All of the other members of the committee, furthermore, reportedly had at least one possible conflict of interest.[17]

Also problematic is the fact that the president also appointed the committee's executive director, Philip Zelikow, who had been deeply enmeshed with the Bush administration. He was appointed to Bush's Foreign Intelligence Advisory Board shortly after 9/11. Back during the administration of the elder George Bush, he served with Condoleezza Rice in the National Security Council, then later collaborated with her on a book.[18] Stephen Push, one of the founders of Families of September 11, commented on the problem of getting "commissioners and staff who are truly independent." He was uncomfortable, he indicated, with the fact "that Philip Zelikow has such a close relationship to Rice and other people the commission is investigating."[19] The Family Steering Committee for the 9/11 Independent Commission has, in fact, called on Zelikow to step down.[20]

Accordingly, given the make-up of the commission, people aware of the issues had reason to suspect that any evidence that the Bush administration itself was complicit in the events of 9/11 would not be impartially and thoroughly explored. Several good people were appointed to the commission, and various issues were assigned to a number of committees, with capable and dedicated staff members. Reports indicated that these committees, under Kean's overall direction, were going somewhat beyond the limited scope originally suggested by Hamilton's statement. But evidently not very far: Even as late as October of 2003, a quotation from one member of the commission seemed to suggest that its most important task would be "making recommendations for the future."[21]

Nevertheless, continued stonewalling by the White House and various agencies led to statements by Kean suggesting that he would be tenacious in obtaining evidence that the Bush administration and its various agencies were trying to withhold. The same month, in fact, Kean's commission issued a subpoena to the FAA, adding that this subpoena would "put other agencies on notice that our document requests must be taken as seriously as a subpoena."[22] He also stated in an interview that he was ready to subpoena the White House itself if necessary. In his strongest statement up to that point, Kean said:

> Any document that has to do with this investigation cannot be beyond our reach.... I will not stand for [stonewalling].... We will use every tool at our command to get hold of every document.... There are a lot of theories about 9/11, and as long as there is any document out there that bears on any of those theories, we're going to leave questions unanswered. And we cannot leave questions unanswered.

Assuming Kean was really serious about taking the various "theories" seriously and obtaining every available document relevant to them, there was the possibility that the commission might uncover evidence suggesting that 9/11 happened more through complicity than incompetence. This possibility was suggested by Max Cleland's statement that, "As each day goes by, we learn that this government knew a whole lot more about these terrorists before Sept. 11 than it has ever admitted."[23]

But there was also the possibility, indeed the probability, that this would *not* happen. And, regardless of people's assessment of Kean's integrity, the fact remains that he was appointed by President Bush. At the time the commission was chosen, of course, the evidence that pointed to complicity by the Bush administration was known by very few people, so acceding to Bush's insistence that he should appoint the commission's leaders did not seem completely absurd. But insofar as there is widespread knowledge of this evidence, the fact that the chairman was appointed by Bush will create suspicion that he, like Kissinger, was chosen for the sake of containing the investigation.

This suspicion might well be misplaced, at least if it is suspicion that Kean would, out of loyalty to his party and the president, deliberately conceal evidence of complicity. Although Kean is, like the president, a Republican, he is "a moderate Republican known for his independence,"[24] who reportedly refused to run for the US Senate because of his disagreement with the direction being taken by his party. The president perhaps selected him to replace Kissinger not because he would be almost as safe but because the administration did not want to risk another embarrassment.

Nevertheless, because Kean, like Zelikow, was appointed by the president, a report by the commission exonerating President Bush and his administration of all wrongdoing would be suspected, by those who know the kinds of questions reported in this book, of contributing to a cover-up, even if only through failure to exert the kind of pressure required to obtain truthful testimony and access to needed documents.

This kind of failure was arguably illustrated, in fact, when in November of 2003 Kean agreed to restrictions demanded by the White House with regard to those intelligence reports for the president known as PDBs, short for Presidential Daily Briefs. (An example would be the PDB for August 6, 2001, which included the memo from British intelligence, discussed in Chapter 5, which reportedly indicated that terrorists planned to use hijacked airliners as missiles to hit targets inside the United States.) According to the agreement accepted by Kean, the White House would be allowed to edit these briefs before sending them to the commission. And then only a few members of the commission would be allowed to see even these edited briefs. Then, besides only being able to take notes on these edited briefs, they would have to show these notes to the White House.[25] As Cleland described the deal that was struck:

> A minority of the commissioners will be able to see a minority of the [PDB] documents that the White House has already said is pertinent. And then a minority of the commissioners themselves will have to brief the rest of the commissioners on what the White House thinks is appropriate.... [B]ut first they have to report to the White House what they're going to tell the other commissioners.[26]

This agreement, continued Cleland, means that the commissioners are not able "to fulfill their obligation to the Congress and the American people." Whereas the commissioners are supposed to get access to all the documents they need, "the president of the United States is cherry-picking what information is shown to what minority of commissioners"—a situation that Cleland labeled "ridiculous."

This decision produced the first public split within the commission. Cleland, a Democrat, called the deal a "bad deal," adding that

> this independent commission should be independent and should not be making deals with anybody.... I don't think any independent commission can let an agency or the White House dictate to it how many commissioners see what.... [W]e shouldn't be dealing. If somebody wants to deal, we issue subpoenas.

In his strongest charge, Cleland said: "[T]hat decision compromised the mission of the 9/11 commission, pure and simple."[27] Fellow Democrat Timothy Roemer also rejected this decision, complaining that the White House might pass along "only two or three paragraphs out of a nine-page report," thereby allowing it to hide any "smoking guns."

This decision was also labeled "unacceptable" by the Family Steering Committee for the 9/11 Independent Commission, which declared: "The commission should issue a statement to the American public fully explaining why this agreement was chosen in lieu of issuing subpoenas to the CIA and executive branch." Spokesperson Kristen Breitweiser added: "This is an independent commission that is supposed to be transparent."[28]

Given these developments, everyone now, including those who fervently want the president and his administration to be freed from any suspicion of complicity in the events of 9/11, should support the authorization of a full investigation led by someone, perhaps a special prosecutor, whose independence cannot reasonably be doubted.[29] Everyone should now favor this regardless of the conclusions of the 9/11 Independent Commission. That is, if the commission's conclusion is that there was, or at least may have been, complicity by the Bush administration, that conclusion would rather obviously require the appointment of a special prosecutor. Alternatively, if the commission denies that there was any complicity, perhaps by failing even to raise the question, a new investigation would be needed for the reason given above—namely, that there will be widespread suspicion that the Bush administration, through its selection of the chairman and executive director combined with its obstructionism, prevented the truth from being discovered.[30]

Recent Events

After the manuscript for this book was essentially finished, several events occurred that drove home even more clearly the need for a new investigation. These events involved publications, two presidential candidates, a lawsuit, and the 9/11 Independent Commission.

Publications: Several recent publications, by raising the kinds of questions dealt with in this book, suggest that these disturbing questions, far from going away, will continue to be raised until credible answers are provided.

One of these publications was an article in the *Guardian* in September of 2003 by former British Minister of the Environment Michael Meacher. Pointing out that the 2000 document produced by the Project for the New American Century (PNAC) says that its agenda will be difficult to implement without "a new Pearl Harbor," Meacher suggested that this document "provides a much better explanation of what actually happened before, during, and after 9/11 than the global war on terrorism thesis." With regard to events prior to 9/11, he said that "US authorities did little or nothing to pre-empt the events of 9/11" even though "at least 11 countries provided advance warning to the US of the 9/11 attacks."[31] With regard to 9/11 itself, he said that with all the advance warnings America had, the slow reaction was "astonishing."

Not a single fighter plane was scrambled to investigate from the US Andrews airforce base, just 10 miles from Washington DC, until after the third plane had hit the Pentagon at 9.38 AM.[32] Why not? There were standard FAA intercept procedures for hijacked aircraft before 9/11.... It is a US legal requirement that once an aircraft has moved signifi- cantly off its flight plan, fighter planes are sent up to investigate.

Meacher then asked the crucial question:

Was this inaction simply the result of key people disregarding, or being ignorant of, the evidence? Or could US air security operations have been deliberately stood down on September 11? If so, why, and on whose authority?

Meacher then quoted the former US federal crimes prosecutor, John Loftus, as having said:

The information provided by European intelligence services prior to 9/11 was so extensive that it is no longer possible for either the CIA or FBI to assert a defence of incompetence.

With regard to the American response after 9/11, Meacher said that

9/11 offered an extremely convenient pretext to put the PNAC plan into action.[33]

Meacher's article evoked much response. The nature of some of it was reflected in the title of an article, "Fury Over Meacher Claims," written by Ewen MacAskill, the *Guardian's* diplomatic editor.[34] As MacAskill reported, a spokesman for the US embassy in London said:

Mr. Meacher's fantastic allegations—especially his assertion that the US government knowingly stood by while terrorists killed some 3,000 innocents in New York, Pennsylvania and Virginia—would be monstrous, and monstrously offensive, if they came from someone serious or credible.

Having made such "fantastic allegations," Meacher could be dismissed as neither serious nor credible, in spite of having been the UK's environment minister for several years (who as such would have known something about internal discussions of coming oil shortages). Equally dismissive was an article in London's *Sunday Times*, which said that Meacher had "lurched into the twilight zone."[35]

At the same time, Meacher's article evoked a remarkable amount of support. One letter to the editor from America said: "It is obvious to me that the 'fury' attributed to representatives of my government derives from their understanding that his views cut close to the bone." Another American wrote: "Please let Mr. Meacher know that, despite howls of outrage and denial at his forthright analysis, there are many of us who have long made the same deductions. My gratitude to the *Guardian* for having the courage to publish it." A writer from England said: "Kudos to Mr. Meacher for being the first prominent British politician to say what many have long known. But when will other senior Labour members have the courage to support him?"[36]

In any case, a week later, Meacher, perhaps rejecting the support he had received as well as the vilification, wrote a second letter, which began:

> Contrary to the wilful misrepresentation by some of my article, I did not say at any point, and have never said, that the US government connived at the 9/11 attacks or deliberately allowed them to happen. It need hardly be said that I do not believe any government would conspire to cause such an atrocity.[37]

He had only, he claims, argued that the US government had exploited 9/11 as a pretext to carry out its already formulated agenda for Iraq and Afghanistan.

However, given Meacher's question whether US security forces were "deliberately stood down" and his rejection of a defense based on "incompetence," the readers could surely be forgiven for having thought that he had charged official complicity.[38] But even if one accepts Meacher's statement that his original article was not meant to "suggest a conspiracy theory," its central point remains valid—that the failure of the US government to give satisfactory answers to the questions it raised "has provided ample ammunition to those who do." Accordingly, his article, along with the positive responses it evoked, points to the increasing sense that we need an investigation aimed at answering these questions.

Shortly after the Meacher flap an article appeared on the front page of the *Wall Street Journal* entitled "Conspiracy Theories About September 11 Get Hearing in Germany."[39] While pointing out that books containing such theories have also become best-sellers in France, Italy, and Spain, this article said that such books have been especially well received in Germany, where a recent public opinion poll showed 20 percent of the citizens believing that "the U.S. government ordered the attacks itself." This article focused in particular on a best-selling book by Andreas von Bülow.[40] Besides pointing out that von Bülow had been a long-time member of parliament after having been "one of the top officials in the West German defense department," this article added that his book was put out by "one of the country's most prestigious publishing houses."

Ian Johnson, the author of this article, suggested that Germany is especially hospitable to 9/11 conspiracy theories, with their "improbable and outrageous assertions," because Germany has become increasingly hostile to American foreign policy. Johnson's article has, nevertheless, alerted a significant readership to the fact that the charge of official US complicity has been made by a highly credible public figure in Germany and is widely believed.

A month after Meacher's original article appeared, freelance journalist Paul Donovan published a criticism of journalists who had attacked Meacher. Complaining that many journalists seemed to be seduced by power, Donovan complained that although the "premier role of the journalist should be as a check on power...many seem to...get greater job satisfaction as parrots of the official truth." After briefly recounting what he called "the staggering story of the events of 9/11," Donovan said:

> No reasons have been given for the Bush administration's conduct on that day, no one has been brought to account. Yet from the tragedy that was 9/11 Bush has been able to deliver for his backers in the arms and oil industries. The President has also been able to portray himself as a wartime leader. This is the real story that journalists should be probing at and uncovering, not decrying the likes of Meacher who has at least had the guts to stand up and say what many have suspected for some time.[41]

During the same period in which the Meacher, Johnson, and Donovan pieces were appearing, a new book by Michael Moore—*Dude, Where's My Country?*—was published. Whatever one thinks of Moore, his books attract a huge readership (his previous book, *Stupid White Men*, was the best-selling nonfiction book of 2002–2003). In this new book's first chapter, entitled "George of Arabia," Moore addresses seven questions to President Bush. One of them asks about Bush's behavior in the classroom on 9/11, but most of them deal with the relationship between him and the Saudi royal family, the bin Laden family, and the

Taliban. Moore's own hunch as to what really happened is evidently reflected in his third question to President Bush: "Who attacked the United States on September 11—a guy on dialysis from a cave in Afghanistan, or your friends, Saudi Arabia?"[42]

Moore's strongest statement is one that provides a possible answer to why the White House has been impeding the 9/11 Independent Commission and also to why the press and the American people in general have been so passive. Having asked why Bush does not "stop prohibiting the truth from coming out," Moore suggests:

> Perhaps it's because George & Co. have a lot more to hide beyond why they didn't scramble the fighter jets fast enough on the morning of September 11. And maybe we, the people, are afraid to know the whole truth because it could take us down roads where we don't want to go.

This latter supposition—which is in harmony with Dan Rather's statement that it is fear that has kept the press from asking the difficult questions—is probably correct.

It is indeed frightening to think that perhaps our government did, Michael Meacher's later statement notwithstanding, "conspire to cause such an atrocity." It is especially frightening to consider the implications of such a conspiracy if it included the FBI, the CIA, the Justice Department, and the Pentagon. It might seem prudent simply to "let sleeping dogs lie." If the suspicions are correct, however, these dogs are not sleeping, but are using the official account of 9/11 for various nefarious purposes, both within our country and the rest of the world. Also, if we suspect foul play but keep silent out of fear, we can say farewell to any pretense to being the "land of the free and the home of the brave." And, in fact, to being a democracy. We may simply have to go "down roads where we don't want to go."

That some members of the American press may be ready to do this is suggested by the publication on September 11, 2003, of an online article by William Bunch of the *Philadelphia Daily News* entitled "Why Don't We Have Answers to These 9/11 Questions?"[43] This is the article, referred to in the Introduction, that asks "why after 730 days do we know so little about what really happened that day?" To illustrate how much is still unknown, Bunch asks 20 questions, about half of which overlap with the central questions of the present book. He then asks why "a docile mainstream media" has not demanded answers to these questions.

Perhaps his article in the United States, like Donovan's article in the United Kingdom, is a sign that the press is ready to become less docile.

A Candidate's Statement about an "Interesting Theory": During an interview on National Public Radio on December 1, 2003, Democratic presidential candidate Howard Dean was asked, "Why do you think he [Bush] is suppressing that [Sept. 11] report?" He replied: "I don't know. There are many theories about it. The most interesting theory that I've heard so far...is that he was warned ahead of time by the Saudis. Now who knows what the real situation is?"[44]

The task of disciplining Dean and warning others not to express such thoughts in public was taken on by Charles Krauthammer. In a *Washington Post* article entitled "Delusional Dean," Krauthammer said that Dean's statement—that "the most interesting" theory...is that Bush knew about Sept. 11 in advance"—is evidence that Dean had been struck by a new psychiatric condition that is abroad in the country. Krauthammer labels this condition BDS, or "Bush Derangement Syndrome," defined as "the acute onset of paranoia in otherwise normal people in reaction to the policies, the presidency—nay—the very existence of George W. Bush."

Krauthammer's piece provides an example of the standard approach taken by defenders of the official account. Rather than dealing with any of the problems in this account, they simply declare that all theories of official complicity are so obviously absurd that anyone taking such theories seriously must have deep psychological problems. Any problem with the official account alleged by critics, such as evidence that the Bush administration had more information about the attacks in advance than it has admitted, is dismissed *a priori.* The official account is thereby protected from scrutiny, and other people are warned not to raise questions.

Although Krauthammer's article was obviously intended to be cleverly humorous, its serious intent was made clear by the following comparison:

> When Rep. Cynthia McKinney (D-GA) first broached this idea [that Bush had advance knowledge] before the 2002 primary election, it was considered so nutty it helped make her *former* representative McKinney. Today the Democratic presidential front-runner professes agnosticism as to whether the president of the United States was tipped off about 9/11 by the Saudis, and it goes unnoticed. The virus is spreading.[45]

Writing several days after Dean's statement was broadcast, Krauthammer appeared alarmed that Dean's statement had not evoked the same outcry that was raised against Congresswoman McKinney. Just as she was convicted in the press and the court of public opinion of being too "nutty" to remain in office, Krauthammer was suggesting, the press and the public should have taken Dean's statement as evidence that he, too, is unfit for public office.

In alluding to Cynthia McKinney's defeat in 2002, Krauthammer was presupposing the conventional wisdom as to the "lesson" to be drawn from it—namely, that it is political suicide for any candidate, even a Democrat, to raise the question of whether the president had prior knowledge about the attacks of 9/11. An examination of the circumstances surrounding McKinney's defeat, however, suggests that this might not necessarily be the case. There are at least three factors to be taken into consideration.

In the first place, McKinney's questions about 9/11 were conflated by the press with her statements about the subsequent wars, with the result that it appeared to most people that she had charged not only that the president had specific foreknowledge of the attacks but that he had allowed them to happen for a very particular reason. A story in the *Orlando Sentinel*, for example, claimed that McKinney had asserted "that President George W. Bush knew about the 9-11 attacks in advance and did nothing to prevent them. Why? So that all his cronies could get rich on the subsequent military buildup."[46] A story in the *New York Times* said: "Ms. McKinney suggest[ed] that President Bush might have known about the September 11 attacks but did nothing so his supporters could make money in a war."[47] As Greg Palast and others have shown, however, the idea that McKinney charged Bush with allowing the attacks for this reason resulted from an illegitimate conflation of some of McKinney's statements. Palast even presents good reason to believe that a similar conflation lay behind the belief that McKinney had charged the Bush administration with having had specific knowledge of the attacks in advance.[48] Palast argues, in fact, that McKinney's real position was similar to his own, according to which several warnings had been given, so that the fact that the attacks were *not* anticipated in time to prevent them pointed to a massive intelligence failure, for which the president's policies were at least partly responsible.[49] In any case, whatever McKinney's actual intent, she was not presented to the public as having simply suggested that there should be an investigation of whether the Bush administration had prior knowledge.

There is, furthermore, a second reason why her electoral defeat does not necessarily mean that making such a suggestion would be political suicide, even for a Democrat. In Georgia, voters in a primary election are allowed to "cross over," so that registered Republicans, for example, can choose to vote in the Democratic primary. According to McKinney's account of what happened, another black woman, with positions closer to those of the Republican party, was urged by Republicans to run against McKinney in the primary, after which "Republicans fed her campaign coffers and then 48,000 of them crossed over and voted for her."[50] Although Georgia's voting laws make it impossible to know how many cross-over voters there actually were, McKinney's general claim is supported by John Sugg, senior editor of Atlanta's weekly paper, who said: "Republicans crossed over in droves to vote in the Democratic primary."[51]

Still another relevant fact concerns an online poll set up on April 17 by the *Atlanta Journal-Constitution*. The poll's question was based on the assumption that McKinney had charged that the president had advance knowledge of the attacks. People were asked: "Are you satisfied the Bush administration had no advance warning of the September 11 attacks?" Given the fact that the *AJC* was one of the newspapers that led the attack on McKinney, the purpose of the poll was evidently to show that McKinney's charge had little if any public support. But according to NewsMax.com—a website that shared the *AJC*'s hostility to McKinney—only 52 percent responded affirmatively. Two percent of the respondents chose the answer, "I'm not sure. Congress should investigate," while the other possible answer, "No, I think officials knew it was coming," was selected by 46 percent of the responders. Hence the title put on the story: "Poll Shocker: Nearly Half Support McKinney's 9/11 Conspiracy Theory." The writer of this story, which was posted shortly after 3:30 PM, added: "Though over 23,000 *Atlanta Journal-Constitution* readers had responded by midafternoon, the poll has been mysteriously withdrawn from the paper's web site."[52]

Such polls are not, of course, scientific. But this one does raise an interesting question, which is what the results of a scientific poll taken in the United States would be. No such poll has been taken—perhaps on the basis of the old advice: "If you don't want to know the answer, don't ask the question." But perhaps if such a poll were to be taken, we would find that public opinion in America regarding the Bush administration's relation to 9/11 is closer to public opinion in Germany than had been assumed. It is, at least, an interesting question, which could be tested.

In any case, these three facts—that Cynthia McKinney's "charge" was distorted, that apart from the cross-over vote she might not have been defeated, and that a remarkable percentage of the people in the Atlanta area evidently believed already in April of 2002 that "officials knew it was coming"—suggest that her defeat does not necessarily prove that it would be political suicide for any politician to point to evidence suggesting that the Bush administration had foreknowledge of the attacks.

Be that as it may, the fact that the question of such foreknowledge was raised by a presidential candidate, whose question was then publicized by a prominent journalist, provides yet further evidence that an investigation into this very question is needed.

Ellen Mariani's Complaint: Still further evidence is provided by another recent event—a lawsuit that makes a charge not wholly unlike the charge Cynthia McKinney was thought to have made.[53] On November 26, 2003, attorney Philip J. Berg held a news conference in Philadelphia to announce that Ellen Mariani, whose husband was on United Airlines Flight 175, had filed a Federal Court Complaint against President Bush and several members of his cabinet under the RICO (Racketeer Influenced and Corrupt Organizations) Act.[54] This Complaint alleges that George W. Bush (GWB) and other officials—including John Ashcroft, Dick Cheney, Condoleezza Rice, Donald Rumsfeld, and George Tenet—are guilty "for 'failing to act and prevent' the murder of Plaintiff's husband, Louis Neil Mariani, for financial and political reasons" and that they "have 'obstructed justice' in the aftermath of said criminal acts and omissions."[55] In elaborating on this summary charge, the Complaint says, among other things:

> Defendant GWB "owed a duty" not only to Plaintiff, but the American People to protect and defend against the preventable attacks based upon substantial intelligence known to Defendant GWB prior to "911" which resulted in the death of Plaintiff's husband and thousands of other innocent victims on "911."...

Defendant GWB has not been forthright and honest with regard to his administration's pre-knowledge of the potential of the "911" attacks and Plaintiff seeks to compel Defendant GWB to justify why her husband Louis Neil Mariani died on "911."...[T]he compelling evidence that will be presented in this case through discovery, subpoena power by this Court and testimony at trial will lead to one undisputed fact, Defendant GWB failed to act and prevent "911" knowing the attacks would lead to our nation having to engage in an "International War on Terror (IWOT)" which would benefit Defendants both financially and for political reasons....

Plaintiff believes, Defendant GWB et al, allowed the attacks to take place to compel public anger and outcry to engage our nation and our military men and women in a preventable "IWOT" for personal gains and agendas....

Special Agent Robert Wright wrote a memo on June 9, 2001, warning his superiors, Defendant DOJ/FBI of the potential of terrorists hijacking aircraft to attack the United States and two (2) months later, Defendant GWB's National Security Advisor, Defendant Condoleezza Rice, acknowledged that on August 6, 2001...she provided a written brief to Defendant GWB at his Texas ranch which warned "OBL" might try to hijack US aircraft. Plaintiff...[has] a "right to know" why these reports provided Defendant GWB were not acted upon to prevent the most deadly attacks against our nation since Pearl Harbor, which led us into World War II, as "911" is now leading us into the never ending "IWOT." From the mountain of evidence and the ongoing "secrecy" of Defendant GWB and his unwillingness to cooperate with the "911 Commission," Plaintiff brings this RICO Act civil action to obtain justice for herself and husband Louis Neil Mariani and to expose the "truth" to the American public as to the great betrayal Defendants have inflicted upon each and every freedom-loving American arising from the crimes prior to, during and after "911."[56]

Besides providing copies of this Complaint, Berg also handed out an open letter to the president from Ellen Mariani. In this letter, she says

Stop blocking the release of certain evidence and documents that were discovered by the 9/11 Investigation Commission if you have nothing to hide proving you did not fail to act and prevent the attacks of 9/11. Your reason for not releasing this material is that it is a matter of "national security."...But...it is your personal credibility/security that you are concerned with....[57]

If this suit is allowed to go forward, which would mean that Mariani and Berg would have subpoena power, it may begin to provide answers to the disturbing questions that have been raised about 9/11.

This suit, along with the Dean–Krauthammer exchange and several recent publications, suggest that these questions will be raised with increasing frequency and intensity. More and more citizens will believe that the official account is a lie. The only solution compatible with a democratic form of government is an investigation that finally provides a credible account of what happened on 9/11. That this may need to be a *new* investigation has been further suggested by recent developments in relation to the 9/11 Independent Commission.

The 9/11 Independent Commission: In spite of all the problems that have hobbled this commission, many people, including leaders of the Family Steering Committee, had long held onto some hope that it would finally provide answers to at least some of the many unanswered questions. But that hope has been undermined by further developments. First, the previously discussed agreement by the commission to work out a deal with the White House, instead of using its subpoena power, gave support to the charge that it should be called "the 9/11 Coverup Commission."[58] Second, the commission lost its most outspoken critical member, Max Cleland.[59] Third, the question of conflicts of interest was raised anew in mid-January by the revelation in a *New York Times* story that the commission had interviewed two of its own members, executive director Philip Zelikow and commissioner Jamie Gorelick (who was a senior member of the Justice Department during the Clinton administration). This revelation raised the question with special intensity because Zelikow and Gorelick are "the only two commission officials with wide access to highly classified White House documents." When asked about the news that Zelikow had been interviewed, Kristen Breitweiser said: "He has a huge conflict of interest," adding: "This is what we've been concerned about from Day 1." Elaborating on this concern, she feared, she said, that the commission report "is going to be a whitewash."[60]

A fourth blow to the hope that the commission's report will answer at least some of the questions will be delivered if the commission's request for additional time is refused. As we saw earlier, commission members had long worried that the obstacles created by the White House would make it impossible for them to complete their work by the end of May. Late in January, the commission formally requested that it be given a few months more so that its work could be, in the words of Timothy Roemer, "credible and thorough." But the initial response to this request was negative. The commission members should "be able to meet that deadline," said a spokesperson for the administration, since "[t]he administration has given them an unprecedented amount of cooperation."[61]

In an article about this response (entitled "What's Bush Hiding From 9/11 Commission?"), Joe Conason said that from the outset "Mr. Bush has treated the commission and its essential work with contempt," continually working "to undermine, restrict and censor the investigation of the most significant event of his Presidency." Referring to a report in *Newsweek* that the administration gave the commission the choice of meeting the May deadline or postponing release of the report until December—which would be, of course, after the November elections—Conason commented: "Mr. Bush doesn't want his re-election subject to any informed judgment about the disaster that reshaped the nation and his Presidency."[62]

Nevertheless, in spite of the continued stonewalling, the commission, according to the most recent reports as this book was going to press, was not planning to issue subpoenas to President Bush, Vice President Cheney, or other administration officials to require them to testify under oath.[63]

These recent developments have evidently been the final straw for at least some members of the Family Steering Committee. According to a story in the *Washington Post*, "The commission's handling of the deadline has angered a group of relatives of Sept. 11 victims, who argue that the panel has not been aggressive enough in demanding more time and in seeking key documents and testimony from the Bush administration." The reporter then quoted Kristen Breitweiser as saying: "We've had it.... It is such a slap in the face of the families of victims. They are dishonoring the dead with their irresponsible behavior."[64] Implicit in her statement would seem to be the conclusion that unless there is a radical change in the attitude and tactics of the 9/11 Independent Commission in its final months, a new investigation will be needed if there is to be any hope for discovering the truth.

A 9/11 Truth Candidate

One more recent event reinforcing the need for a full investigation is the emergence of a presidential candidate running on this issue. This candidate, a Republican named John Buchanan, has said in a stump speech:

> I stand here as a 9/11 Truth Candidate and some may thus dismiss me as a single-issue candidate and in a narrow sense that is true. But if you consider that 9/11 has led us into fiscal ruin, endless war and constitutional twilight, my issue is the mother issue of our age.

Saying that "[w]e have all been lied to about 9/11," Buchanan recited many of the facts reported in the present book. He then closed his speech by urging his hearers to support Ellen Mariani as "one of the heroes of this cause" and to read Nafeez Ahmed's *The War on Freedom* and Paul Thompson's 9/11 timeline.[65]

Buchanan is highly critical of the mainline press for not questioning "the scores of 9/11 lies and contradictions" or even telling the public that there are "still unanswered questions." This same press may now be reluctant to tell the public about the existence of "a 9/11 truth candidate." But his very existence, combined with the fact that millions of Americans will know about him through other sources, provides yet another reason for concluding that a full investigation, one that examines the evidence for official complicity, is a necessity.

NOTES

Frequently Cited Works

Ahmed, Nafeez Mosaddeq. *The War on Freedom: How and Why America Was Attacked September 11, 2001.* Joshua Tree, Calif.: Tree of Life Publications, 2002.

Chossudovsky, Michel. *War and Globalisation: The Truth Behind September 11.* Canada: Global Outlook, 2002.

Meyssan, Thierry. *9/11: The Big Lie.* London: Carnot, 2002 (translation of *L'Effroyable imposture* [Paris: Les Editions Carnot, 2002]).

——. *Pentagate.* London: Carnot Publishing, 2002 (translation of *Le Pentagate* [Paris: Les Editions Carnot, 2002]).

Thompson, Paul. "September 11: Minute-by-Minute," Center for Cooperative Research. After the first citation in a chapter, this timeline will be cited simply as Thompson, followed by the time. For example: Thompson (8:55 AM) or Thompson, 8:55 AM, depending how he marks it on his website.

——. "Was 9/11 Allowed to Happen? The Complete Timeline," Center for Cooperative Research. After the first citation in a chapter, this timeline will be cited simply as "Timeline," followed by the date under which the information is found. Both timelines are available on the website for the Center for Cooperative Research (www.cooperativeresearch.org).

Introduction

[1] James Bamford, *Body of Secrets: Anatomy of the Ultra-Secret National Security Agency* (New York: Anchor Books, 2002), 633.

[2] *Washington Post,* January 27, 2002.

[3] Henry Kissinger, "Destroy the Network," *Washington Post,* September 11, 2001 (washingtonpost.com), quoted in Thierry Meyssan, *9/11: The Big Lie* (London: Carnot, 2002), 65.

[4] Lance Morrow, "The Case for Rage and Retribution," *Time,* September 11, 2001.

[5] The Project for the New American Century, *Rebuilding America's Defenses: Strategy, Forces and Resources for a New Century* (www.newamericancentury.org), 51. This document will be discussed further.

[6] John Pilger, *New Statesman,* December 12, 2002.

[7] Leonard Wong, Institute of Strategic Studies, *Defeating Terrorism: Strategic Issues Analysis,* "Maintaining Public Support for Military Operations" (http://carlisle-www.army.mil/usassi/public.pdf), quoted in *9/11: The Big Lie,* 127.

[8] On these restrictions and their consequences, see Nancy Chang, *Silencing Political Dissent: How Post-September 11 Anti-Terrorism Measures Threaten Our Civil Liberties,* Foreword by Howard Zinn (New York: Seven Stories, 2002).

[9] Phyllis Bennis, *Before and After: US Foreign Policy and the September 11th Crisis,* Foreword by Noam Chomsky (Northampton, Mass.: Olive Branch Press, 2003).

[10] See Richard W. Van Alstyne, *The Rising America Empire* (1960; New York: Norton, 1974); Walter LaFeber, *The New Empire: An Interpretation of American Expansion 1860–1898* (1963; Ithaca: Cornell University Press, 1998); Thomas J. McCormick, *China*

Market: America's Quest for Informal Empire, 1893–1901 (Chicago: Quadrangle Books, 1967); Lloyd C. Gardner, Walter F. LaFeber, and Thomas J. McCormick, *Creation of the American Empire* (Chicago: Rand McNally, 1973); Laurence Shoup and William Minter, *Imperial Brain Trust: The Council on Foreign Relations and United States Foreign Policy* (New York: Monthly Review Press, 1977); Anders Stephanson, *Manifest Destiny: American Expansion and the Empire of Right* (New York: Hill and Wang, 1995).

[11] "More than any single policy," says Bennis, "the biggest cause of international anger against the United States is the arrogance with which US power is exercised" (*Before and After*, xv).

[12] "Resisting the Global Domination Project: An Interview with Prof. Richard Falk," *Frontline*, 20/8 (April 12–25, 2003).

[13] For example, Rahul Mahajan, *The New Crusade: America's War on Terrorism* (New York: Monthly Review, 2002), 7.

[14] *New York Times*, September 11, 2002.

[15] William Bunch, "Why Don't We Have Answers to These 9/11 Questions?" *Philadelphia Daily News* online posting, September 11, 2003.

[16] The media in several other countries have, by contrast, presented investigative reports. In Canada, for example, journalist Barrie Zwicker presented a two-part examination, entitled "The Great Deception: What Really Happened on September 11th," on January 21 and 28, 2002 (*MediaFile*, Vision TV Insight [www.visiontv.ca]). In Germany, the public discussion has been such that a poll in July of 2003 revealed that 20 percent of the German population believed that "the US government ordered the attacks itself" (Ian Johnson, "Conspiracy Theories about September 11 Get Hearing in Germany," *Wall Street Journal*, September 29, 2003, A1).

[17] *Press Gazette*, August 15, 2002.

[18] Rather's remarks, made in a interview on Greg Palast's BBC television show *Newsnight*, were quoted in a story in the *Guardian*, May 17, 2002. This statement is quoted in Greg Palast, "See No Evil: What Bush Didn't (Want to) Know about 9/11," which is contained in Palast's *The Best Democracy Money Can Buy: The Truth about Corporate Cons, Globalization, and High-Finance Fraudsters* (Plume, 2003), which is the Revised American Edition of his 2002 book (with a different subtitle). This essay was also posted March 1, 2003, on TomPaine.com.

[19] "Remarks by the President in Photo Opportunity with the National Security Team" (www.whitehouse.gov/news/releases/2001/09/20010912-4.html).

[20] "President's Remarks at National Day of Prayer and Remembrance" (www.whitehouse.gov/news/releases/2001/09/20010914-2.html).

[21] The material in notes 19–21 is quoted in *9/11: The Big Lie*, 77, 76–77, 79.

[22] Jean Bethke Elshtain, *Just War Against Terror: The Burden of American Power in a Violent World* (New York: Basic Books, 2003), 2–3.

[23] See Michel Chossudovsky, *War and Globalisation: The Truth Behind September 11* (Canada: Global Outlook, 2002), and John McMurtry, *Value Wars: The Global Market Versus the Life Economy* (London: Pluto Press, 2002), Preface.

[24] Elshtain, 9.

[25] To some extent, this fact reflects a matter of principle—a concern that devoting attention to possible conspiracies is diversionary. Some of the reasons for this wariness are

valid. One concern is that a focus on exposing conspiratorial crimes of present office-holders may reflect the naive assumption that if only we can replace those individuals with better ones, things will be fine. Underlying that worry is the concern that a focus on conspirators can divert attention from the more important issue of the structural problems in the national and global order that need to be overcome. But although those dangers must be guarded against, we should also avoid a too strong dichotomy between structural and conspiratorial analysis. For one thing, although structural analysis is essential for any deep understanding of social processes, structures as such, being abstractions, do not enact themselves. They are influential only insofar as they are embodied in agents—both individual and institutional—who act in terms of them. These agents, furthermore, are not fully determined by the dominant values of their societies. They have degrees of freedom, which they can use to act in ways that are more or less wise, more or less just, and more or less legal. When political leaders enact policies that are egregiously unjust, dangerous, and even illegal, it is important to replace them with leaders who are at least somewhat better. Finally, and most important, the exposure of a conspiracy may, rather than diverting attention from a society's problematic structures, turn attention to them. For example, if it became evident that our national political leaders caused or at least allowed the attacks of 9/11 and that they did so partly because they had deeply embodied certain values pervasive of our society, we might finally decide that a society-wide reorientation is in order.

[26] This practice is, of course, not unique to America. It is generally agreed, for example, that the "Mukden incident," in which an explosion destroyed part of the Japanese railway in Manchuria, was engineered by Japanese army officers "as an excuse to conquer Manchuria" (Walter LaFeber, *The Clash: US–Japanese Relations Throughout History* [New York: Norton, 1997], 166).

[27] Rahul Mahajan, *Full Spectrum Dominance: US Power in Iraq and Beyond* (New York: Seven Stories, 2003), 59, 50, 48.

[28] Paul Thompson's main timeline, entitled "Was 9/11 Allowed to Happen? The Complete Timeline," lists possibly relevant events extending over many years and fills some 200 single-spaced pages.

[29] This is one respect in which Thompson sees himself as differing from some other researchers, such as Michael Ruppert, mentioned in note 36, below.

[30] Gore Vidal, *Dreaming War: Blood for Oil and the Cheney-Bush Junta* (New York: Thunder's Mouth/Nation Books, 2002); Nafeez Mosaddeq Ahmed, *The War on Freedom: How and Why America Was Attacked September 11, 2001* (Joshua Tree, Calif.: Tree of Life Publications, 2002). Vidal, one prominent member of the American left who has rejected the official account of 9/11, endorses Ahmed's book—calling it "the best, most balanced report, thus far" (14)—and summarizes some of its argument.

[31] See *Breakdown: How America's Intelligence Failures Led to September 11* (Washington: Regnery, 2002), by Bill Gertz, a journalist for the *Washington Times*. A more recent version of this thesis is provided in Gerald Posner, *Why America Slept: The Failure to Prevent 9/11* (New York: Random House, 2003). Posner attributes the failure to breakdowns (xi), blunders (xii, 169), missed opportunities (xii, 146), investigative mix-ups (34), mistakes (150, 155, 169), incompetence and bad judgment (142, 167), stifling bureaucracy (173), and especially the failure of agencies to share information with each other (35, 44–47, 59, 178). "The failure to have prevented 9/11," asserts Posner, "was a systemic one" (xii). The task before us, therefore, is simply to fix the system. As Walter Russell Mead says (without criticism) in a book review, "the message of *Why America Slept* is on balance a hopeful one.

Incompetence in our security establishment is something we can address" ("The Tragedy of National Complacency," *New York Times*, October 29, 2003).

[32] A Joint Inquiry into the attacks was carried out in 2002 by the intelligence committees of the US Senate and House of Representatives. Although this Joint Inquiry had completed its final report by December of 2002, the Bush administration long refused to allow it to be released. Only a very brief summary of this final report was made public (it can be read at http://intelligence.senate.gov/ press.htm under December 11, 2002). Finally, late in July 2003, the final report itself was released. Although discussions in the press described the report as surprisingly critical, the criticism was limited to charges of incompetence. Significant portions of the final report were, to be sure, deleted in the name of national security, but I see no reason to believe that these deletions—which reportedly involved foreign countries, especially Saudi Arabia—contained any accusations of complicity in 9/11 by US officials. Possible reasons for the inadequacy of the Joint Inquiry's report are discussed in Chapter 10.

[33] Although its official name is the National Commission on Terrorist Attacks upon the United States, it is informally known as the 9/11 Independent Commission. President Bush had long opposed the creation of any such commission, claiming that it would take resources away from the war on terrorism. But embarrassing revelations from the Joint Inquiry (see previous note) reportedly left him little choice (*Newsweek*, September 22, 2002). In November of 2002, Bush signed a bill establishing the commission (the website of which is www.9-11commision.gov). Problems in relation to this commission are discussed in Chapter 10.

[34] In the meantime, Thompson has been developing articles in which the material is organized in terms of a large number of topics, which continues to grow. He also has a growing number of articles in which he discusses various dimensions of the controversies about 9/11. His website is therefore becoming increasingly easy to use.

[35] Implicit in this statement is the fact that I do not endorse all arguments in the main sources I employ. Meyssan, for example, has some theories that I find implausible and others that seem at least insufficiently supported by evidence.

[36] One failing of this book is that I have usually made no effort to discern, with regard to various stories and facts reported, which investigator or researcher was first responsible for reporting them. This means that I have surely in many cases failed to give proper credit. One example involves the fact that I cite Paul Thompson's timelines abundantly while citing Michael Ruppert's website, From the Wilderness (www.fromthewilderness.com or www.copvcia.com), relatively rarely. And yet Ruppert was one of the earliest major critics of the official account of 9/11. In fact, in Thompson's statement of "credits and sources," he says: "This timeline started when I saw the excellent timeline at the From the Wilderness website and began adding to it. I found that timeline to be a great resource, but it wasn't as comprehensive as I wanted. My version has since grown into something of a monster, but the inspiration still lies with From the Wilderness" (www.cooperativeresearch.org/timeline/index.html). Ruppert, furthermore, is simply one example of several researchers, such as Jared Israel, who were publishing information challenging the official account almost immediately after 9/11. To try to sort all of this out in order to assign proper credit, however, would detract from the task of getting the challenge to the official account into the public discussion. Most researchers, as far as I can tell, seem more interested in this than in receiving credit. The question of proper credit, in any case, is one that would appropriately be answered by some historian of this movement if it is successful.

[37] In suggesting that there are many disturbing questions that have thus far not been answered, I am to some extent reflecting the attitude of the organizations formed by families of the victims of the attacks, one of which is, in fact, called "Unanswered Questions" (see www.UnansweredQuestions.org). Other organizations with websites include Family Steering Committee for the 9/11 Independent Commission (www.911independentcommission.org), Voices of September 11th (www. voicesofsept11.org), 9-11 Citizens Watch (www.911Citizenswatch.org), and the 9/11 Visibility Project (www.septembereleventh.org).

[38] This book, cited in previous notes, is a translation of Meyssan's *L'Effroyable imposture* (Paris: Les Editions Carnot, 2002).

[39] This view of the White House could be combined with any of the previous five views insofar as those views deal only with the involvement of other US agencies. This sixth view, therefore, has five possible versions. The same is true of the seventh and eighth views.

[40] Elshtain, 2–3.

[41] Michael Parenti, *The Terrorism Trap: September 11 and Beyond* (San Francisco: City Lights, 2002), 69, 70.

[42] Parenti, 70–71, citing Patrick Martin, "US Planned War in Afghanistan Long Before September 11," World Socialist Conference, November 20, 2001 (www.wsws.org/articles/2001/nov2001/afghn20.html); the quoted words, which summarize Martin's position, are Parenti's.

[43] I emphasize this point because some polemicists, when confronted by a book whose conclusion they do not like, seek to undermine this conclusion by focusing on the few points that they believe can be most easily discredited. That tactic, assuming that good evidence is really presented against those points, is valid with regard to a deductive argument. In relation to a cumulative argument, however, it is tactic useful only to those concerned with something other than truth.

[44] Michael Moore, *Dude, Where's My Country?* (New York: Warner Books, 2003), 2.

[45] To refine the point a little more: There are some conspiracy theories that, although we may not be convinced of their truth, we find at least *plausible*, so we are willing to entertain the possibility that they might be true. We are open, accordingly, to reading and hearing evidence intended to support them. There are other conspiracy theories, by contrast, that we find completely *implausible*, so we tend to suspect the intelligence or sanity of people who believe them or who even entertain the possibility of their truth. Whatever facts they offer as evidence we reject out of hand, holding that, even if we cannot explain these facts, the true explanation cannot be the one they are offering. But the question of what we find completely implausible—"beyond the pale"—is seldom determined simply by a dispassionate consideration of empirical evidence. Plausibility is largely a matter of one's general worldview. We are also influenced to some degree by wishful-and-fearful thinking, in which we accept some ideas partly because we hope they are true and reject other ideas because we would find the thought that they are true too frightening. At least sometimes, however, we are able, in spite of our prejudgments, to revise our prior ideas in light of new evidence. Most revisionists about 9/11, in presenting their evidence, seem to be counting on this possibility.

Chapter 1: Flights 11 and 175: How Could the Hijackers' Missions have Succeeded?

[1] Paul Thompson explains: "The transponder is the electronic device that identifies the jet on the controller's screen, gives its exact location and altitude, and also allows a four-digit

emergency hijack code to be sent." See Thompson, "September 11: Minute-by-Minute" (After 8:13 AM).

[2] That Rumsfeld made this statement was reported by Republican Representative Christopher Cox on September 12, according to an Associated Press story of September 16, 2001, quoted in Thompson, 8:44 AM. Incidentally, as one becomes familiar with the vast amount of material about 9/11 available on the Internet, one learns that there is little about the official account that is uncontested. Even the idea that what hit the North Tower of the WTC was AA Flight 11 has been challenged. In note 32, below, I mention this and some other theories not discussed in the text.

[3] The FAA's *Aeronautical Information Manual: Official Guide to Basic Flight Information and Air Traffic Control (ATC) Procedures* (www.faa.gov), quoted in Thompson, "September 11," introductory material.

[4] Congressional testimony by NORAD'S commander, General Ralph E. Eberhart, made in October 2002, and *Slate* magazine, January 16, 2002, both quoted in Thompson, "September 11," introductory material. Although both statements were preceded by "now," suggesting a speed-up in procedure since 9/11, there seems to be no evidence that response times were different prior to that date. That should, in any case, be easy enough for investigators to determine.

[5] Nafeez Mosaddeq Ahmed, *The War on Freedom: How and Why America Was Attacked September 11, 2001* (Joshua Tree, Calif.: Tree of Life Publications, 2002), 151. (A nautical mile is a little longer than a statute mile.) Since this book by Ahmed is the only writing by him that I use, it will henceforth be cited simply as "Ahmed."

[6] MSNBC, September 12, 2001, quoted in Thompson, "September 11," introductory material.

[7] Ahmed 146, citing the FAA's *Aeronautical Information Manual*, "Interception Signals" (www.faa.gov).

[8] Glen Johnson, "Facing Terror Attacks Aftermath," *Boston Globe*, September 15, 2001, quoted in Ahmed, 148.

[9] Ahmed, 157–58, and Illarion Bykov and Jared Israel, "Guilty for 9-11: Bush, Rumsfeld, Myers, Section 1: Why Were None of the Hijacked Planes Intercepted?", both referring to the interview with Vice President Cheney on NBC's "Meet the Press," September 16, 2001. The article by Bykov and Israel, along with several other articles on 9/11 by Israel, can be found at www.emperors-clothes.com/ indict/911page.htm. This particular article is listed in the Table of Contents under "Evidence of high-level government conspiracy in the events of 9-11."

[10] General Henry Shelton was still the chairman, but on 9/11 he was reportedly out of the country. Myers, who was vice chairman, had just been named as Shelton's replacement and was functioning as the acting chairman.

[11] Myers Confirmation Testimony, Senate Armed Services Committee, Washington, DC, September 13, 2001, cited in Thompson (After 8:48 AM).

[12] Ahmed, 167.

[13] Chairman of the Joint Chiefs of Staff Instruction 3610.01A, June 1, 2001, "Aircraft Piracy (Hijacking) and Destruction of Derelict Airborne Objects" (www.dtic.mil), referred to in Thierry Meyssan, *Pentagate* (London: Carnot Publishing, 2002), 147.

[14] *Pentagate*, 110–11, quoting Department of Defense Directive 3025.15, February

18, 1997, "Military Assistance to Civil Authorities" (www.nci.org). Meyssan hence disagrees with researchers who have accepted the view that, in Ahmed's words, "only the President had the authority to order the shooting down of a civilian airliner" (167).

[15] Thompson, 8:43 AM.

[16] *New York Times*, September 11, and *USA Today*, September 3, 2002, quoted in Thompson (8:55 AM).

[17] *Newhouse News*, January 25, 2002, quoted in Thompson, 8:43 AM.

[18] "US Senator Carl Levin (D-MI) Holds Hearing on Nomination of General Richard Myers to be Chairman of the Joint Chiefs of Staff," Senate Armed Services Committee, Washington DC, September 13, 2001, quoted in Ahmed, 150.

[19] Glen Johnson, "Otis Fighter Jets Scrambled Too Late to Halt the Attacks," *Boston Globe*, September 15, and NBC's "Meet the Press," September 16, 2001, quoted in Ahmed, 150. Cheney made no reference to jets being only a few minutes late.

[20] Israel and Bykov, "Guilty for 9-11," quoted in Ahmed, 168.

[21] Although this new version was in the air a few days earlier, NORAD made it official on September 18 in a press release, in which it gave the times at which, it said, it was notified by the FAA and at which it gave scramble orders (available at www.standdown.net/noradseptember182001pressrelease.htm).

[22] Allan Wood and Paul Thompson, "An Interesting Day: President Bush's Movements and Actions on 9/11," Center for Cooperative Research (www.cooperativeresearch.org), under "Bush is Briefed as the Hijackings Begin."

[23] *Aviation Week and Space Technology*, June 3, 2002, cited in Thompson, 8:52 AM.

[24] George Szamuely, "Scrambled Messages," *New York Press*, 14/50 (www.nypress.com/14/50/taki/bunker.cfm), cited in Ahmed, 151–52.

[25] Thompson, 8:52 AM, citing NORAD, September 18, 2001.

[26] Ahmed, 151.

[27] Stan Goff, "The So-Called Evidence is a Farce," Narco News #14: October 10, 2001 (www.narconews.com), quoted in Ahmed, 173 n. 313.

[28] Andreas von Bülow, *Tagespiel*, January 13, 2002, quoted in Ahmed, 144. Von Bülow later came out with a book, *Die CIA und der 11. September: Internationaler Terror und die Rolle der Geheimdienste* (Munich: Piper Verlag, 2003), which is briefly discussed in the final chapter.

[29] Anatoli Kornukov, *Pravda Online*, September 13, 2001 (http://english. pravda.ru), quoted in Ahmed, 163–64.

[30] Ahmed, 164, 167.

[31] Israel and Bykov, "Guilty for 9-11," quoted in Ahmed, 169.

[32] There are, furthermore, many questions that I have not broached in the text. One of these is whether the airplanes that crashed into the towers were really being flown by hijackers, or were instead being guided by remote control, perhaps using the Global Hawk technology developed by the Defense Department, which has been functioning at least since 1997 and enables an airplane to fly itself, from takeoff through landing (Thompson, "Timeline," 1998 [A] and April 23, 2001). Meyssan believes that this is likely, partly because he considers it improbable that amateur pilots could have hit those

relatively narrow targets so accurately with Boeing airliners, which have low maneuverability. He finds this especially improbable with regard to Flight 175, which "was forced to execute a complex rotation maneuver, particularly difficult facing the wind." Professional pilots he consulted, he reports, "confirmed that few amongst themselves could envisage performing such an operation and completely ruled it out in the case of amateur pilots" (*9/11: The Big Lie*, 33–34).

In relation to this theory, Thompson reports that Flights 11, 175, and 77, all of which had surprisingly few passengers for transcontinental flights (81, 56, and 58, respectively), each had at least one passenger who was a senior official in Raytheon's division of Electronics Warfare, which developed the Global Hawk technology ("Timeline," September 25, 2001). Since such officials would presumably not have sacrificed themselves willingly, this curious fact would seem to make sense only in conjunction with the view, held by some revisionists mainly on the basis of video evidence, that the Twin Towers were not hit by Flights 11 and 175 but instead by military planes. Some who hold this theory believe that the purpose of turning off the transponders was to allow the switch to be made. In any case, this theory would raise the question of what really happened to these two flights and their passengers (just as the theory that the Pentagon was not really hit by Flight 77, to be discussed in Chapter 2, raises the question of what happened to this flight and its passengers). This theory would also seem to imply that the flight training undergone by the alleged hijackers, to be discussed in Chapters 6 and 8, was for the sake of creating a plausible cover story. (On the reason for referring to the *alleged* hijackers, see the section on "The Question of the True Identity of the Hijackers" in Ch. 6.) In any case, the fact that I have not discussed these more radical challenges to the official account in the text does not necessarily reflect my judgment that they are not true. It simply reflects my judgment that, whatever their merits, they are not necessary for the purpose of this book, which is not to explain "what really happened" but merely to summarize what seem to be the strongest reasons that have been given for considering the official account to be false (so as to show the need for a full investigation to *find out* what really happened). And the evidence against the official account of the failure to prevent the attacks on the WTC is very strong independently of any of these more radical challenges. (In the latter part of this chapter and in the following chapter, by contrast, I do deal with the question of what really happened insofar as it is integral to the critics' challenges to the official account.)

[33] Throughout most of the period during which I was working on this book, I had ignored this issue, having decided on the basis of an early, cursory reading of some of the arguments that the evidence against the official view was not strong enough to include. As with other matters, however, I eventually found that my initial impression was faulty. When I finally took a serious look at the case that has been marshalled against the official account of the collapse of the WTC buildings, I found this case, especially with regard to WTC-7, to constitute one of the strongest arguments on behalf of the need for a new investigation.

[34] See FEMA's Report #403, *World Trade Center Building Performance Study* (May, 2002; available at www.fema.gov/library/wtcstudy.shtm).

[35] Bill Manning, "$elling Out the Investigation," *Fire Engineering*, January, 2002, quoted in *The New York Daily News*, Jan. 4, 2002, and in Thompson, "Timeline," January 4, 2002.

[36] The NOVA show "Why the Towers Fell" appeared on PBS April 30, 2002 (www.pbs.org/wgbh/nova/transcripts/2907_wtc.html). Matthys Levy, author of *Why Buildings Fall Down* (New York: Norton, 1994), said on this show: "As the steel began to

soften and melt, the interior core columns began to give." The idea that steel melted has also been stated elsewhere, such as "The Physics of the 2001 World Trade Center Terrorism" (www.jupiterscientific.org/sciinfo/sot.html).

[37] "The Collapse: An Engineer's Perspective," NOVA interview with Thomas Eagar (www.pbs.org/wgbh/nova/wtc/collapse.html).

[38] Perhaps as an overreaction, some critics of the official account, in rejecting what they call the "truss theory," seem to affirm that the core and perimeter columns were connected by full-fledged beams instead of thinner trusses. The history of the construction of the Twin Towers, however, reveals that they were unique (at the time) in this respect. For this history, see James Glanz and Eric Lipton, *The Rise and Fall of the World Trade Center* (New York: Times Books/Henry Holt & Company, 2003). Glanz is a science writer for the *New York Times*.

[39] *Scientific American*, October, 2001. The statements by both McNamara and FEMA are quoted in Eric Hufschmid, *Painful Questions: An Analysis of the September 11th Attack* (Goleta, Calif.: Endpoint Software, 2002), 17. This beautifully self-published book can be purchased at PainfulQuestions@aol.com.

[40] In an article headed "Preliminary Tests Show Steel Quality Did Not Contribute to Towers' Collapse" (Associated Press, August 27, 2003), Devlin Barrett quoted Frank Gayle, who is leading the review of the WTC collapses by the National Institute of Standards and Technology (NIST), as saying that all the steel tested at least met the requirement to bear 36,000 pounds per square inch and that it was often capable of bearing as much as 42,000 pounds.

Incidentally, as Glanz and Lipton explain (*The Rise and Fall of the World Trade Center*, 333), Sherwood Boehlert, the (Republican) Chair of the House Science Committee, got the US Congress in October of 2002 to pass the National Construction Safety Team Act, which authorized an investigation of the collapse of the WTC by NIST, which is a nonpolicy-making part of the US Commerce Department's Technology Administration (its Fact Sheet on the WTC investigation can be seen at www.nist.gov/public_affairs/factsheet/nist_investigation_911.htm).

[41] Thomas Eagar and Christopher Musso, "Why Did the World Trade Center Collapse? Science, Engineering, and Speculation," *JOM* 53/12 (2001), 8-11. Musso was at the time a Ph.D. student. *JOM* is the journal of the Minerals, Metals, and Materials Society.

[42] Hufschmid (see note 39), 27-30.

[43] "The Collapse: An Engineer's Perspective."

[44] Ibid. This point is likewise emphasized in Hufschmid, 32-33, who also makes the next point, about the length of time.

[45] See note 39, above.

[46] Hufschmid, 35.

[47] See Hufschmid, 39. Indeed, a third photograph, looking directly into the hole created by the airplane, reveals two people standing in a room, far removed from any of the flames (27).

[48] Technically, as Hufschmid points out (30), the South Tower had two or even three fireballs.

[49] For a picture of the North Tower fireball, see Hufschmid, 30.

[50] In Hufschmid's words, "that jet fuel burned so rapidly that it was just a momentary

blast of hot air. The blast would have set fire to flammable objects, killed people, and broken windows, but it could not have raised the temperature of a massive steel structure by a significant amount. A fire will not affect steel unless the steel is exposed to it for a long...period of time" (33).

[51] Hufschmid, 38.

[52] With regard to the fire in the South Tower in particular, Hufschmid asks, rhetorically: "How could a fire produce such incredible quantities of heat that it could destroy a steel building, while at the same time it is incapable of spreading beyond its initial starting location? The photos show that *not even one floor* in the South Tower was above the ignition temperature of plastic and paper!...The photos show the fire was not even powerful enough to crack glass [windows]!...Why is there no evidence of an intense fire in *any* photograph? How can anybody claim the fires were the reason the South Tower collapsed when the fires appear so small?" (38)

[53] Quoted in Hufschmid, 38. Evidence against the fire theory is even presented in Appendix A of FEMA's report on the WTC, which says: "In the mid-1990s British Steel and the Building Research Establishment performed a series of six experiments at Cardington to investigate the behavior of steel frame buildings.... Despite the temperature of the steel beams reaching 800–900° C (1,500–1,700° F) in three of the tests..., no collapse was observed in any of the six experiments."

[54] Eagar and Musso; Eagar, "The Collapse."

[55] "The Collapse."

[56] Eagar and Musso.

[57] Quoted in Hufschmid, 42–43.

[58] Hufschmid, 42.

[59] This objection is raised, in slightly different form, in Peter Meyer, "The World Trade Center Demolition and the So-Called War on Terrorism" (www.serendipity.li/wtc.html), section entitled "Evidence for Explosives in the Twin Towers."

[60] Hufschmid, 73.

[61] Eagar and Musso.

[62] Meyer, "The World Trade Center Demolition," section entitled "Evidence for Explosives in the Twin Towers."

[63] This point is emphasized in Fintan Dunne, "The Split-Second Error: Exposing the WTC Bomb Plot" (www.psyopnews.com or www.serendipity.li), section entitled "The Wrong Tower Fell First." Some defenders of the official account have suggested that the fact that the South Tower collapsed more quickly could be explained by the fact that it was struck at the 81st floor and hence about 15 floors lower than the North Tower, which was struck at the 96th floor. Because there were more floors above the weakened portion of the South Tower, accordingly, the additional weight would have led to its faster collapse. The problem with this theory, Hufschmid says, is that "the steel columns in the crash zone of the South Tower were thicker in order to handle the heavier load above them" (41).

[64] Meyer, "The World Trade Center Demolition and the So-Called War on Terrorism," section entitled "Evidence for Explosives in the Twin Towers."

[65] Ibid., section entitled "Did the Twin Towers Collapse on Demand?"

[66] Hufschmid, 45.

[67] Jeff King, "The WTC Collapse: What the Videos Show," Indymedia Webcast News, Nov. 12, 2003 (http://ontario.indymedia.org/display.php3?article_id=7342&group=webcast).

[68] Hufschmid, 50, 80. On the amount of the dust, see www.public-action.com/911/jmcm/usyd/index.htm#why. Mike Pecoraro, quoted in note 74, below, wrote about his experience of walking down the street: "When I tell you the stuff (dust) on the street was a foot deep, that's conservative. I'd say over a foot deep. It was like walking through a blizzard of snow" (quoted in "We will Not Forget: A Day of Terror," *The Chief Engineer* (www.chiefengineer.org/article.cfm?seqnum1=1029).

[69] King, "The WTC Collapse."

[70] Hufschmid, 78.

[71] See especially the photographs on 52-55, 57, 60, and 74.

[72] See especially the photographs on 60 and 61.

[73] Hufschmid, 50.

[74] One of the firefighters in the South Tower, Louie Cacchioli, told *People Weekly* on Sept. 24: "I was taking firefighters up in the elevator to the 24th floor to get in position to evacuate workers. On the last trip up a bomb went off. We think there were bombs set in the building." Kim White, an employee on the 80th floor, said: "All of a sudden the building shook, then it started to sway. We didn't know what was going on.... We got down as far as the 74th floor.... [T]hen there was another explosion" (http://people.aol.com/people/special/0,11859,174592-3,00.html; quoted in Meyer's section "Evidence for Explosives in the Twin Towers"). Construction worker Phillip Morelli reported that while he was in the fourth subbasement of the North Tower, he was thrown to the floor twice. Whereas the first of these experiences apparently occurred at the time of the plane crash, the second one involved a more powerful blast, which blew out walls (http://ny1.com/pages/RRR/911special_survivors.html). Stationary engineer Mike Pecoraro, who was working in the sixth subbasement of the North Tower, reported that after feeling and hearing an explosion, he and his co-worker found the parking garage and the machine shop, including a 50-ton hydraulic press, reduced to rubble. They also found a 300-pound steel and concrete fire door wrinkled up "like a piece of aluminum foil." These effects were, he said, like the effects of the terrorist bombing of 1993 ("We will Not Forget: A Day of Terror," *The Chief Engineer* (www.chiefengineer.org/article.cfm?seqnum1=1029). These latter two stories are contained in "First-hand Accounts of Underground Explosions in the North Tower" (www.plaguepuppy.net/public_html/underground/underground_explosions.htm).

[75] Hufschmid, 73; Christopher Bollyn, "New Seismic Data Refutes Official WTC Explanation," American Free Press, September 3, 2002 (www.rense.com/general28/ioff.htm). Columbia University's data can be seen at www.ldeo.columbia.edu/LCSN/Eq/20010911_wtc.html; it is partially reproduced in Hufschmid, 73 and 78.

[76] Hufschmid, 73, 77.

[77] Likewise Peter Tully, president of Tully Construction of Flushing, reportedly said that he saw pools of "literally molten steel." Both statements are quoted in Bollyn, "New Seismic Data Refutes Official WTC Explanation."

[78] See Hufschmid, 70, 78, 80.

[79] *The New York Times*, Dec. 25, 2001, and *Fire Engineering*, January 2002, quoted in Thompson, December 25, 2001, and January 4, 2002, respectively.

[80] The official investigators found that they had less authority than the clean-up crews, a fact that led the Science Committee of the House of Representatives to report that "the lack of authority of investigators to impound pieces of steel for examination before they were recycled led to the loss of important pieces of evidence" (see the report at www.house.gov/science/hot/wtc/wtc-report/WTC_ch5.pdf).

[81] Meyer, "The World Trade Center Demolition and the So-Called War on Terrorism," section entitled "Evidence for Explosives in the Twin Towers." However, as James Glanz has reported ("Reliving 9/11, With Fire as Teacher," *New York Times*, Science Section, January 6, 2004), it turns out that 236 major pieces of steel were recovered by NIST (see note 40, above). Whether any of these pieces show signs of explosives is presumably something that we will learn near the end of 2004, when NIST's report is due.

[82] Those who accept this theory of controlled demolition are made additionally suspicious by the report that Marvin P. Bush, the president's younger brother, was a principal in a company called Securacom, which provided security for the World Trade Center (as well as United Airlines), especially when this news is combined with testimony from WTC personnel that after the security detail had worked 12-hour shifts for the previous two weeks because of threats, five days before 9/11 the security alert, which had mandated the use of bomb-sniffing dogs, was lifted ("The World Trade Center Demolition: An Analysis" [www.whatreallyhappened.com/shake2.html]).

[83] FEMA's report on WTC-7 is found in Chapter 5 of FEMA's *World Trade Center Building Performance Study*. For a copy of this report with critical commentary interspersed, see "The FEMA Report on the Collapse of WCT Seven is a Cruel Joke" (http://ontario.indymedia.org/display.php3?article_id=14727&group=webcast). The same article is published elsewhere as "Chapter 5-WTC Seven-the WTC Report" (http://guardian.911review.org/WTC/WTC_ch5.htm).

[84] See the report at www.house.gov/science/hot/wtc/wtc-report/WTC_ch5.pdf.

[85] Hufschmid, 62, 63.

[86] See Hufschmid, 68-69.

[87] Some people, to be sure, have spread the idea that tremors created by the collapse of the Twin Towers caused Building 7 to collapse. But even the most powerful earthquakes have not caused the complete collapse of steel-framed buildings. And how would one explain the fact that the Verizon, Federal, and Fiterman Hall Buildings, all right next to WTC-7, did not collapse?

[88] Scott Loughrey, "WTC-7: The Improbable Collapse" (http://globalresearch.ca/articles/LOU308A.html).

[89] Hufschmid, 64.

[90] Hufschmid, 64, 65.

[91] Hufschmid, 70, 78.

[92] Bollyn, "New Seismic Data Refutes Official WTC Explanation."

[93] FEMA, *World Trade Center Building Performance Study*, Ch. 5, Sect. 6.2, "Probable Collapse Sequence."

[94] NOVA, "Why the Towers Fell."

Chapter 2: Flight 77: Was it really the Aircraft that Struck the Pentagon?

[1] Meyssan, *Pentagate*, 88. That there was concern in the Bush administration to squelch this rumor is suggested by the fact that Vice President Cheney, in his appearance on "Meet the Press" on September 16, took time to refute it even though he had not been asked about it. In response to a simple comment about Flight 77, Cheney said that the terrorists, after capturing this plane, "turned off the transponder, which led to a later report that a plane had gone down over Ohio, but it really hadn't. Of course, then they turned back and headed back towards Washington" (quoted in Meyssan, *9/11: The Big Lie*, 165).

[2] *USA Today*, August 13, 2002, quoted in Ahmed, 44.

[3] Meyssan, *Pentagate*, 96.

[4] ABC News, September 11, 2002; see also *Pentagate*, 94.

[5] *Boston Globe*, November 23, cited in Thompson, "September 11" (9:33–9:38 AM).

[6] CBS News, September 21, 2001, quoted in Thompson (9:33–9:38 AM).

[7] *Telegraph*, December 16, 2001, quoted in Thompson (9:38 AM).

[8] ABC News, October 24, 2001, quoted in *Pentagate*, 96–97.

[9] "Extensive Casualties in Wake of Pentagon Attack," *Washington Post*, September 11, 2001, quoted in *Pentagate*, 38–39.

[10] Quoted under "What about All the Witnesses?" in Killtown's "Did Flight 77 Really Crash into the Pentagon?" (thewebfairy.com/killtown/flight77).

[11] CNN, September 12, 2001, quoted in *Pentagate*, 48. The person to whom this statement about "a cruise missile with wings" was attributed was Mike Walter of *USA Today*. But he has also been quoted as saying that it was "an American Airlines plane." Walter's testimony is discussed further in note 55.

[12] "Minute by Minute with the Broadcast News," PoynterOnline, September 11, 2001, cited in *Pentagate*, 88.

[13] *Guardian*, April 1, 2002, quoted in Thompson, "Timeline," early March 2002. Thompson reports—citing the European version of *Time*, May 20, 2002—that Meyssan's first book on this subject, *l'Effroyable imposture* (Paris: Les Editions Carnot, 2002), while being widely denounced by the French media, set a French publishing record for first-month sales. (This is, as mentioned earlier, the book translated as *9/11: The Big Lie*.)

[14] Victoria Clarke, Department of Defense News Briefing, June 25, 2002, quoted on Thierry Meyssan's website (www.effroyable-imposture.net or www. reseauvoltaire.net).

[15] This would be one possible translation of the title of Meyssan's first book on the issue, mentioned in note 13, *l'Effroyable imposture*.

[16] Meyssan, *Pentagate*, 92.

[17] Gerry J. Gilmore, "Alleged Terrorist Airliner Attack Targets Pentagon," *American Forces Information Service*, Defense Link, DoD, September 11, 2001 (www.defenselink.mil/news/Sep2001/n09112001_200109111.html), quoted in *Pentagate*, 96.

[18] "Hijacked Jets Fly into Trade Center, Pentagon," *Los Angeles Times*, September 11, 2001, quoted in *Pentagate*, 96.

[19] *Washington Post*, September 12, and *Newsday*, September 23, 2001, cited in Thompson (Between 8:55–9:00 AM).

[20] *Pentagate*, 89.

[21] *Pentagate*, 98–99, citing *Sydney Morning Herald*, March 20, 2002. Olson's statement, made before the Supreme Court, was also quoted in Jim Hoagland, "The Limits of Lying," *Washington Post*, March 21, 2002.

[22] Thompson (9:25 AM) and (After 9:30 AM).

[23] Thompson (9:30 AM), citing stories from *Scotland Sunday Herald*, September 16, and *Cox News*, October 21, 2001. Anyone who questions the reality of the reported call from Barbara Olson, of course, would probably also question the reported statement by the hijackers, but that does not undermine the validity of Thompson's question. His question merely points out that although these two elements are crucial to the official account, because they reputedly provide evidence that Flight 77 was still aloft, there is a tension between these two elements.

[24] See "Hunt the Boeing. Test Your Perceptions" (www.asile.org/citoyens/ numero13/pentagone/erreurs_en.htm).

[25] This photograph, taken by Jason Ingersoll of the US Marine Corps, is available in Meyssan's *Pentagate* and on the "Hunt the Boeing" website. The quotation is from Marc Fisher and Don Phillips, "On Flight 77: 'Our Plane is Being Hijacked,'" *Washington Post*, September 12, 2001. In an e-mail letter, I asked Mr. Fisher is he knew where he got that information and also if he had "seen any reason in the intervening time to question whether the hole was this big." On January 16, 2004, he replied, saying: "I don't know where that detail came from and I don't know the size of the hole in the building, but that information could be obtained from the Pentagon easily enough."

[26] A photograph by Mark Faram and distributed by the Associated Press shows a little piece of twisted sheet metal colored red and white. Although this photo has been widely published as evidence of debris from Flight 77, the piece of metal it shows does not, points out Meyssan, correspond with any part of a Boeing 757 and was not included by the Department of Defense in the material said to have come from Flight 77 (*Pentagate*, page XVI of the photo section).

[27] This point is important in light of the claim of some defenders of the official account that the reason the plane did not cause much damage to the Pentagon is that it hit the ground first, thereby being greatly slowed down before it hit the Pentagon's facade. That claim co-exists rather uncomfortably, incidentally, with another claim meant to support the official account, which is that the reason the jet engines were not spotted by anyone is that they were pulverized when they hit the facade (see *Pentagate*, 14–17).

[28] This photograph, with the superimposition, is provided in *9/11: The Big Lie*, 22. A clearer version is included among the photos provided on the "Hunt the Boeing" website.

[29] *9/11: The Big Lie*, 22.

[30] This answer is given on a debunking website, Urban Legends (http://urbanlegends.about.com/library/blflight77.htm), which seeks to provide answers to the various questions posed in the "Hunt the Boeing" website, cited above. This answer is provided in response to the third question it lists.

[31] Urban Legends website, in response to the fifth question it lists.

[32] *Pentagate*, 33–34.

[33] Ibid., 54–55, 36.

[34] *9/11: The Big Lie*, 19.

[35] *Pentagate*, 53, 55, 60, 62.

[36] For these photos, which were provided by the Associated Press, see *Pentagate*, pages II and III of the photo section.

[37] *9/11: The Big Lie*, 27–28, 27

[38] *Pentagate*, 112.

[39] Ibid., 116, referring to the presentation of the AN/APX-100(V) transponder at www.globalsecurity.org.

[40] This question is raised, for example, in Thompson (9:33–9:38 AM).

[41] "DoD News Briefing," Defense Link, Department of Defense, September 12, 2001 (www.defenselink.mil/news/Sep2001/t09122001_t0912asd.html), quoted in *Pentagate*, 17.

[42] *Pentagate*, 19.

[43] "DoD News Briefing on Pentagon Renovation," Defense Link, Department of Defense, September 15, 2001, quoted in *Pentagate*, 18.

[44] *NFPA Journal*, November 1, 2001, cited in Thompson, "Timeline," November 21, 2001 (C). As Meyssan points out (*Pentagate*, 14–17), this argument has been articulated by many defenders of the official account.

[45] *Washington Post*, November 21, 2001, and *Mercury*, January 11, 2002, cited in Thompson, "Timeline," November 21, 2001 (C). An alternative version of the official account has the passengers identified by their DNA, but this version would face a similar difficulty.

[46] *Pentagate*, 175.

[47] "Pourquoi la démonstration de Meyssan est cousue de très gros fils blancs' blancs,'" *Libération*, March 30, 2001, quoted in *Pentagate*, 20.

[48] *Pentagate*, 20–21.

[49] Thompson, "Timeline," October 16, 2001, citing *New York Times*, October 16, 2001.

[50] Thompson, "Timeline," September 21, 2001, quoting the *Richmond Times-Dispatch*, December 11, 2001. It should be added that the reporter who wrote this story, Bill McKelway, accepted the official account, according to which it was Flight 77 that hit the Pentagon. He raised no questions as to why the FBI would have confiscated the video or how they could have gotten there "within minutes." We have no reason, therefore, to suspect that he fabricated this story.

[51] Jon Ungoed-Thomas, "Conspiracy Theories about 9/11 are Growing and Getting More Bizarre," *Sunday Times*, September 14, 2003.

[52] *Pentagate*, 42–46.

[53] Meyssan, *9/11: The Big Lie*, 27–28. One website (http://www.fas.org/man/ dod-101/sys/smart/bgm-109.htm) carries photographs of cruise missiles that show how similar they can look to small military planes.

[54] See urbanlegends.about.com/library/blflight77.htm.

[55] As mentioned in note 11, Walter at first said that it was like "a cruise missile with wings." He also made conflicting statements about whether he saw the aircraft (whatever it was) hit the Pentagon. The first quotations from him indicate that he did not—that the aircraft disappeared from his view behind a hill, after which he heard the explosion and saw the ball of fire. When he was interviewed by Bryant Gumbel on CBS September 12, he first

said that he saw an American Airlines jet and saw it hit the Pentagon. Under questioning from Gumbel, however, he said that his view was obstructed. An hour later on NBC, he repeated this latter affirmation, saying: "It kind of disappeared over this embankment here for a moment and then a huge explosion." All these statements are quoted in Gerard Holmgren, "Did F77 Hit the Pentagon? Eyewitness Accounts Examined," NYC IndyMediaCenter (http://nyc.indymedia.org/front.php3?article_id=25646).

[56] Holmgren, "Did F77 Hit the Pentagon? Eyewitness Accounts Examined."

[57] Dick Eastman, "What Convinced Me that Flight 77 Was Not the Killer Jet," Part 1, American Patriot Friends Network (http://www.apfn.org/ apfn/77_deastman1.htm). Incidentally, although Eastman supposes that the American airplane was Flight 77, his thesis would be consistent with its having been a different airplane. In any case, Eastman also discusses five frames from the Pentagon's security camera video that were released shortly after Thierry Meyssan's missile theory was published. Although the Pentagon meant for these frames to prove that a plane rather than a missile really was involved in the attack, Eastman reports that it was his scrutiny of these frames that first convinced him that the official story was false, because the aircraft on the video was much too short to have been a Boeing 757.

[58] Holmgren has said (personal correspondence on November 29, 2003) that he has tentatively accepted Eastman's two-aircraft hypothesis.

[59] *9/11: The Big Lie*, 19.

[60] *Los Angeles Times*, September 16, 2001, quoted in Thompson, 9:38 AM.

[61] Ahmed, 299–300.

[62] *9/11: The Big Lie*, 20.

[63] Thompson (9:33–9:38 AM).

[64] Ibid.

[65] Ahmed, 161–62, quoting Stan Goff, "The So-Called Evidence is a Farce," Narco News #14: October 10, 2001 (www.narconews.com).

[66] *New York Times*, May 4, 2002, and CBS News, May 10, 2002, quoted under "Was Hani Hanjour Even on Flight 77 and Could He Have Really Flown It to Its Doom?" in Killtown's "Did Flight 77 Really Crash into the Pentagon?" (thewebfairy.com/killtown/flight77), October 19, 2003.

[67] "Air Attack on Pentagon Indicates Weaknesses," *Newsday*, September 23, 2001, quoted in *Pentagate*, 112.

[68] Thompson, 9:33 AM.

[69] *Pentagate*, 91.

[70] Ahmed, 153.

[71] *Pentagate*, 115 (see also 174), quoting "PAVE PAWS, Watching North America's Skies, 24 Hours a Day" (www.pavepaws.org). "PAWS" stands for Phased Array Warning System.

[72] Ahmed, 153.

[73] *Washington Post*, September 12, NORAD, September 18, and Associated Press, September 19, 2001, cited in Thompson, 9:24 AM.

[74] Ahmed, 153–54.

[75] Thompson, 9:24 AM.

[76] *USA Today*, September 17, 2001, cited by Ahmed, 154, and Bykov and Israel, "Guilty for 9-11" (see note 9 of Ch. 1). General Larry Arnold said: "We [didn't] have any aircraft on alert at Andrews," MSNBC, September 23, 2001, quoted in Thompson (After 9:38 AM).

[77] Bykov and Israel, "Guilty for 9-11," and Ahmed, 154–55, citing DC Military (www.dcmilitary.com). Bykov and Israel report that, having found this website on September 24, 2001, they discovered a month later that the address had been changed, that the information about Andrews had been put in the smallest possible type, and that the official Andrews AFB website was "down" (although, they add, it could still be accessed through www.archive.org by entering www.andrews.af.mil). Bykov and Israel report that they maintain backups of the DC Military web pages for September and November at www.emperors-clothes.com/9-11backups/dcmilsep.htm and www.emperors-clothes.com/9-11backups/dcmil.htm.

[78] Thompson (After 9:03 AM).

[79] Ahmed, 155–56.

[80] Thompson (After 9:03 AM). This change is also reported by Bykov and Israel, "Update to Guilty for 9-11: Bush, Rumsfeld, Myers: Section 1," The Emperor's New Clothes (www.emperors-clothes.com).

[81] Thompson, 9:30 AM. Thompson's statement about the earliest "claim" as to when the crash occurred reflects the fact that the time has been placed variously between 9:37 and 9:45, with NORAD listing the earliest possible time, which would have given the fighter jets less time to get there. Thompson's own time, 9:38, differs little from NORAD's time, so his calculations would not be seriously changed by adopting NORAD's time.

[82] George Szamuely, "Nothing Urgent," *New York Press*, 15/2 (www.nypress.com/15/2/taki/bunker.cfm), quoted in Ahmed, 152.

[83] *Aviation Week and Space Technology*, June 3, CNN, September 4, and ABC News, September 11, 2002, cited in Thompson (After 8:46 AM).

[84] Thompson (9:03–9:08 AM), citing *USA Today*, September 12 and 13, 2002.

[85] *Telegraph*, September, 16, 2001, cited in Thompson, "Timeline," October 24–26, 2000.

[86] *Newsday*, September 23, 2001, cited in Thompson, 9:24 AM.

[87] *Washington Post*, September 12, 2001, *Guardian*, October 17, 2001, and Associated Press, August 19, 2002, cited in Thompson, 9:24 AM.

[88] Thompson, citing *New York Times*, September 15, 2001.

[89] The FBI statement was issued April 2, 2002. Victoria Clarke's statement was made at a Department of Defense News Briefing on April 24, 2002. Both statements are printed on Meyssan's website (www.effroyable-imposture.net).

[90] Barrie Zwicker, "The Great Deception: What Really Happened on September 11th Part 2," *MediaFile*, Vision TV Insight, January 28, 2002 (www.visiontv.ca), quoted in Ahmed, 169.

[91] Zwicker, "The Great Deception: What Really Happened on September 11th Part

1," January 21, 2002, quoted in Ahmed, 169–70.

[92] Gore Vidal, *Dreaming War: Blood for Oil and the Cheney-Bush Junta* (New York: Thunder's Mouth/Nation Books, 2002), 32.

[93] Parenti, *The Terrorism Trap: September 11 and Beyond* (San Francisco: City Lights, 2002), 93–94; Ahmed, 168 (emphasis original).

[94] Kristen Breitweiser appeared on Phil Donahue's show on August 13, 2002.

[95] The interview, conducted by *Parade* magazine, is available at www.defenselink.mil/news/nov2001/t11182001_t1012pm.html

Chapter 3: Flight 93: Was it the One Flight that was Shot Down?

[1] Thompson, "September 11" (8:42 AM), (9:27 AM), (9:36 AM), and (9:37 AM).

[2] Thompson, 9:45 AM.

[3] Thompson, 9:47 AM. Thompson says that of the numerous calls, only the first call (9:27 AM) from Tom Burnett mentioned guns—and this only in one of the versions, a fact that suggests that it may have been doctored.

[4] 9:54 AM, quoting *Toronto Sun*, September 16, and *Boston Globe*, November 23, 2001.

[5] 9:54 AM, quoting Jere Longman, *Among the Heroes: United Flight 93 and the Passengers and Crew Who Fought Back* (New York: HarperCollins, 2002), 118.

[6] (Between 10:00–10:06 AM).

[7] 9:58 AM.

[8] 9:58 AM, citing *Pittsburgh Post-Gazette*, September 28, 2002, and Longman, *Among the Heroes*, 180.

[9] 9:58 AM, quoting ABC News, September 11, and Associated Press, September 12, 2001.

[10] 9:58 AM, citing Longman, *Among the Heroes*, 264, and *Mirror*, September 13, 2002.

[11] (Between 10:00–10:06 AM), quoting *San Francisco Chronicle*, September 17, 2001.

[12] (Between 10:00–10:06 AM), quoting *Mirror*, September 13, 2002.

[13] 10:03 AM, citing *Philadelphia Daily News*, September 16, 2002.

[14] Thompson, "Timeline," October 16, 2001 (B), citing *New York Times*, October 16, 2001.

[15] Thompson (After 9:56 AM), citing *USA Today*, September 16, 2001, *Washington Post*, January 27, 2002, and ABC News, September 11, 2002.

[16] (After 9:56–10:06 AM), citing *Pittsburgh Post-Gazette*, October 28, 2001, and *Washington Post*, January 27, 2002.

[17] (After 9:56–10:06 AM), citing *Washington Post*, January 27, 2002.

[18] (After 9:56–10:06 AM), quoting ABC News, September 15, 2002.

[19] (10:08 AM), quoting *Washington Post*, January 27, 2002.

[20] (Before 10:06 AM), quoting Associated Press and *Nashua Telegraph*, both September 13, 2001.

[21] (Before and After 10:06 AM), quoting *Independent*, August 13, 2002.

[22] (Before and After 10:06 AM), citing *Indepedent,* August 13, 2002.

[23] (Before and After 10:06 AM), quoting *Mirror,* September 13, 2002.

[24] (Before 10:06 AM), citing *Philadelphia Daily News,* November 15; *Pittsburgh Post-Gazette,* September 12; *St. Petersburg Times,* September 12; and Cleveland Newschannel 5, September 11, 2001.

[25] (Before 10:06 AM), citing *Independent,* August 13, 2002, and quoting *Philadelphia Daily News,* November 15, 2001.

[26] (Before 10:06 AM), citing Reuters, September 13, and *Pittsburgh Tribune-Review,* and quoting *Pittsburgh Post-Gazette,* September 13, 2001.

[27] (Before 10:06 AM), quoting Reuters, September 13, 2001, and CBS News, May 23, 2002.

[28] (2:00 PM), citing *Aviation Week and Space Technology,* June 3, and *Cape Cod Times,* August 21, 2002.

[29] This interchange is quoted in *9/11: The Big Lie,* 162.

[30] Ahmed, 160, quoting *Boston Herald,* September 15, 2001.

[31] Thompson (After 9:56 AM).

[32] We do not know about the passengers on Flight 77. Revisionists can speculate that they too tried to gain control of their plane, which could explain its momentary deviation from course as well as its crash in Ohio or Kentucky—if that indeed is what happened to it.

[33] Thompson, 9:48 AM, citing Associated Press, August 19, 2002. That might have been the case, of course, only if both the Senate and the House were in session so that most senators and representatives would have been in the Capitol Building.

[34] *New York Times,* September 16, 2001, and ABC News, September 11 and 14, 2002, cited in Thompson (After 9:03 AM).

[35] CNN and *New York Times,* September 12, 2001, and *Washington Post,* January 27, 2002, cited in Thompson (9:45 AM).

[36] *Scotland Sunday Herald,* September 16, and Cox News, October 21, 2001, cited in Thompson (9:30 AM).

Chapter 4: The President's Behavior: Why Did He Act As He Did?

[1] Allan Wood and Paul Thompson, "An Interesting Day: President Bush's Movements and Actions on 9/11," Center for Cooperative Research (www.cooperativeresearch.org), under "When Did Bush First Learn of the Attacks," citing *New York Times,* September 15, and CNN, September 11, 2001. (This article will henceforth be cited simply as "Wood and Thompson," followed by the heading under which the material is found.)

[2] Barrie Zwicker, "The Great Deception," Vision TV Insight, *MediaFile* (www.visiontv.ca), February 18, 2002, cited in Ahmed, 166.

[3] Thompson, "September 11" (After 8:46 AM), quoting "Meet the Press," NBC News, September 16, 2001.

[4] CNN, December 4, 2001, *Daily Mail,* September 8, 2002, and ABC News, September 11, 2002, cited in Thompson (Between 8:55–9:00 AM).

[5] Thompson (Between 8:55–9:00 AM).

[6] *Time*, September 12, and *Christian Science Monitor*, September 17, 2001, cited in Thompson (Between 8:55–9:00 AM). A few minutes after 8:46, CIA Director Tenet reportedly learned from a cell phone call that the WTC had been "attacked" by an airplane, after which he said to Senator Boren, with whom he was having breakfast: "You know, this has bin Laden's fingerprints all over it" (ABC News, September 14, 2002, cited in Thompson [After 8:46 AM]).

[7] Associated Press, August 19, 2002, quoted in Thompson (Between 8:55–9:00 AM).

[8] Wood and Thompson, introductory discussion.

[9] *Sarasota Herald-Tribune*, September 10, 2002, quoted in Thompson (9:30 AM).

[10] *New York Times*, September 16, 2001, *Telegraph*, December 16, 2001, ABC News, September 14, 2002, and *Washington Post*, January 27, 2002, quoted in Thompson (After 9:30 AM).

[11] Thompson (After 9:30 AM) and (9:06 AM), quoting *Globe and Mail*, September 12, 2001.

[12] Wood and Thompson, under "Why Stay?"

[13] James Bamford, *Body of Secrets: Anatomy of the Ultra-Secret National Security Agency* (New York: Anchor Books, 2002), 633, cited in Thompson (9:06 AM).

[14] Bamford, 633.

[15] Bamford, 633, and *Time*, September 9, 2001, cited in Thompson (9:06–9:16 AM).

[16] Gail Sheehy, "Four 9/11 Moms Battle Bush," *New York Observer*, August 21, 2002.

[17] Sammon's sympathies are further shown by another book published at about the same time, *At Any Cost: How Al Gore Tried to Steal the Election* (Washington: Regnery, 2002).

[18] Bill Sammon, *Fighting Back: The War on Terrorism: From Inside the Bush White House* (Washington: Regnery, 2002), 89–90, quoted in Wood and Thompson, under "When Did Bush Leave the Classroom?"

[19] *Tampa Tribune*, September 1; *St. Petersburg Times*, September 8; and *New York Post*, September 12, 2002, cited in Wood and Thompson, under "when Did Bush Leave the Classroom?"

[20] Sammon, *Fighting Back*, 90, quoted in Wood and Thompson, under "When Did Bush Leave the Classroom?" and "Rewriting History."

[21] *San Francisco Chronicle*, September 11, 2002, quoted in Wood and Thompson, under "Rewriting History."

[22] MSNBC, September 9, 2002.

[23] Wood and Thompson, under "Rewriting History."

[24] Thompson, 9:29 AM.

[25] Wood and Thompson, under "Why Stay?", citing MSNBC, October 29, 2002, and ABC, September 11, 2002.

[26] Thompson (9:34 AM) and (9:56 AM). Air Force One took off at 9:35 AM. It would be at least 90 minutes before it had an escort (Wood and Thompson, under "When Does the Fighter Escort Finally Arrive?").

[27] Thompson (9:30 AM) and (10:42 AM), citing *Time*, September 14, *Los Angeles Times*, September 17, 2001, and *USA Today*, August 13, 2002.

[28] *New Yorker*, October 1, 2001, cited in Wood and Thompson, under "Air Force One Departs Sarasota." As Wood and Thompson also point out (under "Were There Threats to Air Force One?"), a little later in the day, Dick Cheney originated, and then Karl Rove and Ari Fleischer spread, a story that a threat against the White House and Air Force One was received from terrorists who used the secret code for Air Force One, which suggested either that there was a mole in the White House or that terrorists had hacked their way into White House computers. This story, first published by William Safire of the *New York Times* (September 13, 2001), spread throughout the media, although there was considerable skepticism, based on suspicion that the story was created to dampen down criticism of Bush for remaining away from Washington for so long (*St. Petersburg Times*, September 13, and *Telegraph*, December 16, 2001). When Ari Fleischer was pressed for credible evidence on September 15, he replied that that topic had already been exhausted. Finally, on September 26, CBS News laid the story to rest with this explanation: "Sources say White House staffers apparently misunderstood comments made by their security detail." *Slate* magazine gave its "Whopper of the Week" award to Cheney, Fleischer, and Rove (*Slate*, September 28, 2001). Unfortunately, Thierry Meyssan, having evidently missed the retraction, based his most speculative theory on this bogus report (*9/11: The Big Lie*, Ch. 3: "Moles in the White House"). But he can perhaps be forgiven, since CBS, evidently forgetting about its own debunking, revived the story a year later (CBS, September 11, 2002, cited in Wood and Thompson, under "Rewriting History").

[29] Wood and Thompson, under "Air Force One Takes Off Without Fighter Escort."

[30] Kristen Breitweiser's comments, made on Phil Donahue's television show on August 13, 2002, are quoted in Thompson, "Timeline," August 13, 2002.

[31] *Washington Post*, September 29, 2001, cited in Wood and Thompson, introductory discussion.

[32] CNN December 4, 2001, quoted in Thompson (9:01 AM).

[33] *Washington Times*, October 7, 2002, quoted in Thompson (9:01 AM).

[34] *Boston Herald*, October 22, 2002, quoted in Thompson (9:01 AM).

[35] Meyssan, *9/11: The Big Lie*, 38–39. Other revisionists have suggested that images of this crash might have been transmitted to the president's limousine, so that he would have seen them before arriving at the school.

[36] President Bush is not the only high official, furthermore, whose reported behavior that day has raised serious questions. Critics have also found the reported behavior of General Richard Myers, then Acting Chairman of the Joint Chiefs of Staffs, suspicious. See Israel and Bykov, "Guilty for 9–11: Bush, Rumsfeld, Myers" (www.emperors-clothes.com), who say that Myers "offered three mutually contradictory cover stories." See also Ahmed, 164–66.

Chapter 5: Did US Officials Have Advance Information About 9/11?

[1] This statement was made in Rice's press briefing of May 16, 2002, which was reported in the *Washington Post*, May 17, 2002. It was quoted by Mary Fetchet, Co-Chair of Voices of 9/11 and a member of the Family Steering Commission for the 9/11

Independent Commission, in testimony to that commission, March 31, 2003 (available at 911citizenswatch.org).

[2] *Sydney Morning Herald,* June 8, 2002, quoted in Thompson, "Timeline," June 4, 2002.

[3] The summary of this final report of the Joint Inquiry can be read at http://intelligence.senate.gov/press.htm under December 11, 2002.

[4] *Newsday,* September 23, 2001, quoted in "Timeline," September 11, 2001 (C).

[5] MSNBC, September 18, 2002, quoted in "Timeline," May 15, 2002.

[6] *Washington Post,* October 2, 2001, quoted in "Timeline," 1993 (C).

[7] *New York Times,* November 3, 2001, and *Time,* April 4, 1995, cited in "Timeline," April 3, 1995.

[8] *New York Times,* June 5, 2002.

[9] *New York Times,* October 3, 2001; Robert Novak, *Chicago Sun-Times,* September 27, 2001; "Western Intelligence Knew of Laden Plan Since 1995," Agence France-Press, December 8, 2001; *Washington Post,* September 23, 2001; and "Terrorist Plan to Use Planes as Weapons Dates to 1995: WTC Bomber Yousef Confessed to US Agents in 1995," Public Education Center Report (www. publicedcenter.org); cited in Ahmed, 83–84, and "Timeline," January 6, 1995.

[10] Ahmed, 84.

[11] Thompson, "Timeline," January 6, 1995, quoting *Washington Post,* September 23, 2001.

[12] Associated Press, April 18, 2002, quoted in "Timeline," September, 1999.

[13] MDW News Service, November 3, 2000, and *Mirror,* May 24, 2002, cited in "Timeline," October 24–26, 2000.

[14] "Timeline," May 21, 2002 (see also September 14, 2001).

[15] "Timeline," September 10, 2001, and June 18, 2002.

[16] "Timeline," May, 2001, citing *Los Angeles Times,* May 18, 2002, and the Senate Intelligence Committee, September 18, 2001.

[17] *Washington Post,* May 17, 2002, quoted in "Timeline," June 28, 2001.

[18] *Independent* and Reuters, both September 7, 2002, cited in "Timeline," late July 2001 (A).

[19] CBS News, July 26, 2001, cited in "Timeline," July 26, 2001.

[20] Associated Press, May 16, 2002, and *San Francisco Chronicle,* June 3, 2002, cited in "Timeline," July 26, 2001; *Washington Post,* May 27, 2002, cited in "Timeline," July 26, 2001.

[21] Agence France-Presse, November 22, 2001, *International Herald Tribune,* May 21, and *London Times,* May 12, 2002, cited in "Timeline," August 2001 (C).

[22] Robert Baer, *See No Evil: The True Story of a Ground Soldier in the CIA's War on Terrorism* (New York: Crown Pub, 2002), 270–71; Bill Gertz, *Breakdown: How America's Intelligence Failures Led to September 11* (Washington: Regnery, 2002), 55–58; and *Financial Times,* January 12, 2002; all cited in "Timeline," August 2001 (E).

[23] MSNBC, September 15, 2001, and Agence France-Presse, September 16, 2001, quoted in "Timeline," August 2001 (D).

[24] *Telegraph*, September 16, 2001, *Los Angeles Times*, September 20, 2001, Fox News, May 17, 2002, *International Herald Tribune*, May 21, 2002, and *New York Times*, June 4, 2002, cited in "Timeline," August 6, August 30–September 4, and late summer, 2001.

[25] David Wastell and Philip Jacobson, "Israeli Security Issued Warning to CIA of Large-Scale Terror Attacks," *Telegraph*, September 16, 2001, quoted in Ahmed, 114.

[26] *Newsweek*, May 27, 2002, *New York Times*, May 15, 2002, and *Die Zeit*, October 1, 2002, cited in "Timeline," August 6, 2001.

[27] *New York Times*, May 16, 2002, quoted in "Timeline," May 15, 2002.

[28] *Guardian*, May 19, 2002, quoted in "Timeline," May 15, 2002.

[29] Michael Moore, *Dude, Where's My Country?* (New York: Warner Books, 2003), 114. Incidentally, although Moore's book has a less than scholarly title and contains much humor, it is also a serious book based on remarkably good research. This is especially true of his first chapter, "George of Arabia," which is discussed at the end of this book.

[30] Ahmed, 118–24.

[31] Michael Ruppert, "Guns and Butter: The Economy Watch," available at "The CIA's Wall Street Connections," Centre for Research on Globalisation (http://globalresearch.ca), quoted in Ahmed, 122.

[32] *San Francisco Chronicle*, September 29, 2001, quoted in Ahmed, 118.

[33] Ahmed, 120, quoting Michael Ruppert, "Suppressed Details of Criminal Insider Trading Lead Directly into the CIA's Highest Ranks," From the Wilderness Publications (www.fromthewilderness.com or www.copvcia.com), October 9, 2001, and United Press International, February 13, 2001. On ECHELON, see Ahmed, 127–30.

[34] *Independent*, October 10, 2001, and Michael Ruppert, "Suppressed Details," cited in Ahmed, 124.

[35] *Newsweek*, October 1, 2001, quoted in Ahmed, 117.

[36] NBC News, October 4, 2001, quoted in Ahmed, 117.

[37] *USA Today*, June 4, 2002, quoted in "Timeline," September 10, 2001 (C).

[38] *Los Angeles Times*, December 22 and 24 and August 1, 2002, and *Independent*, June 6, 2002, cited in "Timeline," January 6, 1995; Knight Ridder, June 6, and *Independent*, June 6, 2002, cited in "Timeline," summer 2001.

[39] *Independent*, September 15, 2002, cited in "Timeline," September 10, 2001 (F).

[40] *Los Angeles Times*, December 12, 2003, reporting findings of the Congressional Joint Inquiry, cited in "Timeline," June 2001 (I).

[41] Associated Press and ABC News, both September 12, 2001, cited in "Timeline," September 11, 2001 (I).

[42] *Newsweek*, September 24, 2001, quoted in Ahmed, 125.

[43] Summary of the Final Report of the Joint Inquiry (http://intelligence. senate.gov/press.htm).

[44] Ahmed, 135 n. 169. Readers familiar with evidence that US intelligence agencies had advance knowledge of the attacks may wonder why I have not included the case of Delmart "Mike" Vreeland. After being jailed in Toronto on charges of fraud in August of 2001, Vreeland claimed to be an officer with US naval intelligence. Evidently in support of

this claim, Vreeland wrote something on a piece of paper, sealed it in an envelope, and gave it to Canadian authorities. Then on September 14, according to a newspaper story, these authorities opened the envelope and found that Vreeland's note had accurately predicted the attacks on the World Trade Center and the Pentagon. Vreeland's lawyers were evidently able to prove that he was indeed a naval officer on active duty. But although there was a lot of bitter controversy about this story, most of it was beside the point, because Vreeland's note could not reasonably be considered a prediction of the attacks of 9/11. Besides listing several sites other than the WTC and the Pentagon (such as the Sears Tower in Chicago and the Parliament Building in Ottawa), it also had no reference to 2001. The only dates on the note were 2007 and 2009. The note has been made available by From the Wilderness Publications (www.fromthewilderness.com/ free/ww3/01_28_02_vreeland.jpg).

[45] Chossudovsky, *War and Globalisation*, 145, 62.

Chapter 6: Did US Officials Obstruct Investigations Prior to 9/11?

[1] *New York Times*, September 18, 2002, cited in Thompson, "Timeline," December 4, 1998.

[2] "Timeline," January 25, 2001.

[3] This man's name is also sometimes spelled Massood, Massoud, Masoud, and Masud. I have followed Chossudovsky's spelling, Masood.

[4] ABC News, February 18, 2002, cited in "Timeline," 2001 (this item is placed at the beginning of the items for 2001).

[5] *Jane's Intelligence Review*, October 5, 2001, quoted in "Timeline," March 7, 2001.

[6] Richard Labeviere, "CIA Agent Allegedly Met Bin Laden in July," *Le Figaro*, October 31; Anthony Sampson, "CIA Agent Alleged to Have Met bin Laden in July," *Guardian*, November 1; Adam Sage, "Ailing bin Laden 'Treated for Kidney Disease,'" *London Times*, November 1; Agence France-Presse, November 1; Radio France International, November 1; and Reuters, November 10, 2001; cited in "Timeline," July 4–14 and July 12, 2001, and in Ahmed, 207–09.

[7] "Timeline," July 4–14, 2001.

[8] This statement (quoted in Ahmed, 209) occurs in Chossudovsky's Introduction to Labeviere's *Le Figaro* article (see note 6), which is on the website of the Centre for Research on Globalisation (www.globalresearch.ca/ articles/RIC111B.html), November 2, 2001.

[9] See the evidence in the section entitled "Bush and Bin Laden Family Ties" in Ahmed, 179–87.

[10] See the section entitled "Osama: Not a Black Sheep," in Ahmed, 178–79.

[11] See the sections entitled "Osama and the Saudis: A Covert Alliance," "The US–Saudi Alliance," and "Osamagate?" in Ahmed, 187–202.

[12] Patrick E. Tyler, "Fearing Harm, Bin Laden Kin Fled from US," *New York Times*, September 30, 2001, and Jane Mayer, "The House of Bin Laden: A Family's, and a Nation's, Divided Loyalties," *New Yorker*, November 12, 2001. (Michael Moore reports that it was reading these stories that first made him suspicious about the official account of 9/11; see *Dude, Where's My Country* [New York: Warner Books, 2003], 3–5.)

[13] *New Yorker*, January 14, 2002, cited in "Timeline," August 22, 2001 (B).

[14] CNN, January 8, 2002, and Lara Marlowe, "US Efforts to Make Peace Summed

Up by Oil," *Irish Times*, November 19, 2001, cited in "Timeline," Mid-July 2001, and Ahmed, 206.

[15] Ahmed, 191–92, quoting Tariq Ali, "The Real Muslim Extremists," *New Statesman*, October 1, 2001. A "Wahhabi" is a follower of Wahhabism, the extreme form of Muslim "fundamentalism" dominant in, and promoted by, Saudi Arabia.

[16] On Posner's general perspective about 9/11, see note 31 of the Introduction, above.

[17] Gerald Posner, *Why America Slept: The Failure to Prevent 9/11* (New York: Random House, 2003), 181–88. Posner's case for the credibility of this account is that, besides the fact that it was provided independently by two informants within the US government, he also had independent confirmation of the described interrogation techniques from a member of the Defense Intelligence Agency (180n.).

[18] Ibid., 188–93.

[19] Ibid., 193.

[20] Gregory Palast and David Pallister, "FBI Claims Bin Laden Inquiry Was Frustrated," *Guardian*, November 7, 2001, quoted in Ahmed, 111.

[21] "Above the Law: Bush's Radical Coup d'Etat and Intelligence Shutdown," *Green Press*, February 14, 2000 (www.greenpress.org), quoted in Ahmed, 186.

[22] Palast and Pallister, "FBI Claims Bin Laden Inquiry Was Frustrated," quoted in Ahmed, 111.

[23] "Excerpts from Report on Intelligence Actions and the September 11 Attacks," *New York Times*, July 25, 2003.

[24] *New York Times*, May 19 and 20, *Fortune*, May 22, and *Los Angeles Times*, May 26, 2002, cited in "Timeline," July 10 and December, 2001.

[25] *New York Times*, February 8, 2002, quoted in "Timeline," August 13–15, 2001.

[26] This warning was reported in Jean-Charles Brisard and Guillaume Dasquié, *Forbidden Truth: US–Taliban Secret Oil Diplomacy and the Failed Hunt for Bin Laden* (New York: Thunder's Mouth Press/Nation Books, 2002), 53–55. Brisard is a former agent of the French secret service. Wayne Madsen, in his introduction to the book, says that when the book was first published in France in November of 2001, "skeptics inside and outside the US government scoffed at the authors' contention that French intelligence had warned the FBI about the terrorist connections and ongoing flight training in the United States of Zacarias Moussaoui," but that they were then confronted with "incontrovertible validation of this information" when Coleen Rowley's memo became public (xv).

[27] *Time*, August 4, 2002, quoted in "Timeline," August 15 and August 22, 2001.

[28] *Newsweek*, May 20, 2002, quoted in "Timeline," August 23–27, 2001.

[29] *Time*, May 21 and May 27, and *New York Times*, August 27, 2002, quoted in "Timeline," August 23–27, 2001.

[30] Senate Intelligence Committee, October 17, 2002, and *Time*, May 21, 2002, cited in "Timeline," August 24–29, 2001.

[31] Senate Intelligence Committee, October 17, 2002, cited in "Timeline," August 28, 2001 (B).

[32] *Time*, July 21 and 27, 2002, and *Sydney Morning Herald*, July 28, 2002, cited in "Timeline," August 23–27 and August 28, 2001.

[33] *Time*, May 21 and 27, and *Sydney Morning Herald*, May 28, 2002, cited in "Timeline," August 23–27 and August 28, 2001.

[34] *Washington Post*, June 6, 2002, quoted in "Timeline," June 3, 2002.

[35] *New York Times*, December 22, 2001, quoted in Ahmed, 95.

[36] Senate Intelligence Committee, September 18, *Time*, May 21, and *New York Times*, May 30, 2002, cited in "Timeline," May 8, 2002.

[37] Ian Bruce, "FBI 'Super Flying Squad' to Combat Terror," *Herald*, May 16, 2002, quoted in Ahmed, 112, who also refers to Brian Blomquist, "FBI Man's Chilling 9/11 Prediction," *New York Post*, May 9, 2002 (www.nypost.com).

[38] *Time*, May 27, 2002, quoted in "Timeline," May 21, 2001 (A).

[39] *New York Times*, May 30, 2002, quoted in "Timeline," May 21, 2001 (A).

[40] United Press International, May 30, 2002, quoted in "Timeline," June 9, 2001.

[41] *LA Weekly*, August 2, 2002, quoted in "Timeline," May 30, 2002.

[42] ABC News, November 26 and December 19, 2002, quoted in "Timeline," October, 1998.

[43] Congressional Intelligence Committee, September 20, 2002, and *New York Times*, September 21, 2002, quoted in "Timeline," August 28, 2001 (A).

[44] *Washington Post*, May 19, Cox News, August 14, and Associated Press, October 18, 2002, cited in "Timeline," March 22, 2002.

[45] Alex Jones Show, October 10; *World Net Daily*, October 21; "David Schippers Goes Public: The FBI Was Warned," *Indianapolis Star*, October 13; and "Active FBI Special Agent Files Complaint Concerning Obstructed FBI Anti-Terrorist Investigations," *Judicial Watch*, November 14, 2001; cited in Ahmed, 107–09, and "Timeline," late July 2001 (B).

[46] William Norman Grigg, "Did We Know What Was Coming?", *New American* 18/5: March 11, 2002 (www.thenewamerican.com), cited in Ahmed, 110–11.

[47] "Catastrophic Intelligence Failure," Accuracy In Media (www.aim.org), September 24, 2001, quoted in Ahmed, 95–97.

[48] *New York Times*, September 21, *Telegraph*, September 23, 2001, and BBC, August 1, 2002, cited in "Timeline," September 16–23, 2001.

[49] Meyssan, *9/11: The Big Lie*, 54.

[50] *London Times*, September 20, 2001.

[51] Associated Press, November 3, 2002.

[52] "Timeline," September 16–23, 2001. One more intriguing bit of information that Thompson gives involves the reported telephone call from Amy Sweeney, a flight attendant on Flight 11, to American Airlines ground manager Michael Woodward, which began shortly after the plane was hijacked and continued until the plane hit the WTC. According to reports, she identified four hijackers, but they were *not* the four said to be on the plane (Thompson [8:21 AM], citing *Boston Globe*, November 23, 2001, and ABC News, July 18, 2002). Thompson adds that the *Boston Globe* says that it has a transcript of the call.

[53] "Timeline," May 2001 [C]), citing *San Francisco Chronicle*, October 4, and *Newsweek*, October 15, 2001.

[54] "Timeline," September 11, 2001 (J), citing Associated Press, October 5, 2001, *Boston Globe*, September 18, and *Independent*, September 29, 2001, along with *New Yorker*, October 1, 2001.

[55] ABC News, September 12 and 16, and Associated Press, September 16, 2001, cited in "Timeline," September 12, 2001.

[56] *Guardian*, March 19, 2002.

[57] *9/11: The Big Lie*, 56.

[58] Ahmed, 132, 110–11, quoting Dennis Shipman, "The Spook Who Sat Behind the Door: A Modern Day Tale," *IndyMedia*, May 20, 2002 (http://portland.indymedia.org), and William Norman Grigg, "Did We Know What Was Coming?" *New American* 18/5: March 11, 2002 (www.thenewamerican.com).

Chapter 7: Did US Officials Have Reasons for Allowing 9/11?

[1] These sources include Jean-Charles Brisard and Guillaume Dasquié, *Forbidden Truth: US–Taliban Secret Oil Diplomacy and the Failed Hunt for Bin Laden* (New York: Thunder's Mouth Press/Nation Books, 2002), and Ahmed Rashid, *Taliban: Militant Islam, Oil and Fundamentalism in Central Asia* (New Haven: Yale University Press, 2000).

[2] Ahmed, 55.

[3] Quoted in Phyllis Bennis, *Before and After: US Foreign Policy and the September 11th Crisis* (Northampton, Mass.: Olive Branch Press, 2003), 129. This quotation occurs in a section of her book headed "Oil, Oil Everywhere."

[4] Ahmed, 46–48, and Thompson, "Timeline," 1994 (B), citing *Times of India*, March 7, 2001, *Asia Times*, November 15, 2001, and CNN, October 5, 1996, and February 27, 2002.

[5] Rashid, *Taliban*, as quoted in Ted Rall, "It's All about Oil," *San Francisco Chronicle*, November 2, 2001.

[6] *Telegraph*, October 11, 1996, quoted in "Timeline," September 27, 1996.

[7] P. Stobdan, "The Afghan Conflict and Regional Security," *Strategic Analysis* 23/5 (August 1999): 719–47, cited in Ahmed, 50.

[8] "Timeline," August 9, 1998, quoting *New York Times*, December 8, 2001.

[9] "Timeline," quoting *Telegraph*, August 13, 1998.

[10] Ahmed, 50–51.

[11] Julio Godoy, "US Taliban Policy Influenced by Oil," Inter Press Service, November 16, 2001, quoted in Ahmed, 58–59.

[12] Jonathan Steele, et al., "Threat of US Strikes Passed to Taliban Weeks Before NY Attack," *Guardian*, September 22, 2001, quoted in Brisard and Dasquié, *Forbidden Truth*, 43, and Ahmed, 60.

[13] George Arney, "US 'Planned Attack on Taleban'," BBC News, September 18, 2001, quoted in Ahmed, 60–61. ("Taleban" is a spelling used by some British writers.)

[14] "Timeline," October 7, 2001 (B).

[15] Michael C. Ruppert, "A Timeline Surrounding September 11th," From the

Wilderness Publications (www.fromthewilderness.com), item 94, citing the account as published on the Common Dreams website (www.commondreams.org/ views02/0614-02.htm).

[16] George Arney, "US 'Planned Attack on Taleban'," BBC News, September 18, 2001, quoted in Ahmed, 60–61.

[17] This statement from the Israeli newspaper *Ma'ariv* was quoted in the *Chicago Tribune*, February 18, 2002, which is in turn quoted in "Timeline," February 14, 2002.

[18] "Timeline," December 22, 2001, and January 1, 2002, and Ahmed, 260.

[19] Ahmed, 227, citing *Frontier Post*, October 10, 2001.

[20] Ahmed, 60–61.

[21] White House, March 13, quoted in "Timeline," March 13, 2002.

[22] In 1992, Wolfowitz and Libby were reportedly the principal authors of a draft of the Defense Planning Guidance document that, having been leaked to the *New York Times*, caused a furor because of its overtly imperialistic language. Although this draft was withdrawn, its main ideas reappeared in the Project for the New American Century's 2000 publication, *Rebuilding America's Defenses: Strategy, Forces and Resources for a New Century* (available at www.newamericancentury.org). On this episode, see Andrew Bacevich, *American Empire: The Realities and Consequences of US Diplomacy* (Cambridge: Harvard University Press, 2002), 43–46 (although Bacevich, referring to this document as the "Wolfowitz Indiscretion," does not mention Libby's participation).

[23] "Timeline," September 2000, citing *Scotland Sunday Herald*, September 7, 2002, which was quoting *Rebuilding America's Defenses* (see previous note).

[24] Edward Herman, "The Manufactured and Real Iraq Crisis," *ZNet Commentary*, February 3, 2003.

[25] This letter, dated January 26, 1998, is available at the website for the Project for the New American Century (www.newamericancentury.org).

[26] Thompson, "September 11" (2:40 PM), quoting CBS News, September 4, 2002.

[27] John Pilger, *New Statesman*, December 12, 2002, citing Bob Woodward, *Bush at War* (New York: Simon & Schuster, 2002), 49. Woodward adds: "Before the attacks, the Pentagon had been working for months on developing a military option for Iraq" and "Rumsfeld was raising the possibility that they could take advantage of the opportunity offered by the terrorist attacks to go after Saddam immediately." Woodward also points out that Rumsfeld was thereby echoing the position of his deputy, Paul Wolfowitz.

[28] Porritt's statement is quoted in James Kirkup, "US, UK Waged War on Iraq Because of Oil, Blair Adviser Says," May 1, 2003 (http://quote.bloomberg.com), which is reprinted on Michael Ruppert's website, From the Wilderness Publications (www.fromthewilderness.com or www.copvcia.com). Paul O'Neill's charge is contained in a book by former *Wall Street Journal* reporter Ron Susskind, *The Price of Loyalty: George W. Bush, the White House, and the Education of Paul O'Neill* (New York: Simon & Schuster, 2004), and in an interview on CBS's "60 Minutes" on January 11, 2004. According to O'Neill, who was a member of the National Security Council, the main topic within days of the inauguration was going after Saddam, with the issue being not "Why Saddam?" or "Why Now?" but merely "finding a way to do it." Susskind, whose book is primarily based on interviews with O'Neill and other officials, says that already in January and February of

2001 the Bush administration was discussing an occupation of Iraq and the question of how to divide up Iraq's oil (see story at www.cbsnews.com/stories/2004/01/09/60minutes/main592330.shtml).

[29] Stephen Gowans, "Regime Change in Iraq: A New Government by and for US Capital," *ZNet*, April 20, 2003, quoting Robert Fisk, *Independent*, April 14, 2003.

[30] Thompson, "Timeline," 59, August 11, 2002, citing *Newsweek*, August 11, 2002.

[31] John Pilger, *New Statesman*, December 12, 2002. Although Perle talks in public about using war to bring democracy to the world, he knows that it has other uses. Shortly before the recent war in Iraq, he gave a talk to clients of Goldman Sachs about moneymaking opportunities that would arise from the imminent invasion. His "total war" vision was suggested by the title of the talk, which was: "Implications of an Imminent War: Iraq Now. North Korea Next?" See Maureen Dowd, "Perle's Plunder Blunder," *New York Times*, March 23, 2003, and Stephen Gowans, "Regime Change in Iraq: A New Government by and for US Capital," *ZNet*, April 20, 2003.

[32] Meyssan, *9/11: The Big Lie*, 130.

[33] Richard Falk, *The Great Terror War* (Northampton, Mass.: Olive Branch Press, 2002), 108, 5.

[34] Bennis, *Before and After*, 163.

[35] Zbigniew Brzezinski, *The Grand Chessboard: American Primacy and Its Geostrategic Imperatives* (New York: Basic Books, 1997), 35–36.

[36] Ibid., 212, quoted in Ahmed, 73–77, and Thompson, "Timeline," 1997.

[37] Ibid., 24–25, quoted in Ahmed, 77.

[38] John Pilger, *New Statesman*, December 12, 2002, quoting the Project for the New American Century, *Rebuilding America's Defenses*, 51. The heading of Pilger's article reads: "Two years ago a project set up by the men who now surround George W. Bush said what America needed was 'a new Pearl Harbor.' Its published aims have, alarmingly, come true."

[39] Ibid.

[40] This document is available at www.spacecom.af.mil/usspace. It is discussed in Jack Hitt, "The Next Battlefield May Be in Outer Space," *New York Times Magazine*, August 5, 2001, and Karl Grossman, *Weapons in Space* (New York: Seven Stories, 2001).

[41] This figure is reported in the *Global Network Space Newsletter #14* (Fall, 2003), which is posted on the website of the Global Network Against Weapons and Nuclear Power in Space (www.space4peace.org).

[42] Falk, *The Great Terror War*, xxvii. Falk continues: "If this project aiming at global domination is consummated, or nearly so, it threatens the entire world with a kind of subjugation, and risks encouraging frightening new cycles of megaterrorism as the only available and credible strategy of resistance."

[43] The developments achieved already by 1998 are described in George Friedman and Meredith Friedman, *The Future of War: Power, Technology and American World Dominance in the 21st Century* (New York: St. Martin's, 1998).

[44] Jack Hitt, "The Next Battlefield May Be in Outer Space."

[45] Ibid. For a brief overview of this project, see Karl Grossman's *Weapons in Space*.

[46] The Project for the New American Century, *Rebuilding America's Defenses*, 54; quoted in Mahajan, *Full Spectrum Dominance: US Power in Iraq and Beyond* (New York: Seven Stories Press, 2003), 53–54.

[47] *The National Security Strategy of the United States of America* (Washington: September 2002), 6. As John Pilger concluded (see note 38, above), most of the suggestions made in the Project for the New American Century's document were enacted by the Bush administration. This is not surprising, of course, given the overlap in personnel.

[48] *Report of the Commission to Assess US National Security Space Management and Organization* (www.defenselink.mil/cgi-bin/dlprint.cgi).

[49] Ibid., quoted in *9/11: The Big Lie*, 151–52.

[50] Department of Defense News Briefing on Pentagon Attack (www.defenselink.mil/cgi-bin/dlprint.cgi), quoted in *9/11: The Big Lie*, 152.

[51] *9/11: The Big Lie*, 154.

[52] "A Program of Covert Operations Against the Castro Regime," April 16, 1961 (declassified CIA document), quoted in *9/11: The Big Lie*, 140.

[53] This plan has come to be somewhat widely known through James Bamford's discussion of it in his *Body of Secrets*.

[54] This memorandum is printed in *9/11: The Big Lie*, 198.

[55] This memorandum is printed in *9/11: The Big Lie*, 199–205. The passages quoted here are on page 199.

[56] Ibid., 202–203.

[57] Ibid., 204.

[58] Ibid., 202.

[59] Idem. The extent to which another precedent was provided by the original Pearl Harbor is a question for another occassion.

[60] See Richard Van Alstyne, *The Rising American Empire* (1960; New York: Norton, 1974), 177–79.

[61] John Pilger points to evidence that President George W. Bush has adopted a plan somewhat reminiscent of Operation Northwoods. Describing a secret army set up by Secretary of Defense Rumsfeld ("similar to those run by Richard Nixon and Henry Kissinger and which Congress outlawed"), Pilger reports that according to a classified document, this secret army, known as "the Proactive Preemptive Operations Group," will provoke terrorist attacks that would then require "counter-attack" by the United States on countries "harbouring the terrorists" (Pilger, *New Statesman*, December 12, 2002, citing a report by military analyst William Arkin, "The Secret War," *Los Angeles Times*, October 27, 2002).

[62] Chossudovsky, *War and Globalisation*, 62.

Chapter 8: Did US Officials Block Captures and Investigations After 9/11?

[1] Thompson, "Timeline," early November 2001 (A), quoting *London Times*, July 22, 2002.

[2] Knight-Ridder, October 20, 2002, quoted in "Timeline," Early November (B).

[3] *Sydney Morning Herald,* November 14, 2001, *Christian Science Monitor,* March 4, 2002, and Knight-Ridder, November 20, 2002, cited in "Timeline," November 10, 2001.

[4] *Newsweek,* August 11, 2002, cited in "Timeline," November 16, 2001 (B).

[5] *Christian Science Monitor,* March 4, 2002, and *Telegraph,* February 23, 2002, cited in "Timeline," early December 2001.

[6] "Timeline," November 28, 2001, citing *Fayetteville Observer,* August 2, and *Newsweek,* August 11, 2002.

[7] "Timeline," November 28, 2001, citing *Independent,* August 2, 2002.

[8] BBC, December 30, 2001, cited in "Timeline," December 30, 2001.

[9] "Timeline," March 13, 2002, quoting the White House, March 13, and the Department of Defense, April 6, 2002.

[10] Ahmed, 78, quoting *Daily Mirror,* November 16, 2001.

[11] George Monbiot, "The Need for Dissent," *Guardian,* September 18, 2001, quoted in Ahmed, 295–96.

[12] Chossudovsky, *War and Globalisation,* 60.

[13] Ibid., 61.

[14] Ibid., 22–23; "Timeline," March 1985, citing *Washington Post,* July 19, 1992, and Rashid, *Taliban: Militant Islam, Oil and Fundamentalism in Central Asia* (New Haven: Yale University Press, 2000).

[15] Ahmed, 177–78, quoting John K. Cooley, *Unholy Wars: Afghanistan, America and International Terrorism* (London: Pluto, 1999), 120, 226. Another thing that the CIA, the ISI, and bin Laden had in common, Thompson reports, is that they all had accounts in the now notorious Bank of Credit and Commerce International (BCCI), which was based in Pakistan ("Timeline" July 5, 1991, citing *Detroit News,* September 30, 2001, and *Washington Post,* February 17, 2002).

[16] *Newsweek,* October 1, 2001, quoted in "Timeline," March 1985.

[17] *Times of India,* March 7, 2001, and CNN, February 27, 2002, quoted in "Timeline," March 1994 (B).

[18] *Time,* May 6, 2002, quoted in "Timeline," 1984; *New Yorker,* October 29, 2001, quoted in "Timeline," October 7, 2001.

[19] Chossudovsky, *War and Globalisation,* 38.

[20] Ahmed, 216, quoting Selig Harrison, "Creating the Taliban: 'CIA Made a Historic Mistake,'" *Rationalist International Bulletin* No. 68: March 19, 2001 (http://rationalist international.net).

[21] Ahmed, 189.

[22] Gerald Posner, *Why America Slept: The Failure to Prevent 9/11* (New York: Random House, 2003), 193.

[23] ABC News, September 30, and *Wall Street Journal,* October 10, 2001, cited in "Timeline," May 2000.

[24] Agence France-Presse, October 10, 2001, cited in Chossudovsky, *War and Globalisation,* 58.

[25] "Timeline," October 12, 1999, citing the *News*, September 10, 2001.

[26] Chossudovsky, *War and Globalisation*, 52–54, 60.

[27] PBS's *Frontline*, October 3, 2002, quoted in "Timeline," August 23, 2001.

[28] Chossudovsky, *War and Globalisation*, 156–58.

[29] Ibid., 58–59, quoting Brian Ross on ABC's "This Week," September 30, 2001.

[30] "Timeline," October 7, 2001.

[31] "Timeline," Septumber 8–11, 2001 (C), citing *Guardian*, October 1, and CNN, October 6, 2001. Thompson adds that although earlier the media had "sometimes made the obvious connection that the paymaster was the British man Saeed Sheikh, a financial expert who studied at the London School of Economics" (see "Timeline," June 1993–October 1994), after October 8, when the story that ISI Director Ahmad ordered Saeed to give Mohamed Atta $100,000 began to break, "References to the 9/11 paymaster being the British Saeed Sheikh...suddenly disappear from the Western media (with one exception [CNN, 10/28/01])." Thompson then documents the fact that the Western media began referring to this individual, under numerous names, as Egyptian or Saudi Arabian, rather than Pakistani. One of the results of this confusion was that, conveniently, the paymaster came to be identified as "Sheikh Saiid," said to be an alias for Sa'd al-Sharif, one of bin Laden's brothers-in-law. For details about the massive confusion in the press about the name of the paymaster, see "Timeline," October 1, October 16, November 11, December 11, 2001, January 23, June 4, June 18, September 4, and December 26, 2002. See also two articles by Chaim Kupferberg (who prefers to call the paymaster Omar Saeed), "Daniel Pearl and the Paymaster of 9/11: 9/11 and the Smoking Gun that Turned on its Teacher," and "There's Something about Omar." These two articles were posted September 21, 2002, and October 21, 2003, respectively, on the website of the Centre for Research on Globalisation (www.globalresearch.ca).

[32] "Timeline," September 8–11, 2001 (C), citing *New York Times*, July 10, 2002, and *Financial Times*, November 30, 2001.

[33] "Timeline," September 8–11, 2001 (C), citing *Guardian* on the relationship between Saeed Sheikh and bin Laden.

[34] Chossudovsky, *War and Globalisation*, 146.

[35] Ibid., 62.

[36] Ahmed, 218, 226, citing Jared Israel, "Did 'Our' Allies, Pakistani Intelligence, Fund the WTC Attackers?" The Emperor's New Clothes (www.emperors-clothes.com), October 15, 2001.

[37] *Pittsburgh Tribune-Review*, March 3, 2002, quoted in Thompson, "Timeline," 1999 (J).

[38] Ahmed, 218–19, citing Manoj Joshi, "India Helped FBI Trace ISI-Terrorist Links," *Times of India*, October 9, 2001.

[39] Ibid., 224, 225.

[40] Chossudovsky, *War and Globalisation*, 62.

[41] *New York Times*, November 4, and Associated Press, August 24, 2002, cited in "Timeline," 1999 (K).

[42] UPI (United Press International), September 30, 2002, cited in "Timeline," June 4,

2002; see also early 1994–January 1995, and December 24, 2001–January 23, 2002.

[43] *Telegraph*, November 11, 2001, cited in "Timeline," November 10, 2001.

[44] "Timeline," January 6 and January 23, 2002, quoting *Washington Post*, February 23, 2002, and citing *Boston Globe*, January 6, *Pittsburgh Tribune-Review*, March 3, and *Vanity Fair*, August, 2002.

[45] "Timeline," January 28, 2002, citing *London Times*, April 21, and *Guardian*, July 16, 2002.

[46] "Timeline," January 28, 2002, citing UPI, January 29, 2002.

[47] "Timeline," February 12, 2002, citing *Boston Globe*, February 7, *Observer*, February 24, 2002, *Newsweek*, March 11, and *Vanity Fair*, August, 2002.

[48] "Timeline," February 6, 2002.

[49] UPI, September 30, 2002; *Vanity Fair*, February, 2002, and Baer, *See No Evil: The True Story of a Ground Soldier in the CIA's War on Terrorism* (New York: Crown Pub, 2002), 270–71, cited in "Timeline," December 1997.

[50] CNN, January 30, 2003, cited in "Timeline," December 22, 2001 (B).

[51] *Time*, January 26, and CNN, January 30, 2003, cited in "Timeline," January 23, 2002.

[52] UPI, September 30, 2002, cited in "Timeline," June 4, 2002.

[53] John J. Lumpkin, "New Theory on Pearl Slaying: 9/11 Mastermind Believed to Have Killed Wall Street Journal Reporter," APAP, October 21, 2003.

[54] "Timeline," February 18, 2002 (B), citing *News*, February 18, *London Times*, April 21, and *Guardian*, July 16, 2002.

[55] "Timeline," March 1, 2002, citing "There's Much More To Daniel Pearl's Murder Than Meets the Eye," *Washington Post*, March 10, 2002.

[56] "Timeline," March 3, 2002.

[57] "Timeline," July 19, 2002 (B), citing *Time*, February 25, 2002, and "Timeline," December 26, 2002, citing *India Express*, July 19, 2002.

[58] "Timeline," March 3, 2002, citing *Dawn*, March 3, 2002, and *Guardian*, April 5, 2002.

[59] "Timeline," March 14, 2002, citing CNN, March 14, and *Los Angeles Times*, March 15, 2002.

[60] WPBF Channel 25, August 5, 2002, Cox News, August 2, 2002, and *Palm Beach Post*, October 17, 2002, cited in "Timeline," July 14, 1999.

[61] *Palm Beach Post*, March 20, 2003 (see also *South Florida Sun-Sentinel*, March 20, 2003), quoted in "Timeline," June 2002.

[62] *Newsweek*, September 15, *New York Times*, September 15, and *Washington Post*, September 16, 2001, cited in "Timeline," September 15–17, 2001.

[63] Gannett News Service and *Pensacola News Journal*, both September 17, 2001, cited in "Timeline," September 15-17, 2001.

[64] *Washington Post*, September 16, 2001, quoted in Ahmed, 97.

[65] Daniel Hopsicker, "Did Terrorists Train at U.S. Military Schools?" *Online Journal*, October 30, 2002, quoted in Ahmed, 98–99. (Hopsicker, who has produced television

business shows, including "Inside Wall Street," is also the author of *Barry and the Boys: The CIA, the Mob, and America's Secret History* [Madcow Press, 2001].)

[66] Hopsicker, "Did Terrorists?" quoted in Ahmed, 98, 99.

[67] Steve Fainaru and James V. Grimaldi, "FBI Knew Terrorists Were Using Flight Schools," *Washington Post*, September 23, 2001, quoted in Ahmed, 99.

[68] Hopsicker, "Did Terrorists?", quoted in Ahmed, 99.

[69] Hopsicker, "What Are They Hiding Down in Venice, Florida?" *Online Journal*, November 7, 2001, quoted in Ahmed, 100. An interesting footnote to this story is provided by the fact that Arne Kruithof and Rudi Dekkers, each of whom owned one of these flight schools, each narrowly escaped dying in a small plane crash. On Kruithof's crash, which occurred on July 26, 2002, see Hopsicker, "Magic Dutch Boy Escapes Fiery Crash," *Mad Cow Morning News*, July 4, 2002 (www.madcowprod.com/index27.html); on Dekkers' crash, which occurred on January 24, 2003, see Hopsicker, "Dekkers' Helicopter Crashed on Way to Showdown over Huffman Aviation," *Mad Cow Morning News*, January 28, 2003 (www.madcowprod.com/index43.html).

[70] "Timeline," November 1999, citing *Sunday Mercury*, October 21, 2001, *Washington Post*, December 29, 2001, and *Newsweek*, September 24, 2002.

[71] James Risen, "Informant for F.B.I. Had Contacts with Two 9/11 Hijackers," *New York Times*, July 25, 2003.

[72] "Timeline," September 21 or 22, 2001, citing *Los Angeles Times* and *Newsweek*, both November 24, 2002.

[73] *Boston Globe*, October 27, 2001, cited in "Timeline," October 24, 2001.

[74] *Washington Post*, September 19, and the BBC, June 21, 2002, cited in "Timeline," August 2002 (B). Bamford, as we saw earlier, wrote *Body of Secrets: Anatomy of the Ultra-Secret National Security Agency* (2001; New York: Anchor Books, 2002).

[75] Michael Ruppert, "A Timeline Surrounding September 11th," From the Wilderness Publications (www.fromthewilderness.com), item 96, citing *Washington Post*, July 3, 2002.

[76] Seymour Hersh, *New Yorker*, September 30, 2002, quoted in "Timeline," September 30, 2002.

[77] Larry Margasak, "Feds Reject Moussaoui Witness," Associated Press, July 14, 2003.

[78] Thompson, "Timeline," October 17, 2002, citing *Washington Post*, September 18, 2002.

[79] "Timeline," December 4, 2002, quoting *Star Tribune*, December 22, 2002.

[80] "Timeline," December 4, 2002, quoting *Time*, December 30, 2002.

Chapter 9: Is Complicity by US Officials the Best Explanation for 9/11?

[1] Ahmed, 290.

[2] Ibid., 290, citing Patrick Martin, "Was the US Government Alerted to September 11 Attack? Part 4: The Refusal to Investigate," World Socialist Web Site (www.wsws.org), January 24, 2002.

[3] Bob Woodward and Dan Balz, "Saturday, September 15, at Camp David, Advise and Dissent," *Washington Post*, January 31, 2002.

[4] Meyssan, *9/11: The Big Lie*, 153.

[5] Phyllis Bennis, *Before and After: US Foreign Policy and the September 11th Crisis* (Northampton, Mass.: Olive Branch Press, 2003), 83.

[6] This fact is included in a document called "Missile Defense Milestones," which is on the website of the Missile Defense Agency (acq.osd.mil/bmdo).

[7] Ahmed, 236–38.

[8] Ibid., 240, 262.

[9] Henry Kissinger, "Destroy the Network," *Washington Post,* September 11, 2001 (http://washingtonpost.com), quoted in *9/11: The Big Lie,* 65.

[10] Richard Perle, "State Sponsors of Terrorism Should Be Wiped Out Too," *Daily Telegraph,* September 18, 2001, quoted in *9/11: The Big Lie,* 169.

[11] Bennis, *Before and After,* 82.

[12] *9/11: The Big Lie,* 129.

[13] John Pilger, *New Statesman,* December 12, 2002.

[14] Bob Woodward, *Bush at War* (New York: Simon & Schuster, 2002), 32.

[15] "Secretary Rumsfeld Interview," *New York Times,* October 12, 2001; quoted in Andrew Bacevich, *American Empire: The Realities and Consequences of US Diplomacy* (Cambridge: Harvard University Press, 2002), 227.

[16] Rice's statement was reported by Nicholas Lemann in the April 2002 issue of the *New Yorker.*

[17] *The National Security Strategy of the United States of America,* September 2002 (www.whitehouse.gov./nssc), 28. At about the same time, Tony Blair, the prime minister of America's junior partner, said to the liaison committee of the British House of Commons: "To be truthful about it, there was no way we could have got the public consent to have suddenly launched a campaign on Afghanistan but for what happened on September 11" (*London Times,* July 17, 2002).

[18] Thomas Omestand, "New World Order," *US News and World Report,* December 31, 2001, quoted in Ahmed, 262.

[19] Walden Bello, "The American Way of War," *Focus on Trade,* No. 72: December 2001, quoted in Ahmed, 279–80.

[20] Karen Talbot, "Afghanistan is Key to Oil Profits," Centre for Research on Globalisation, November 7, 2001 (globalresearch.ca), quoted in Ahmed, 280.

[21] William Pfaff, "Will the New World Order Rest Solely on American Might?" *International Herald Tribune,* December 29, 2001, quoted in Ahmed, 274.

[22] Ahmed, 279, quoting John McMurtry's statement in *Economic Reform,* October, 2001.

[23] Ibid., 290–93.

[24] Ibid., 291.

[25] Gore Vidal, *Dreaming War: Blood for Oil and the Cheney-Bush Junta* (New York: Thunder's Mouth/Nation Books, 2002), 72.

[26] *9/11: The Big Lie,* 10, 25.

[27] See The Emperor's New Clothes (www.emperor-clothes.com).

[28] *9/11: The Big Lie*, 10.

[29] Ahmed, 291–92.

Chapter 10: The Need for a Full Investigation

[1] *Washington Post*, August 2, 2002, cited in Thompson, "Timeline," August 2, 2002.

[2] *Washington Post*, August 3 and 24, and Associated Press, August 29, 2002, cited in "Timeline," August 2, 2002.

[3] "Bush asks Daschle to Limit September 11 Probes," CNN, January 29, 2002, quoted in Ahmed, 133.

[4] *Newsweek*, September 22, 2002.

[5] Associated Press, January 27, 2003, cited in "Timeline," January 27, 2003.

[6] *Time*, March 26, 2003, quoted in "Timeline," March 26, 2003.

[7] *Seattle Times*, March 12, 2003, quoted in "Timeline," March 12, 2003.

[8] Philip Shenon, "9/11 Commission Could Subpoena Oval Office Files," *New York Times*, October 26, 2003.

[9] UPI, February 6, 2003.

[10] David Corn, "Probing 9/11," *Nation*, 277/1 (July 7: 2003): 14–18, at 15.

[11] CNN, November 30, *Pittsburgh Post-Gazette*, December 3, *Washington Post*, December 1, and *Chicago Sun-Times*, December 13, 2002, cited in "Timeline," November 27, 2002.

[12] *New York Times*, November 29, 2002, cited in "Timeline," November 27, 2002.

[13] *Newsweek*, December 15, 2002, cited in "Timeline," December 13, 2002.

[14] *Washington Post*, October 5, 1998, and Salon.com, December 3, 2002, cited in "Timeline," December 13, 2002.

[15] *New York Times*, December 12, MSNBC, December 13, and *Seattle Times*, December 14, 2002, cited in "Timeline," December 13, 2002.

[16] *Multinational Monitor*, November 1997, and Associated Press, January 20, 2003. On Hess-Delta, see *Boston Herald*, December 11, 2001, cited in "Timeline," December 16, 2002.

[17] CBS, March 5, 2003, and Associated Press, December 12, 2002, January 1, 2003, February 14, 2003, and March 27, 2003, cited in "Timeline," December 13, 2002.

[18] Associated Press, December 27, 2003; The 9/11 Independent Commission (www.9-11commision.gov), March, 2003; Corn, "Probing 9/11," 16.

[19] Corn, "Probing 9/11," 16.

[20] This call, made earlier, was implicitly repeated in the Family Steering Committee's press release of December 1, 2003, involving conflicts of interest (see the website at www.911independentcommission.org). This committee's concern about Zelikow was discussed in Philip Shenon, "Terrorism Panel Issues Subpeona to City for Tapes," *New York Times*, November 21, 2003.

[21] Timothy J. Roemer, a former congressman from Indiana, quoted in Shenon, "9/11 Commission Could Subpoena Oval Office Files."

[22] "White House Accused of Stalling 9-11 Panel," Associated Press, October 26, 2003.

[23] Shenon, "9/11 Commission Could Subpoena Oval Office Files."

[24] Ibid.

[25] Philip Shenon, "Deal on 9/11 Briefings Lets White House Edit Papers," *New York Times*, November 14, 2003; Tim Harper, "Did Bush Know Before 9/11? Briefing Notes May Hold Key to Crucial Question," *Toronto Star*, November 14, 2003. According to later stories (Philip Shenon, "Terrorism Panel Issues Subpeona to City for Tapes"; Eric Lichtblau and James Risen, "Two on 9/11 Panel are Questioned on Earlier Security roles," *New York Times*, January 15, 2004), the only commission officials to have access to highly classified White House documents would be Zelikow and Jamie Gorelick, who was a top member of the Justice Department during the Clinton administration.

[26] Eric Boehlert, "The President Ought to be Ashamed: Interview with Max Cleland," Salon.com, November 13, 2003.

[27] In the same interview, Cleland also, after saying that "the Warren Commission blew it," added: "I'm not going to be part of that. I'm not going to be part of looking at information only partially. I'm not going to be part of just coming to quick conclusions. I'm not going to be part of political pressure to do this or not do that. I'm not going to be part of that." Less than a month later, it was announced that Cleland was going to resign from the commission to accept a position on the board of the Export-Import Bank. Philip Shenon of the *New York Times* wrote:

> Mr. Cleland's intention to resign from the 10-member commission has been known since last summer, when Senate Democrats announced that they had recommended him for a Democratic slot on the board of the Export-Import Bank. But the timing of his departure became clear only last week, when the White House formally sent the nomination to the Senate.

> His imminent departure from the panel has created concern among victims' family groups, because Mr. Cleland has been one of the commission's most outspoken members and has joined with advocates for the families in their criticism of the Bush administration. (Philip Shenon, "Ex-Senator Will Soon Leave 9/11 Panel," *New York Times*, December 5, 2003.)

Suspicious minds might, of course, speculate that the White House speeded up the nomination process because it would rather have the outspoken Cleland on the board of the Export-Import Bank than on the commission investigating 9/11. In any case, a few days later it was announced that Tom Daschle, the leader of the Senate's Democrats, had selected Bob Kerrey, the former Democratic senator from Nebraska (who had been vice chairman of the Senate Intelligence Committee), to replace Cleland (Philip Shenon, "Ex-Senator Kerrey Is Named to Federal 9/11 Commission," *New York Times*, December 9, 2003).

[28] Shenon, "Deal on 9/11 Briefings Lets White House Edit Papers."

[29] In saying that "everyone" should favor this, I mean, of course, everyone innocent of complicity in the attacks of 9/11.

[30] The suspicious attitude toward the 9/11 Independent Commission held by many of those who have studied the evidence for official complicity is illustrated by an article that refers to it as "the 9-11 Coverup Commission." With regard to Kean himself, this article predicted: "To ensure that the 9-11 Coverup Commission projects an image of at least 'trying,' the commission's chairman Thomas H. Kean...publicly stated that the presence of

so-called agency 'minders' (or coaches) was the same as 'intimidation' of witnesses called before the Commission.... Rest assured, however, Thomas Kean will do the Bush Cabal's bidding and keep it all covered up" (Conspiracy Planet, "9-11 Commission Covers Up Bush Family Ties," www.conspiracyplanet.com/channel.cfm?ChannelID=75). Kean's agreement, after threatening to subpoena the White House, to allow it to edit the presidential briefs could be seen as a fulfillment of this prediction, so this agreement probably increased the suspicion.

[31] Michael Meacher, "This War on Terrorism is Bogus," *Guardian*, September 5, 2003.

[32] In response, one debunker, Jon Ungoed-Thomas, wrote: "However, logs compiled by the North American Aerospace Defense Command record that it learnt of a possible hijacking at 8.40 AM. F-15 fighters were alerted immediately, were scrambled at 8.46 AM and were airborne by 8.52 AM" (Conspiracy Theories about 9/11 are Growing and Getting More Bizarre," *Sunday Times*, September 14, 2003). This conflict of opinion reflects the fact, of which most people still seem unaware, that there have been two versions of the official account on this matter. Meacher cited the first account (whether because it was the account he accepted or the only one he knew), then Ungoed-Thomas "refuted" him by citing the second (perhaps because it was the only one *he* knew). That issue aside, there are several other problems with Ungoed-Thomas' attempt to defend the official account. First, in citing NORAD'S logs, he is relying on an account provided by one of the agencies that, according to most conspiracy theories, would have been party to the conspiracy. Second, he repeats NORAD's claim that it was not notified until 8:40 without mentioning the fact that this would mean that the FAA would have flagrantly violated regulations by not notifying NORAD until 26 minutes after Flight 11's radio and transponder went off. Third, he evidently sees no tension between claiming that NORAD responded "immediately" and pointing out that it was 12 minutes until any planes were airborne. Fourth, he does not even mention the fact that NORAD, according to this second version of the official account, gave the scramble order to Otis rather than to the much nearer McGuire Air Force Base. Fifth, he seems not to realize that even planes coming the 170 miles from Otis should have reached New York City in plenty of time—he simply repeats the standard line that it "was already too late to stop the hijackers flying into the World Trade Center." This article illustrates a widespread tendency of debunkers to regard 9/11 "conspiracy theorists" with such disdain (Ungoed-Thomas speaks of their "bizarre" theories and "grotesque distortions") that they can be easily refuted even by someone largely ignorant of the facts. Then, having provided this refutation, at least to his own satisfaction, Ungoed-Thomas asks: "Why do so many people cleave to these theories when there are such discrepancies and perfectly reasonable explanations?" He answers this question by citing a psychologist who explains that adherents of conspiracy theories "are driven by a thirst for certainty in an uncertain world." We can ignore 9/11 conspiracy theories, in other words, because they are simply products of pathetic minds—not of minds that have noticed conflicts between the official account and the facts.

[33] Michael Meacher, "This War on Terrorism is Bogus," *Guardian*, September 5, 2003.

[34] Ewen MacAskill, "Fury Over Meacher Claims," *Guardian*, September 6, 2003.

[35] This statement is in the article by Jon Ungoed-Thomas quoted in note 32, above.

[36] The letters all appeared in the *Guardian* on September 8, 2003; they were accompanied by many letters denouncing Meacher.

[37] Michael Meacher, "Cock-Up Not Conspiracy," *Guardian*, September 13, 2003.

[38] That this was a natural interpretation of his article is suggested by the fact that Ian Johnson, whose *Wall Street Journal* article is discussed next, said that Meacher had written "a blistering attack...implying that Washington was involved in the attacks to justify a more interventionist foreign policy."

[39] Ian Johnson, "Conspiracy Theories About September 11 Get Hearing in Germany," *Wall Street Journal*, September 29, 2003.

[40] The English translation of the title of Andreas von Bülow's book would be "The CIA and the 11th of September: International Terror and the Role of the Secret Services" (Munich: Piper Verlag, 2003). In Chapter 1, I quoted a 2002 statement by von Bülow.

[41] Paul Donovan, "Why Isn't the Truth Out There?" *Observer*, October 5, 2003 (http://observer.guardian.co.uk/comment/story/0,6903,1054495,00.html).

[42] Michael Moore, *Dude, Where's My Country?* (New York: Warner Books, 2003), 15.

[43] William Bunch, "Why Don't We Have Answers to These 9/11 Questions?" *Philadelphia Daily News* online posting, September 11, 2003.

[44] "Diane Rehm Show," National Public Radio, December 1, 2003, quoted in Charles Krauthammer, "The Delusional Dean," *Washington Post*, December 5, 2003.

[45] Krauthammer, "The Delusional Dean."

[46] This story, written by Kathleen Parker, appeared in the *Orlando Sentinel* on April 17, 2002; it is available at www.osamaskidneys.com/mckinney.html.

[47] This story, written by Lynette Clemetson, appeared in the *New York Times* on August 21, 2002. For Greg Palast's criticism, see his "The Screwing of Cynthia McKinney," AlterNet, June 13, 2003 (www.alternet.org/story. html?StoryID=16172). Palast quotes Clemetson as saying, in response to his question as to where McKinney said this: "I've heard that statement—it was all over the place."

[48] On Pacifica radio on March 25, 2002, McKinney read a prepared statement, after which she was interviewed (the transcript is available at www.freerepublic.com/focus/news/665750/posts). In her prepared statement, after saying that the US government had received numerous warnings prior to 9/11, she asked: "What did this Administration know, and when did it know it, about the events of September 11? Who else knew and why did they not warn the innocent people of New York who were needlessly murdered?" She also said, in a different paragraph, that "persons close to this Administration are poised to make huge profits off America's new war." These statements contain three distinct elements: (1) the question of what the Bush administration knew—which referred back to her statement that "[w]e know there were numerous warnings of the events to come on September 11. Vladimir Putin, President of Russia, delivered one such warning"; (2) the suggestion that *some people* had foreknowledge of the attacks of 9/11 and failed to issue a warning—which referred to her earlier statement that "[t]hose engaged in unusual stock trades immediately before September 11 knew enough to make millions of dollars from United and American airlines, certain insurance and brokerage firms' stocks"; and (3) her assertion that some persons close to the Bush administration would profit financially from the US war on terrorism. However, as her statements were repeated in the mainline press (after they were publicized by an April 12 story in the *Washington Post* under the headline "Democrat Implies September 11 Administration Plot"), these three elements became conflated. The conflation made by Kathleen Parker of the *Orlando Sentinel* on April 17 was

quoted in the text. On June 16, a show on NPR (National Public Radio) claimed that McKinney "suggested the Bush Administration may have known in advance about the September 11 attacks and allowed them to happen in order for people close to the President to profit." To back up this claim, NPR played these words from the Pacifica broadcast: "What did this administration know, and when did it know it, about the events of September 11th? Who else knew, and why did they not warn the innocent people of New York who were needlessly murdered?...What do they have to hide?" The problem here is that the final question, "What do they have to hide?", came later in the program, during the interview, while McKinney was discussing the requests by both the president and the vice president to Tom Daschle that he not have a Senate investigation. By quoting that statement out of context, NPR made it appear that the "they" in the prior sentence—the "they" who had specific knowledge about the events in advance—referred to members of the Bush administration. NPR then played another statement made during the interview— "And so we get this presidency...requesting a nearly unprecedented amount of money to go into a defense budget for defense spending that will directly benefit his father." By conflating this statement with the earlier one, NPR made it sound as if McKinney was charging that this was the president's motive for allowing the attacks to proceed. For Palast's analysis of this conflation, see his "Re-Lynching Cynthia McKinney," July 21, 2003 (www.gregpalast.com/detail.cfm?artid=232&row=0). Palast's analysis is supported by John Sugg. Having said that the most infamous assault against McKinney "was the claim that she had questioned whether Dubya had knowledge of 9-11 before it happened, and that he didn't act because his dad and cronies were going to make bundles off the war machine," Sugg adds: "The truth was that McKinney quite accurately predicted—months before it broke in the press—that Bush had extensive intelligence on likely terrorist attacks and failed to act. And McKinney was equally accurate in saying that Bush insiders would reap windfalls from slaughter. However, nowhere did McKinney ever link the two statements" (John Sugg, "Truth in Exile: US Reporter Breaks Bush Blockbusters—on English TV," Creative Loafing, April 9, 2003 [http://atlanta.creativeloafing.com/suggreport.html]).

[49] Palast, "Re-Lynching Cynthia McKinney." Palast agrees, incidentally, that McKinney's statement is sufficiently ambiguous to be read in more than one way, but he argues that this fact provides no excuse for the way it was used: "Can you read an evil accusation into McKinney's statement—Bush planned September 11 attacks to enrich his daddy? Oh, yes, if that's what you want to read. But reporters are not supposed to play 'Gotcha!' with such serious matters. If a statement can be read two ways—one devastating—then journalists have an obligation to ask and probe, and certainly not spread an 'interpretation' as a quotation."

[50] Cynthia McKinney at Project Censored! October 4, 2003, available at www.oilempire.us/cynthiamckinney.html.

[51] John Sugg, "Truth in Exile." Sugg, whose Creative Loafing is one of the five largest weekly newspapers in the nation, has added, in personal correspondence, "With no big GOP race [that year], I'd guess the cross-over tally approached McKinney's estimate" (e-mail message of December 22, 2003).

[52] "Poll Shocker: Nearly Half Support McKinney's 9/11 Conspiracy Theory," Newsmax, Wednesday, April 17, 2002 (www.newsmax.com/showinside.shtml?a=2002/4/17/144136).

[53] One big difference is the fact that in discussing motive, Mariani's Complaint speaks of political (as well as financial) reasons.

[54] Berg's press release was reported at Scoop Media (http://www.scoop.co.nz/mason/stories/WO0311/S00261.htm). I have learned from sources in Philadelphia that Berg, formerly Deputy Attorney General of Pennsylvania, is a highly respected lawyer. He has established a website for this case at www.911forthetruth.com.

[55] This Complaint is available at http://nancho.net/911/mariani.html (as well as www.911forthetruth.com).

[56] This is actually an "Amended Complaint." The initial one, which was noted in a brief story in the *Philadelphia Inquirer* on September 23, 2003, had been filed on September 12. The Amended Complaint of November provides, it says, "newly discovered substantial additional facts." While being interviewed on Pacifica Radio on December 14, Mariani and Berg announced that due to still more facts and potential witnesses that had been brought to their attention, they would be filing yet another version of the Complaint.

[57] Mariani's letter is available at Scoop Media (www.scoop.co.nz/mason/stories/WO0311/S00262.htm) as well as www.911forthetruth.com.

[58] See note 30.

[59] See note 27.

[60] Eric Lichtblau and James Risen, "Two on 9/11 Panel Are Questioned on Earlier Security Roles," *New York Times*, January 15.

[61] Dan Eggen, "9/11 Panel Unlikely to Get Later Deadline," *Washington Post*, January 19, 2004.

[62] Joe Conason, "What's Bush Hiding From 9/11 Commission?" *The New York Observer*, January 21, 2004.

[63] Timothy J. Burger, "Condi and the 9/11 Commission," *New York Times*, December 20, 2003; Dan Eggen, "9/11 Panel Unlikely to Get Later Deadline"; Philip Shenon, "9/11 Commission Says It Needs More Time," *New York Times*, January 28, 2004.

[64] Dan Eggen, "9/11 Panel Unlikely to Get Later Deadline."

[65] John Buchanan, "Speech to Manchester Support Group, 1/7/04" (johnbuchanan.org/news/newsitem.php?section=INF&id=1154&showcat=4). Information about this campaign is available at http://johnbuchanan.org and buchanan@nancho.net.

INDEX OF NAMES